STREETWISE®

BUSINESS MANAGEMENT

Books in the Streetwise® series include:

Streetwise® 24 Hour MBA
Streetwise® Achieving Wealth Through Franchising
Streetwise® Business Forms (with CD-ROM)
Streetwise® Business Letters (with CD-ROM)
Streetwise® Business Tips
Streetwise® Complete Business Plan
Streetwise® Customer-Focused Selling
Streetwise® Direct Marketing
Streetwise® Do-It-Yourself Advertising
Streetwise® Finance and Accounting
Streetwise® Get Your Business Online
Streetwise® Hiring Top Performers
Streetwise® Independent Consulting
Streetwise® Internet Business Plan
Streetwise® Low-Cost Web Site Promotion
Streetwise® Managing People
Streetwise® Marketing Plan
Streetwise® Maximize Web Site Traffic
Streetwise® Motivating and Rewarding Employees
Streetwise® Relationship Marketing on the Internet
Streetwise® Sales Letters (with CD-ROM)
Streetwise® Small Business Start-Up
Streetwise® Small Business Success Kit (with CD-ROM)
Streetwise® Small Business Turnaround
Streetwise® Time Management

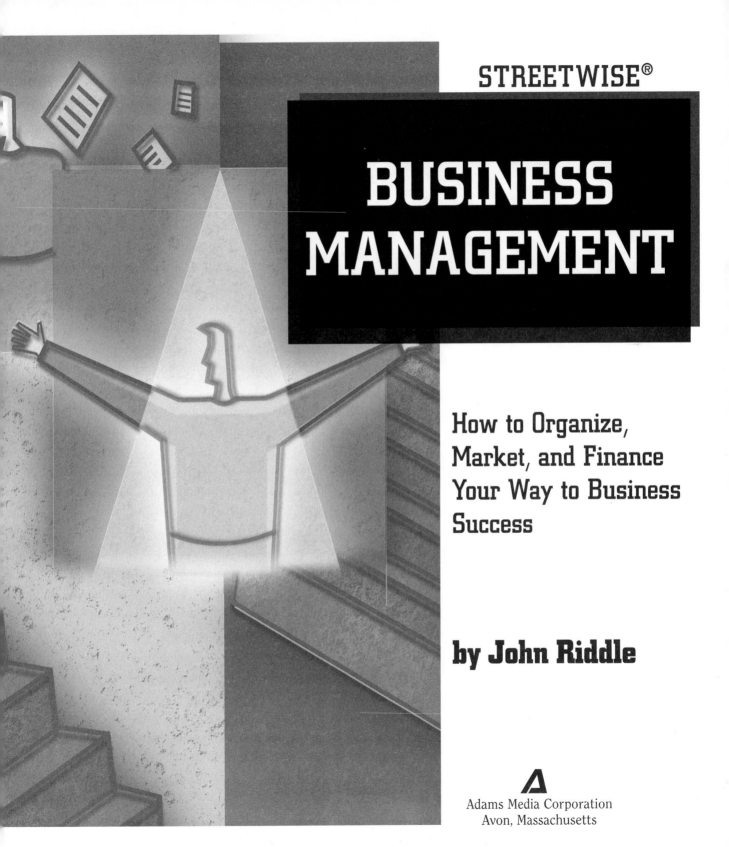

STREETWISE®

BUSINESS MANAGEMENT

How to Organize,
Market, and Finance
Your Way to Business
Success

by John Riddle

Adams Media Corporation
Avon, Massachusetts

A Streetwise® Publication.
Streetwise® is a registered trademark of Adams Media Corporation.

Published by Adams Media Corporation
57 Littlefield Street, Avon, MA 02322. U.S.A.
adamsmedia.com

ISBN: 1-58062-540-1

Printed in the United States of America.

J I H G F E D C B A

Library of Congress Cataloging-in-Publication Data
Riddle, John.
Streetwise business management : how to organize, market,
and finance your way to business success / John Riddle.
p.   cm.
Includes bibliographical references and index.
ISBN 1-58062-540-1
1. Industrial management. 2. Small business–Management. 3. Office management.
4. Marketing-Management. 5. Corporations–Finance. 6. Success in business. I. Title.
HD31 .R496   2001
658.02'2-dc21   2001041274

Cover illustration by Eric Mueller.

This book is available at quantity discounts for bulk purchases.
For information, call 1-800-872-5627.

Visit our exciting small business Web site: www.businesstown.com

Contents

SECTION I: MANAGEMENT BASICS

SECTION II: SMALL BUSINESS: START-UPS, FAMILY BUSINESS, AND MORE

SECTION III: THE MANAGER'S ROLE IN MARKETING

SECTION IV: THE MANAGER AND MONEY

SECTION V: MANAGERS AND COMMUNICATION

SECTION VI: THE MANAGER, TECHNOLOGY, AND THE FUTURE

Management Basics

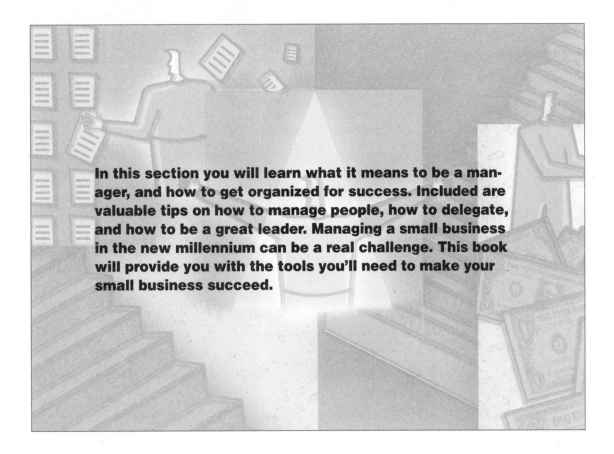

In this section you will learn what it means to be a manager, and how to get organized for success. Included are valuable tips on how to manage people, how to delegate, and how to be a great leader. Managing a small business in the new millennium can be a real challenge. This book will provide you with the tools you'll need to make your small business succeed.

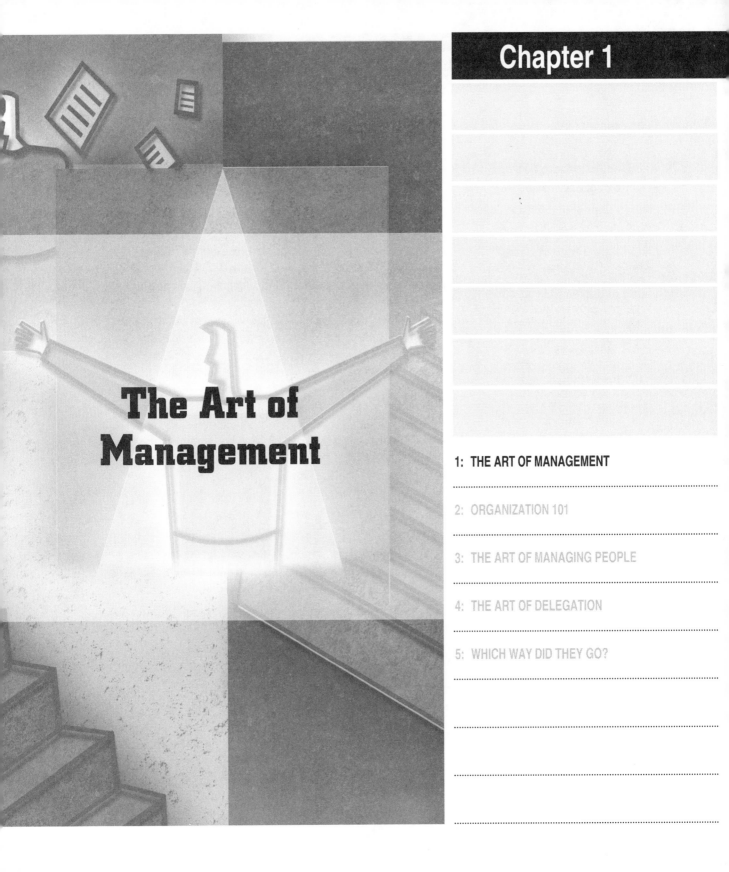

Chapter 1

The Art of Management

What Is Management?

Why is management such a hot topic? Well, consider that there are millions of people who work as managers every day of their lives. Whether they are in control of their own small business, manage one for someone else, or are a manager of a specific department or function of a company, managing people can be very simple one day and overwhelmingly complex the next. In addition, there is the whole aspect of being responsible for the day-to-day operations of your business or department. A lot can ride on a manager's every little decision.

Don't feel bad if you haven't had much luck in the past with the whole management thing. Most managers would admit that dealing with people is their biggest headache. Because people are human, there will always be problems to deal with. But like any other problem on the planet, if it is broken down into little sections, it can be fixed. All it takes is time, patience, and a little knowledge.

This book will provide you with all the necessary information to help you manage your business in the ever-changing corporate environment. Management, like life, can be filled with ups and downs. You never know what the next day will bring.

Rate Yourself in the Following Areas

Values—How do your values stack up against the rest of the business world? If everyone else is doing the wrong thing, do you have what it takes to do the right thing?

Vision—How well can you see the big picture? Is it easy for you to step back, glance around, and be the first to admit that you're not sure what you see? Many managers fail the vision test because they refuse to delegate tasks to people who have valuable talents.

Action—How well do you perform in the action arena? If you compared your management skills to the athletic prowess of a boxer, would you be knocked out in the first round? Or have you learned to "float like a butterfly and sting like a bee"?

Self-awareness–How smart are you? Are you smart enough to know that one person can't do it all? Too many businesses fail simply because the person at the top refused to admit he or she needed help. Do you think Bill Gates could run Microsoft by himself? He's smart enough to hire and surround himself with enough talent to help his business soar.

Finances–Okay, here's one that most people think they know everything about, but in reality, it's where most businesses begin to fail. Why? Because they failed to understand the A-to-Z of finances when it comes to running a successful small business. How about you? How's your knowledge of finances these days? If you're not the financial wizard that you think you should be, at least recognize that you need help, and that it's okay to get some (reread the previously listed self-awareness section).

Stress Management–How's your blood pressure? Have you had it checked lately? Or a better question might be: how well do you handle stress? Stress is one of the leading causes of problems in businesses, not only for employees, but for the business owners as well. Have you read any good books on stress management lately? Or attended a good stress management seminar? Have you learned the art of relaxation? If not, you'd better brush up, because to be an effective business manager in the new century, you're definitely going to need some topnotch stress management skills.

While many people want to become good managers, only a handful will end up eventually succeeding. Sometimes it's a matter of choice, but more often than not, it's because they didn't have the right stuff.

> Finances—Okay, here's one that most people think they know everything about, but in reality, it's where most businesses begin to fail.

The Right Stuff: What Makes a Great Manager

Great managers are great leaders. History is filled with examples of great leaders, not only in the business world, but in all facets of human existence. Think about your favorite leaders, and why they are your favorites. What characteristics do they portray? How do you compare to them? If you find yourself not measuring up, what do you need to do to reach the high standards their examples have set for you?

Great managers believe in themselves. If you don't believe in yourself, how can you expect others to? In order to be a great manager, you have to lead from the inside. Be confident that you can do the job, and you will inspire others.

Great managers are organized. If you have trouble finding your car keys every day, it doesn't mean you are not organized. But a great manger must have excellent organization skills in order to lead others.

Great managers respect others. A good manager will just tolerate the people around him or her, but a great manager will embrace others, show the utmost respect for them, and even rely upon them for support.

Great managers know their business. Great managers will take the necessary time to learn as much as possible about how the business operates. But they will not interfere with the people whom they have hired to do a particular job.

> A great manager will embrace others, show the utmost respect for them, and even rely upon them for support.

Management Means Constant Change

There's an old saying that goes something like this: A baby is the only person who likes change. And there is a lot of truth in that statement, because many people don't normally accept change with grace and excitement. Lots of us would rather keep things "status quo" and not rock the boat. Change? Are you kidding?

Change does happen. It happens every minute of every hour of every day of the year. Change is constantly happening, and it takes a great manager to stare change in the face and know what to do with it. An employee may see change and not know how to handle it, but as a great manager it is your job to guide that employee and help him or her make the necessary adjustments to meet the challenges associated with change.

Dealing with change may not always make you the most popular person on the job, however. You have to remember that being a great manager means grabbing the constant change by the horns and letting it know who's in charge. Sometimes you have to make a decision that goes against what everyone else is wanting. It won't win you any friends, but it will reaffirm your skills as a manager.

Take This Quiz to See How You Rate When It Comes to Dealing with Change

1. I recognize that change is a fact of life.
2. I know that people, as a rule, don't deal well with change.
3. I will do what it takes to help people cope with change.
4. I stare change in the face and only blink when necessary.
5. I understand that dealing with change is part of what makes a great manager.

If you answered "Yes" to all five questions, congratulations, you have the potential for being a great manager who is ready to deal with any type of change on the job. If you answered "No" to any of the questions, don't worry, these concepts can be acquired simply through recognizing their value and lots of practice and experience.

Setting and Reaching Goals

As a manager, where do you stand on the issue of goals? Are you willing to sit around and watch people go through the paces of work each day, with no real goals in mind? Or are you the type of manager who really doesn't have any goals for yourself?

The Secret to Implementing Change

Employees will almost always reject change in the workplace. It doesn't matter how or why a change will take place. It's just human nature, and workers will cringe when they find out a procedure has been changed, or a new policy has been adopted. The secret to successfully implementing change in the workplace is to involve the employees at every level. Sit everyone down in a brainstorming session, and ask for their input. When they feel they have a part in the change, it will be easier for them to accept it.

If you happen to have set goals, and you run into a few speed bumps along the way, do those goals often seem to fall by the side of the road and die by themselves?

Walt Disney had a goal when he was young. He thought he wanted to work at a newspaper. When Walt Disney tried to get a job as a newspaper reporter, he was told he wasn't creative enough and that he lacked imagination. Can you imagine? The man who brought the world Mickey Mouse, Donald Duck, and Disneyland was told he lacked ideas. Luckily for the world, Walt didn't let his failure to reach his initial goal discourage him.

How about you? If you were in Walt's shoes way back then, and someone told you that you lacked the right stuff, would you have thrown in the towel and settled in for a long life of mediocrity? Hopefully not. In order to be a great manager, you can't let failures, setbacks, disappointments, heartaches, or any other problem keep you from rising to the top.

> Do you keep a written record of what it is you are trying to accomplish?

When Setting Goals Ask Yourself Several Questions

1. Have I recorded my goals? Do you keep a written record of what it is you are trying to accomplish? Many successful managers actually keep a goal log, where they can record their goals, and what it takes to reach them.
2. How often do I reassess my goals? Sometimes goals will change as time goes by. Make sure you re-examine your goals to see if any changes are necessary.
3. Do my goals match the goals of everyone else in the business? Is everyone on the same track? Are we all working toward the same result?
4. Am I prepared to do whatever it takes to meet my goals? When the going gets rough, will you hang on and make necessary course adjustments? Or will you get off course, and end up somewhere else?
5. What steps am I taking to help others in the business meet their goals? A great manager is also a great encourager, so make sure you are helping others meet their goals as well.

When big goals are reached, it's a cause for a celebration. Break out the champagne, blow up the balloons, push back the desks, and turn on the music and dance. Or, if you prefer, you can celebrate in a less flashy method. Whatever you do, it's important to celebrate when the big goals are met. Why? Because it gives everyone a sense of a job well done and it makes people feel like all of the toil they went through to meet that goal was worth all of their hard work and effort.

If you don't celebrate goals, then it will be more difficult to encourage and inspire others—even yourself for that matter—to move on to the next level. How can you expect anyone to reach for the stars and want to keep reaching higher if you don't acknowledge their accomplishments with a little fanfare?

Remember, too, that a happy employee is a motivated employee. So make sure you communicate your approval whenever a goal is accomplished.

Ways to Communicate Goals

Memos—You can send a written memo, or even an e-mail, letting the person know how pleased you are with his or her recent performance on a particular task or project.

In-person—Stop by their office, desk, or whatever their work area is and shake their hand. Make sure you smile and make eye contact. Above all, be sincere. You're bound to brighten their day.

Telephone call—Let your fingers do the walking, pick up the receiver, and say "thanks" and "congratulations."

Let the world know—Send out press releases, add something to your company's Web site, or hang a poster in the lobby. When people see how much they are appreciated, they will be encouraged to do their very best, all the time.

> When people see how much they are appreciated, they will be encouraged to do their very best, all the time.

Strategies for Reaching and Surpassing Goals

A great manager who wants involved and active workers needs to understand what real participation is all about. You need a plan, and you also need some strategies to help everyone reach and surpass their goals (don't forget to include yourself, as well). When workers feel they are participating, and that management is working with them, instead of against them, they will move forward with a better attitude.

Today, a company's workforce is more important to its profits and success than ever before. Better use of human resources is critical at a time when all other resources—energy, capital, equipment— cost more and more.

Worker participation can lead to positive results. Worker participation begins with a simple but powerful recognition by management that someone doing a particular job knows more about that job than the boss does. It continues with the understanding by both management and the worker that he or she wants to help solve the problems that stand in the way of doing the job well. With that recognition comes the most important motivation for enlarging a workers role: to make the business more successful.

And participation depends on information. What kind of a manager are you? Do you share information openly with other employees so that they are able to effectively do their jobs? Or are you the type of manager who goes by the old saying "information is power"? Information may indeed be power, but it's how that information is used and shared that makes the difference between a successful business and one that fails.

A common complaint among employees at many small businesses is that information doesn't sift down to them from the top, which makes them in turn fail in their efforts to share information with other workers. When workers lack information, it becomes a struggle between what they think they are supposed to do and what they are expected to do. How can you possibly expect employees to solve problems without all the facts?

Solving problems as part of a team is a key aspect of participation. It doesn't matter how small your business is. Employees want to be a vital part of the management team, so it's your job to help them

> Better use of human resources is critical at a time when all other resources—energy, capital, equipment—cost more and more.

meet that goal. Worker participation is a powerful motivating and learning experience for both employees and management. They can see immediately the results of their efforts, and they can respond faster with even better results the next time.

If you are having problems trying to figure out ways to set goals for yourself and your employees, why not invite everyone in for a brainstorming session? One of the most effective ways to find creative solutions is by brainstorming. Walt Disney was a strong believer in the process, so why not give it a try?

Basic Brainstorming Rules

- Limit your first brainstorming session to thirty minutes or less.
- Have someone write all ideas on a chalkboard or dry-erase board.
- Remember, there are no "bad ideas." Anything goes, and every idea is worth mentioning and recording.
- Even if you have only a partial solution to a problem, write it down. It could spark someone else in the group to come up with the rest of the idea or solution.
- It is difficult to work with a short list of ideas, so remind everyone that in the rules of brainstorming, quantity, not quality, is the rule of thumb.
- The latter half of the brainstorming session is usually better than the first half. It normally takes the first half of the session to get all the usual responses and habitual solutions out of the way. When these are removed, you are left with new and creative ideas and solutions.

Why not schedule a brainstorming session soon? You'll be pleasantly surprised at how everyone will want to participate and help the business succeed and move forward.

What is Your Management Style?

If you want to be a successful manager of your small business, you need the right management style. But what exactly is the right management

Goals Are for Winners

If you learn how to set goals, you are following in the footsteps of winners. Walt Disney had a goal: he wanted to build Disneyland, and wouldn't let anything get in his way. How about you? What goals have you set for yourself? If you haven't set goals in a while, start with small ones, and slowly increase as time goes on. As you see your goals being met, you will feel like a winner.

What if your management style doesn't mesh with the employees in your business?

style for you? And what if your management style doesn't mesh with the employees in your business?

First of all, realize that your particular management style is unique to you. It doesn't mean that you are the only person on the planet using that particular management style, it just means it's part of what makes you who you are. It determines whether or not the people around you will respond to your wishes and commands.

There are a variety of management styles, just like there are a variety of television shows. Let's take at a closer look:

Sitcom—Is your management style like a half-hour sitcom you watch every week? Are you running your business as if it were an episode of *Friends*? Is it complete with a laugh track, slap stick, and corny jokes? In other words, is your management style one that incorporates humor into everything you do with your business? Don't laugh, because many successful business mangers have modeled their management style after a sitcom.

Drama—Is your management style more in line with an hour-long drama series, like *NYPD Blue*? Do you operate your small business like a weekly drama? Are you too serious? And do you come across in an authoritative manner when you really don't mean to?

Mini-series—Is your management style more in line with a mini-series, like *Lonesome Dove?* In other words, do people have to keep coming back every week or every few days to get more information from you before they can do their jobs?

Soap opera—Is your management style more in line with a soap opera, like *General Hospital?* In other words, do you have so many plot lines going on at one time that it's difficult for employees to keep up with the information they really need to get their jobs done?

News program—Is your management style more in line with one of those twenty-four-hour-a-day news shows, like you see on CNN? In other words, can your employees tune in any time and within a few minutes know what is going on within your organization?

No matter what your management style is, you will always have to keep adapting your style to keep up with changes in the work-place (remember our section on changes earlier?), and with changes in your employees. When it really gets down to it though, there are really two types of management styles: old school and new school.

An example of an old-school management style would be a company that has plenty of rules that date back to the beginning of the organization. The company will be filled with middle managers, junior mangers, and vice presidents in charge of managers . . . the list goes on and on. Old-school management likes strict rules that can never be broken or bent, for any reason at all. They like meetings, and take pride in the number of meetings they can schedule each week. And in companies where old-school management is in charge, everyone knows their place. It's like a caste system; no one dares to venture into a place where they are not worthy. Old-school management also seems to frown on creativity. You would be hard pressed to find many brainstorming sessions taking place there.

New-school management tries to be: fresh, new, creative, innovative, cutting edge, and exciting. Have you figured out the difference yet? Old-school management style thinking had its place in history. But with the new century comes new rules, and new rules call for a new style of management. Which style do you think will lead your small business down the path to success?

Characteristics of New-School Managers

Successful small business managers who strive to be new-school managers exhibit these character traits:

> **Desire for responsibility**—New-school managers feel a personal responsibility for the businesses they manage. They are not afraid of responsibility, and are not afraid of delegating tasks when it becomes necessary.

Learn How to Duplicate Success

Everyone wants to be successful, so why not duplicate successful management styles that you have learned and have been exposed to over the years? Think about the managers you have worked under. There have no doubt been good ones, bad ones, and down right ugly ones. Learn how to duplicate the successful management style of the good ones. Also, take care not to duplicate the habits of the poor managers.

Openness to risk taking—New-school managers aren't afraid to take risks. That doesn't mean they are reckless with resources and people; it just means they are willing to venture outside their comfort zone to make things happen.

High energy level—New-school managers have more energy than the average person. They have the incredible ability to work long hours and never seem to get tired. However, the really smart new-school managers have also learned to take care of themselves by eating right, sleeping enough, and exercising.

Flexibility—New-school managers could have the nickname "Gumby" because of their ability to be as flexible as they need to be. They are able to adapt to the changing demands of the business and the economy.

The right attitude—New-school managers are known to be upbeat and positive. In other words, they have the right attitude. They are always optimistic, and wouldn't hesitate to hunt down Moby Dick in a rowboat armed with only a harpoon and a fresh container of tartar sauce.

Managing in the New Millennium

Small business owners are in for a wild ride. But it's a ride that is filled with exciting times as the new century unfolds. Who can predict what the future will hold for you and your small business? Have you given it much thought? Do you have a plan in place? If that plan fails, do you have a backup?

As a small business owner, you are part of a majority. Did you know that over 95 percent of the businesses in the United States today are small businesses? And their contributions to the economy are important, not only in terms of the gross national product, but in the numbers of people they employ. Small businesses create more jobs than big businesses do, and in the mid-1990s they created 75 percent of the nation's new jobs.

> New-school managers aren't afraid to take risks. They are willing to venture outside their comfort zone to make things happen.

You should learn as much as you can about your business, your competitors, and most importantly of all, your employees. Working together as a team, you and your loyal employees have the ability to make things happen in a positive and winning manner. And when you combine that with a little common sense, you have no place to go but up. Yes, I did say common sense. Believe it or not, for some reason many small business owners seem to toss out their common sense when they open a business.

Listen to that inner voice, the one that is talking to you when you are not reading this book. It is the voice of reason, your intuition, your gut instinct—whatever you want to call it. Just make sure you listen to it.

Learn how to manage people effectively, and the majority of your problems will never materialize at all. But realize, too, that no business owner can do everything on their own. So, take a lesson from other successful small business owners and surround yourself with the people you need to make your business succeed in the new millennium.

Achieving business success takes time, effort, and a lot of imagination. Make sure you have the right combination and you will be doing everything possible to make your business a winner.

> Learn how to manage people effectively, and the majority of your problems will never materialize at all.

For more information on this topic, visit our Web site at www.businesstown.com

Organization 101

Chapter 2

Try a Thirty-Day Experiment

If procrastination has been a problem for you, then try a thirty-day experiment. Behavior experts have proved that if people can change their behavior for thirty days in a row, then that behavior will become the norm. In other words, if you have been procrastinating really badly, pick one or two areas that have been bugging you, and for thirty days make a concentrated effort to "get the job done." At the end of the thirty days you will no doubt feel good that you have put that area of procrastination to rest.

Stop Procrastinating and Start Managing

Procrastination gets every small business owner into trouble sooner or later, and it's also one of the top stress producers in your life. Oh, but how easy it is to put things off. See how taking the attitude of "I'll deal with it tomorrow" is so easy to do? The problem is, however, unlike Little Orphan Annie's famous song, "Tomorrow," the procrastinator's tomorrow never really gets here. And procrastinating can become a very bad habit.

Why Small Business Owners Might Procrastinate:

- It is easier to think about dealing with an unpleasant problem or situation later, rather than tackling it head on, and handling it when it warrants attention.
- By putting off a decision, you don't have to face rejection if someone doesn't like your idea or performance.
- You feel as if you shouldn't have to do the task, and that someone else should be responsible for getting it done.

The list goes on and on. What's your reason for procrastinating, and were you even aware that it's affecting your business—and your bottom line? Remember the old saying, "The longest journey begins with the first step?" Well, the same principle applies to overcoming the problems of procrastination. You have to start at the beginning. You need to adopt the attitude of "be faithful, start now." In other words, you need to put aside your procrastination habit NOW. There is no other way to put it, other than by saying "just do it."

Tips to Help Overcome the Procrastination Bug

- Reward yourself when you complete a task that you have been procrastinating doing. Treat yourself to something special like a movie. Find something that motivates you, and use it.
- If rewarding yourself doesn't seem to work for you, try the other end of the spectrum: punish yourself. Tough love

sometimes works for different people. Tell yourself that unless you complete that task you've been putting off lately, that you won't be able to watch your favorite television show. Or you will have to pay a fine. Or come up with something else that you can use as your punishment. In other words, whatever works for you, use it.

- Use the "I Can" approach. The "I Can" approach will help boost your self-esteem and make you put the tasks you have been procrastinating about down on paper. Buy yourself a small notebook that will fit into your pocket, briefcase, or purse. Or use an index card, or even one of those new, fancy electronic organizers. Make two columns; in the left column, record the task you have been putting off completing. In the right column, record when you completed the task. Check your "I Can" notebook daily, and make sure you take whatever steps are necessary to get the job done.

No More Messy Desks

What does your desk look like these days? Is it nice and neat, with everything filed and organized the way it should be? Or has it been days, or even weeks, since you've seen the desk top? You are not alone, my friend. The messy desk syndrome has been around for some time now, and it's striking when you least suspect it would.

Sooner or later it happens. You pile up a few pieces of paper on your desk. Then the mail arrives, and you toss in into yet another pile, promising yourself, "I'll look at that later today." Add some catalogs, files, purchase orders, your beeper, several magazines that you need to read to catch up on what's happening in your line of business, and you have the average business owner's desk.

Sooner or later, clutter and disorganization invades everyone's life. Face it, we live in a world filled with stuff and things, and when stuff and things are allowed to pile up, disorganization is the result. All of a sudden, when you're in a hurry and need an important telephone number, or a file with the latest sales projection figures, you won't be able to lay your hands on them.

> The "I Can" approach will help boost your self-esteem and make you put the tasks you have been procrastinating about down on paper.

Excuses for a Messy Desk

- I can't file this right now, because I know I'll need to review the information really soon.
- There's an important article in this trade journal that I just have to read later today.
- I have got to keep this important telephone number handy.
- I'll just stack these purchase orders here and review them as soon as I have time.

And the list of excuses goes on and on. What's your favorite excuse for having a messy desk? Let's review the list, and offer some solutions that would have nipped the "messy desk syndrome" in the bud.

There Are No Excuses

- In the case of the "I can't file this right now, because I'll need to review the information really soon," get *real*. The solution: Do it now, because if you don't, before you know it, there will be six other files waiting in line. Then what will you do?
- In the case of "There's an important article in this trade journal that I just have to read later today," then for crying out loud, tear out the article and throw away or file the rest of the publication. One article takes up a lot less room than an entire magazine or trade journal. (Slip the article you want to read into a special folder in your brief case, and if you commute to work on the train or bus, it will give you something to read.)
- In the case of "I have got to keep this important telephone number handy," how handy do you think it will be when it becomes buried under a pile of debris later on in the day as other files and papers become stacked on your desk? If you have an "important" telephone number, take time NOW to place it in your Rolodex, Palm Pilot, or address book. And later when you need to retrieve it in a hurry, you won't have

> Do it now, because if you don't, before you know it, there will be six other files waiting in line. Then what will you do?

to sift through dozens of phone messages, Post-it notes, and memos that will have found their way to your desktop.

- In the case of "I'll just stack these purchase orders here and review them as soon as I have time," make time NOW. There's no time like the present. Remember, "be faithful, start now." Get it done while it is fresh in your mind. If you put off this important task now, how will you ever be able to handle it later when other important tasks are all shouting, "handle me now!"?

Just How Organized Are You? Take Our Quiz and Find Out

Do you consider yourself an organized business owner? Well, take our quiz and discover just how organized or unorganized you really are. Answer "Yes" or "No" to the following questions:

1. I file things immediately when I receive them.
2. I know exactly where everything is in my office.
3. I can find important telephone numbers in sixty seconds or less.
4. I regularly weed through useless papers that come across my desk each day.
5. I plan ahead and am always on time for appointments.
6. I schedule some free time each and every day.
7. I never let procrastination affect my work or personal life.
8. I am a wizard of time management.
9. I am always writing myself notes and lists so I do not forget anything.
10. I delegate tasks that can be delegated to free up time for me to handle other issues at my business.

If you answered "Yes" to all ten questions, congratulations, you are a very organized person. If you are like most business owners, however, it is doubtful that you got 100 percent correct.

If you answered "No" to five or more questions, you need some help becoming organized. There's no shame in being unorganized. The real shame, however, comes if you fail to act upon it.

File It Now

If you are suffering from the "messy desk syndrome," chances are you are handling mail, memos, faxes, reports, etc., more than one time. As soon as you get a document, assign it a resting place. File it, read it, pass it on, toss it out, or sign it. Do something about the paperwork that attacks you everyday.

Tips for Becoming a More Organized Business Owner:

- Don't put off becoming organized any longer.
- Do your worst job first, and it will be downhill from there.
- If you are faced with an overwhelming task, remember the saying "Inch by inch, it's a cinch." Break large jobs down into smaller, more manageable tasks, and they will be easier to accomplish.
- Stop hoarding papers. Read them once, and file them, or pass them on to someone else to handle.
- Get your employee files updated; and keep them updated.
- Have your accountant go through your files and put records into storage that are no longer considered active and that don't need to be lying around the office, getting in the way of everything.
- Empty your IN basket each day.
- Empty your OUT basket each day.
- Delegate tasks whenever possible.
- Remember to schedule some free time for yourself each and every day.
- Keep a positive attitude.
- Get rid of gadgets and gizmos that are just cluttering up your workspace.
- Handle a piece of paper only once.
- Review subscriptions to magazines and trade journals, and cancel any ones that you really don't need. (Remember that many publications now have Web sites with current issues posted.)
- Read a book on how to get better organized.
- Return telephone calls the same day you receive them.
- Return e-mail messages that need a response. Delete others that are just of an informational nature, otherwise, your inbox will become cluttered and unorganized.
- Don't pout over any mistakes you make. Learn from them, but keep looking forward.
- Take a day off now and then.
- Learn how to listen to other people without interrupting.
- Set goals.
- Dream a little each day, and enjoy your life.

> Stop hoarding papers. Read them once, and file them, or pass them on to someone else to handle.

How to Organize Your Business for Success

The best way to help your small business to succeed is to become as organized as possible. Organization is a key to your success, so it's imperative that you strive to find a way to organize your business so that you can enjoy the fruits of your labor.

One way to organize your business is to develop a short-range plan and a long-range plan. With both plans, you can spell out step-by-step what will take place, what your goals are, and how you plan to meet them. By putting your short-range and long-range plans down on paper, you are getting a chance to see the big picture. You can look for possible "speed bumps" that may become obstacles to your success, and then come up with creative solutions to destroy those speed bumps before they materialize.

Put together a team to help you create both plans. The team can be made up of your most creative and imaginative employees. Hold brainstorming sessions to develop the plans you feel will benefit your small business. Proper planning takes time, but don't fall into the trap of holding meeting after meeting without moving forward. If you don't move forward with your plans, your employees will quickly get bored and wonder why their time is being wasted.

So organize yourself and your small business for success. Take whatever steps are necessary to see your plan through. Don't let anything get in your way.

> Organization is a key to your success, so it's imperative that you strive to find a way to organize your business so that you can enjoy the fruits of your labor.

Time Management Techniques for Super Managers

How are your time management techniques these days? Are you one of those rare people who seem to have it all together, and get everything done that needs to be accomplished—and still have time left over at the end of the day?

Or are you like one of the millions of business owners who frantically goes from task to task, wondering just where in the heck the time went? Small business owners have a lot of responsibility these days, just keeping their company in the black. Every day brings new

Background Noise

Did you know that some people actually get more work done when there is music playing softly in the background? But other people find that same music so distracting they find it difficult to concentrate. If you have employees who work well with music in the background, encourage them to play a radio, but not loud enough to disturb others around them. Corporations have experimented with so-called "elevator" music for years, and have found that some employees can listen and work at the same time.

challenges, and every day it seems as if there's never enough time to meet those challenges.

Solutions for Managing Your Time

So what's the solution? Do more at a faster pace? Do you do your job while walking the baby, drive while talking on your cell phone, or eat lunch at your desk while holding a meeting and reviewing paperwork in front of you?

Actually, the best advice is just the opposite of what you would expect: do less, and slow down. Yes, you read that correctly. Before you reach for that cell phone the next time you're in the car, think twice. If you slow down, you will actually be more productive, more creative, and even healthier. You see, to beat the clock on the wall, our biological clocks speed up in ways that could lead to heart disease, high blood pressure, high cholesterol, depressed immunity, headaches, and stomach problems. In short, the faster you work, the harder it is on you and your health.

It's really your attitude about time that is the problem. People who are time-pressured are probably at risk for heart disease because they are no doubt angry and hostile as they race to beat the clock and meet yet another impossible deadline. Even Type A personalities (you know, the ones who aren't happy unless they're racing at breakneck speed) can be trained to slow down. A critical insight for stressed-out, time-pressured business owners is to realize that their sense of time urgency does not help them succeed. Instead, it actually works against them, and when they fail, they continue on with their cycle of misery.

Perceptions of Time

How well do you perceive time? Time orientation is one of the most influential factors in human behavior, yet most people are unaware of it. Here's a test for you: Sit back, relax, close your eyes, and have someone say "go." Now see if you can determine how long it takes for a minute to pass. You can time yourself, but it's better if you have someone else do it for you. Go ahead. Try it. Then come back to this passage.

If you're like many small business owners, you probably didn't even make it to thirty seconds before you thought a minute had passed. In fact, if you put ten busy people to this test, I'm willing to bet that most of them wouldn't even last for fifteen seconds before they thought that a minute had passed.

Think about it. At this very moment, in businesses everywhere, men and women are checking their watches and glancing at the clock on the wall—only to discover that they are late for their next appointment. If you race the clock, you are certain to lose. But you can turn time from an enemy into a friend by simply slowing down. We'll address some additional time management techniques in Chapter 19.

Personal Planners: The Good, the Bad, and the Ugly

Do you make a plan each and every day? Or are you one of those business owners who fails to plan? Failing to plan translates into "planning to fail." That's right. If you don't start out each day with a plan of action as to what will take place, you will end up going from task to task, never really accomplishing anything.

Not everyone will plan the same way, or even at the same pace. But the important thing is to PLAN. Put your thoughts down on paper. Or add them to your Palm Pilot. Or maybe you prefer to use different colored Post-it notes. Whatever works for you, just make sure that you do something.

There are so many personal planners on the market today, it would take an entire book just to feature them. So take a trip to your local office supply store, and check out their inventory. Find a personal planner that you think will work for you. Buy it. Use it. Experiment with it. If it doesn't work, don't whine, just pick up a new one. Just remember to plan. You'll be glad you did.

Personal Planners

The best advice you can find about personal planners is to ask other people what types of planners they are using, and why they like them. There's nothing better than a word-of-mouth recommendation to find one that you will enjoy using. But, just like with movie reviews, heed advice carefully, and also remember that the final decision rests with you.

For more information on this topic, visit our Web site at www.businesstown.com

The Art of Managing People

People Skills
Rank High

Did you know that people skills
rank very high on a scale of
traits that executives look for in
their managers? If you think
your people skills are a bit rusty,
consider reading a book or
attending a workshop or seminar to learn new ways to become
a "people person." Once you've
honed those people skills, you'll
be ready for anything.

Without People Skills, You're Dead in the Water

Have you ever considered yourself to be an artist? Now, that might be a strange thing for a small business owner or manager to think about, but in reality, you are an artist who is in control of a business. And that business is made up of people. So it's very important that you, as an artist, can paint the right strokes on your canvas to come up with the finished picture that you have been hoping for.

As an artist, you have the ability to create a successful business environment that will allow everyone to work together toward a common goal. Hopefully, that goal is the success of your small business.

The law of cause and effect tells us that for every action there is an equal and opposite reaction. We only get back what we put in. The same rule can be applied to managing people. As you probably know by now, managing people can be a real challenge. In fact, I'm willing to be that 90 percent of the problems you encounter each week in your business are people problems.

Unfortunately, it's a fact of life when working with people. Some people will be happy, some people will be sad. Some people will be cooperative, while some people will work against you. Some people will be hard workers, and some people will hardly work.

It's your job to determine what makes those people tick, and do everything in your power to help them do their job the way they are supposed to. It takes psychological effort to learn how to manage people, that's for sure.

Things a Good Manager Needs to Be or Have

Understanding–You must learn what it is like to walk in someone else's shoes before you can judge them. So keep that in mind when dealing with people at your own small business.

Listening skills–When is the last time you really listened to someone when they were talking to you? Did you give them your full, undivided attention, or was your mind thinking about five other different things? And if you are listening, do you know what it is that those people are really trying to tell you?

Leadership—If you are not an effective leader, how do you expect to ever be able to manage people? People are looking for good leaders to help guide them, so make sure your leadership skills are topnotch and in order.

A sense of humor—Let's face it, no one likes working for a sourpuss, so don't be one. Make sure your sense of humor is in good working order if you expect to be a good people manager. Before you know it, your sense of humor will rub off onto your employees, and your working environment will be a fun and happy place.

Common sense—You'll need more than your fair share of common sense if you ever expect to be a good manager of people. For some unknown reason, many small business owners and managers seem to toss their common sense out of the window, and then when things go wrong, they wonder what happened. Use common sense and you will prevail.

A sense of fairness—This is an important aspect and should never be overlooked or tossed aside. Employees all want to be treated fairly when they are at work. Think of them as if they were your own small children.

Honesty—No one wants to work for a dishonest boss, so be honest and ethical in all of your business dealings. Think about your own situation; would you want to stay and work for a boss who is not an honest one?

Communication skills—In addition to being a great listener, as mentioned previously, you will also need to be a great communicator. People thrive on information these days, and in order to keep the flow of information moving forward, you need to be a communicator of that information. Use memos, meetings, and e-mail to pass this information along.

Use common sense and you will prevail.

A sense of encouragement–You need to play the role of the encourager in your small business. Employees will need your input and encouragement from time to time in order to be successful, so be prepared to fill that role.

Ability to delegate–There will be times in the life of your small business when you will need to delegate tasks to some of your employees. Be prepared for that day, and be prepared to turn over responsibility to others when it is called for. (See Chapter 4 for additional information on the art of delegation.)

Organizational skills–While it is true that some people will thrive on chaos, most people prefer to work in an organized environment. How are your organizational skills? Do you consider yourself organized? If not, take whatever steps are necessary to organize yourself, and success will follow.

Creativity–How creative are you? The more creative you are, the easier it will be to be a good people-manager. Creativity will help you problem solve by coming up with several solutions to the same problem. And because many of your problems will be people related, it's good to have a sense of creativity to help you out.

Positive attitude–Let's face it, no one wants to work for a doom-and-gloom type of manager. So when is the last time you had an attitude check? Is your attitude a positive one, or does it need some work? People respond better to a positive attitude than a negative one, so start wearing your positive one to work NOW.

> You need to play the role of the encourager in your small business.

Why Employees Do What They Do

Ever wonder why your employees act the way they do? Well, it should come as no surprise to you that because people are people, they all come with their own agenda. Some agendas will be proudly displayed, while others will be kept hidden.

It's these agendas that often motivate people to act the way that they do. Your job, then, as a super manager, is to take their agenda and make sure it meshes with your own company's agenda. In other words, you need to make sure that everyone is working together toward a common goal. When everyone is busy with their own agenda, then the only things that get taken care of are those things they are interested in.

Sometimes employees will do things that will absolutely drive you crazy and you'll wonder why you ever hired them in the first place.

Some Behavioral Traits of Which You Should Be Aware

They are jealous—Sometimes one employee may be jealous of another employee who recently received a promotion. Or it can even be unrelated to work. Maybe they are jealous of a coworker's new car.

They have low self-esteem—Employees with behavior problems often have low self-esteem. They don't think they are worthy, and have a "why bother?" attitude when it comes time to doing their work.

They are critical of others—Sometimes employees will be too critical of everything at work. They will constantly berate other employees and the work they have completed. Or they will be critical of the boss, which is not a very smart thing for them to be doing.

They are feeling guilty—For some unknown reason, some employees who exhibit bad behavior feel guilty about something else they have done in their past. Until they get over that feeling of guilt and move on with their lives, they will probably always have problems.

They are angry—Many people have anger management problems, and when those problems follow them into their place of employment, trouble is sure to surface sooner or later. Angry employees can affect your bottom line, as well

Be a Friend and a Leader

If you think an employee is behaving badly because of a personal problem, it's best to let the employee know you do sympathize with his or her problem, but you also must stress that he or she has a job to accomplish. Be supportive, but be a leader at the same time. Offer any creative solutions that you can think of to help employees in their times of distress, no matter how small you think their personal problems may be. Remember, to the person who is having a problem, it is a very big deal.

as making it uncomfortable for everyone else who has to work with them.

They are depressed–Depression is a problem for many people, and depressed people are not productive employees. Unless they seek treatment for their problems, don't expect things to get better.

They have health issues–Unfortunately, people with health issues may have problems getting their job done. If an employee is having a health problem, do what you can to help him or her get help.

> Why do some employees seem as if they are always putting in the extra effort, going the extra mile to get their job done, while other employees barely get by?

What Motivates Employees to Excel

Have you ever given any thought to what actually motivates an employee to excel? In other words, why do some employees seem as if they are always putting in the extra effort, going the extra mile to get their job done, while other employees barely get by? The reason employees, or any people for that matter, behave in a particular way is called their motive. So it's your job to help provide a motive for your employees to want to do their very best.

Throughout history there have been many explanations as to what really motivates employees, and one of the more popular theories was developed by the psychologist Abraham Maslow.

In Maslow's theory, which he called his hierarchy of needs, he determined that when one level of a person's needs is satisfied, then the next level has the greatest influence on that person's behavior. This theory has helped many small business owners and managers have a better understanding of their employees' behavior in the work place.

Maslow's Theory of the Hierarchy of Needs

Physiological needs must be met–Includes food, water, air, rest, sex, and shelter

Safety needs must be met–Includes protection from physical harm, and freedom from fear of deprivation

Social needs must be met–Includes friendships, affection, and acceptance

Esteem needs must be met–Includes self-respect, respect of others, recognition, and achievement

Self-actualization needs must be met–Includes a person's realization of their own individual potential, creative talents, and personal future fulfillment

How to Implement Maslow's Theory of the Hierarchy of Needs

If you were to use Maslow's theory, how would it compare to how you are meeting the needs of your employees? Let's look at each one and see how you can use them to help motivate your workers.

1. Hopefully, you are providing a working environment that meets all of their physiological needs. It doesn't take much to provide a cafeteria or lunch room, along with adequate restroom facilities.
2. The safety issue is just basic common sense. If your employees can't feel safe at work, then you must be doing something wrong. Over the past few years there has been an increase in the number of workplace shootings and violence. Make sure your workplace is a safe one.
3. The social needs can be tricky. You want your employees to have a sense of social acceptance, but you don't want them to be socializing all of the time instead of working. So make sure you provide special times when socializing can take place. For example, you can have a gathering in the lunch room or cafeteria to celebrate someone's birthday, or other special event, such as a wedding or a birth.
4. The esteem needs should be an easy one for small business managers. If people want to have a sense of self-respect,

> How are you meeting the needs of your employees?

recognition, and achievement, then it's your job to provide just that. Treat your employees with respect, let them know when they have done a good job, and reward them for their achievements, and they will return the favor by being loyal and hard-working employees for you.

5. The self-actualization needs can also be easy for you to fulfill. When you see a person who is having difficulty performing his or her job, ask yourself this question: Does that person really have the skills and interest level in order to be able to perform that task well? For example, if you have a payroll clerk who is having trouble working with numbers, but seems to be a creative person, then move that person to a more creative position. Creative people cannot stand to work at the same job, day in and day out, all year round. So a creative person who is forced to work in accounting is really like a fish out of water. Throw that person back into the water, and let him or her experience the opportunity to be a loyal and hard-working employee.

> When you see a person who is having difficulty performing his or her job, ask yourself this question: Does that person really have the skills and interest level in order to be able to perform that task well?

Other Motivational Factors

Frederick Herzberg, another psychologist, also developed his own explanations as to what motivates employees. He suggested that satisfaction and dissatisfaction on the job come from two different sets of factors. One set is refereed to as the "motivating" factors and the other set is called the "hygiene" factor.

The motivating factors include the following:

- Recognition
- Achievement
- Responsibility
- Opportunity for advancement
- The job itself

He theorized that those motivating factors were all related to internal satisfaction, and that they had the power to influence the employees to improve their performance.

The hygiene factors include the following:

- Salary
- Company policies
- Working conditions
- Relationships with other employees

Herzberg theorized that the hygiene factors must be present in order to prevent job dissatisfaction, but that it is really the motivating factors that influence the employees to do the best job that they possibly can.

Your job is to develop a work environment where the employee meets the needs of your business, and your business meets the needs of the employee. When that happens, a successful business environment results, and everyone is working towards the same common goal.

Incentives and Rewards

What can your small business do to help your employees want to put forth their best effort? For one, you can use a system of incentives and rewards, which has helped many a small business owner in the past.

Suggestions to Consider as Incentives and Rewards

Profit sharing–They say that money isn't everything, but there's nothing like good old-fashioned profit sharing to motivate employees to perform at their best. Come up with a profit sharing plan that works best for your small business. The first step is to gather input from your employees themselves. Ask them how they feel about such a plan, and ask them for their ideas to help make it succeed and be profitable for both themselves and the business.

Time off–There isn't an employee on the planet who isn't always looking forward to his next day off (with pay, that is). So why not build in some time off as a reward and incentive for doing well? Again, ask for input from your employees to

Survey Your Employees

If you want to know what the majority of your employees feel would be a good incentive and reward, consider drafting a questionnaire. Keep it simple; just a few questions should give you the results you are looking for. You will end up with a very good list to choose from to create an incentive and reward program that will work at your business.

see what they feel is a good plan (tied into employee performance) for offering a day or two off with pay.

Trips to exotic locations–People who work in sales for major corporations are used to this type of incentive and reward. Many of the big companies send their best salespeople on a paid vacation to some exotic destination. And it's those annual vacations that those salespeople look forward to, so it works as a powerful motivating factor to make them want to do their best and excel at their job. So what can your small business do? You can come up with a plan that works for your budget and corporate culture. Remember to include your employees in any discussion, because they will feel twice as motivated if they know they had a hand in creating this type of an incentive and reward plan.

Free merchandise–Who doesn't like to receive something that's free? So make sure you come up with a plan to give your employees some type of free merchandise. It can be something that your small business makes, or it can be something from an outside vendor. There are plenty of companies that specialize in employee incentive plans by offering a wide variety of merchandise in their catalogs. Survey your employees to see what it is that they would like as an incentive, then put your plan into action.

Employee of the month–Or employee of the quarter. Whatever works for your corporate culture, make sure you reward employees who excel above and beyond the call of duty by having a special award. For example, you can reward them with a special parking place, or hang their picture on a wall. Some companies even offer extra time off for employees who receive an employee of the month award. Again, you need to sit down and brainstorm with your employees to see what they would like, and then go from there.

> Remember to include your employees in any discussion, because they will feel twice as motivated if they know they had a hand in creating this type of an incentive and reward plan.

Money Isn't Everything

Remember the old joke about money not being everything? Well, here's a real puzzle for you. To an employee, money isn't everything, but at the same time, money is everything. Confused? You should be, because any time you factor money into an equation that concerns employee motivation and satisfaction, confusion is bound to result.

Employees want to feel as if they are being adequately rewarded for the job they are performing for your small business. But in addition to earning a fair hourly wage or salary, other factors are important to your employees. These include the following:

> These days health insurance is a very important benefit, and the more you can help your employees afford it, the more loyal and hard-working they might be for you.

Pension plans—Who doesn't worry about their financial future when they reach retirement age? Well, your employees are no different, and many will seek out a small business that can offer a pension or retirement plan. Pension plans are subject to approval by the Internal Revenue Service since they represent a business expense, so make sure you are doing things by the book before you proceed. You can get information about pension plans from local banks and other financial institutions.

Health insurance—These days health insurance is a very important benefit, and the more you can help your employees afford it, the more loyal and hard-working they might be for you. Small business owners can provide health insurance without going broke. Make sure you compare several plans before choosing the right one for you and your employees. And when rates go up each year (as they most surely will), shop around and see what type of deals another health insurance company might be willing to work out with you in order to get your business.

Life insurance—Life insurance is also an important benefit to many employees, especially ones that are working at small businesses. Make sure you shop around and compare plans carefully before signing on the dotted line.

Tuition refund—Some small businesses feel that it is important for their employees to be able to continue with their education. As an incentive, consider refunding all or part of the employees' tuition when they finish taking a course.

Paid vacations—Let's face it, we all need a vacation at least once a year. And if that vacation is a paid one, then it becomes a real benefit and a real incentive for an employee to work toward making that goal become a reality. Some businesses offer paid vacations that are based on the length of service of the employee. Ask your employees for their input and see what they think.

Leave of absence—In addition to complying with the Family Medical Leave Act, you might consider offering additional time off in the form of a leave of absence if special circumstances call for it. Survey your employees and seek their input on this topic, and see what type of program they think would work well for your small business.

> If you want your employees to excel, then be prepared to manage them for success, and not for failure.

Manage People for Success, Not Failure

If you want your employees to excel, then be prepared to manage them for success, and not for failure. Here are some tips to help you meet that goal:

Be a fair supervisor—Employees want to be treated fairly, and you must take the necessary steps to make sure they feel as if they are being treated fairly.

Keep an eye on morale—Morale at the workplace can be affected positively or negatively by an incident that might seem insignificant to you, but can be very important to your employees. Remember, a happy group of employees will do more and better work than an unhappy group.

Set an example—If you want your employees to work hard and succeed, then set an example by doing so yourself. Be a good role model and you will be doing your part.

Take responsibility for your actions—This means don't try and pass the buck. If something goes wrong and it's your fault, step up to the plate and take full responsibility for whatever it is that went wrong.

Maintain a positive attitude—They say that attitudes are contagious, so why not have a positive one that will be passed on to your employees? Keep a can-do type of spirit at all times, and you will be an inspiration to your workers.

Maintain your sense of humor—It doesn't mean you have to dress up like a clown to come to work (but it might help now and then), but keeping your sense of humor will go a long way in helping your employees to do well.

Acknowledge good work through praise—Everyone wants to hear "well done" now and then, so make sure you acknowledge any good work your employees have accomplished by telling them what a great job they are doing. Remember, when a worker feels good about himself and the job he is performing, he tends to do it better than an employee who hasn't been given any accolades in some time.

Give credit for ideas—If one of your employees comes up with a great idea, then by all means give that person the credit she deserves. Don't steal your employees' ideas and try and pass them off as your own. That type of behavior will surely backfire and cause more problems on the job than its worth.

> Attitudes are contagious, so why not have a positive one that will be passed on to your employees?

Managing people can be challenging, but at the same time it can be fulfilling and rewarding, both for you and your small business's bottom line.

The Right Attitude

If you want your employees to have the right attitude, make sure that yours is in check. Many employees will simply wonder, "Why should I worry about my attitude, when my manager has a lousy one?" Attitudes are contagious, so make sure you have one that is worth catching.

What's Your People Style? Take This Quiz and Find Out

1. I enjoy meeting new people and am at ease in new social situations.
2. People tell me I have a great sense of humor.
3. I always look for the best in people.
4. I believe that attitude is important in everyone.
5. I tend to lead by example.
6. People feel they can trust me.
7. I don't mind listening to people's problems.
8. I consider myself a fair supervisor.
9. I believe people are a company's biggest and best asset.
10. I believe that people should take responsibility for their actions.

If you said "Yes" to all ten statements, congratulations, because you are a certified People Person. If you said "No" to four or more statements, then you might need to brush up on your people skills in order to be a successful manager of people. Remember, people respond better to managers who are "people oriented." So if your skills need a little refresher course, then get your act together.

For more information on this topic, visit our Web site at www.businesstown.com

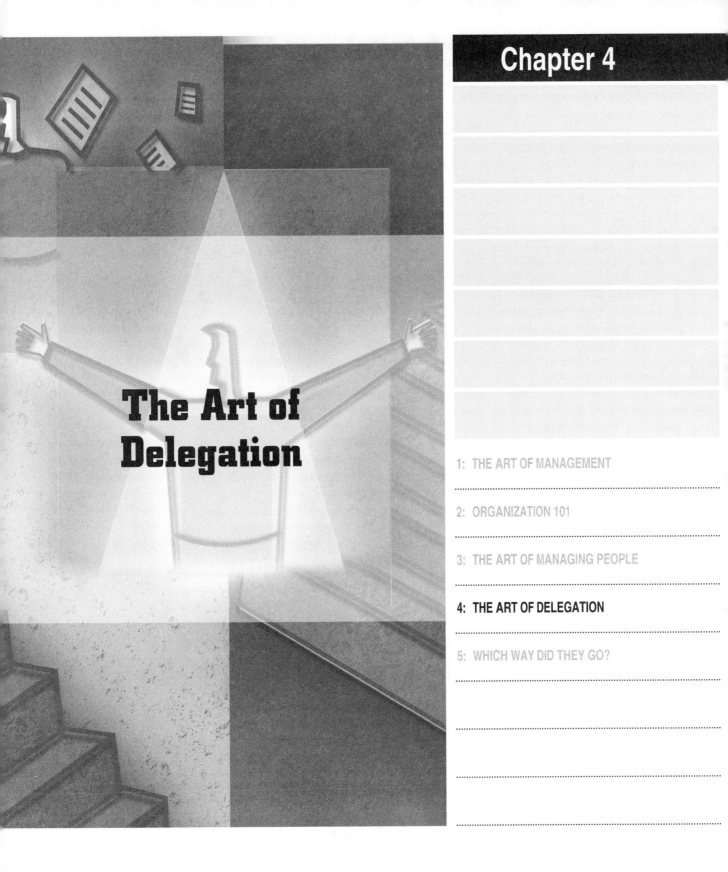

The Art of Delegation

Test Your Delegation Skills

When it comes to the fine art of delegation, most managers of small businesses fail miserably? Why? There are a variety of reasons why many small business managers are afraid to delegate. The most common ones include the following:

- Fear that the task will not be done right
- Fear that the task will not be done at all
- Fear that they will lose control of the project or task at hand
- Fear that no one will understand how complicated the task really is
- Fear that they will be perceived as a failure if the task doesn't get accomplished on time

Have you noticed the one common denominator yet? It's fear, plain and simple. Well, if you want to succeed in today's business climate, learning the fine art of delegation is a non-negotiable assignment. But delegating requires a manager to realize that there is more than one way to accomplish a task, and that sometimes an employee may have valuable input that will help everyone work toward a common goal.

As a busy manager you no doubt have many responsibilities and shouldn't expect to have to carry them all out all by yourself. You must guard against wasting your time when it can be spent on something more cost and time efficient. In other words, you must learn how to delegate.

> Delegating requires a manager to realize that there is more than one way to accomplish a task.

How Are You When It Comes to Delegating? Take This Quiz and Find Out

1. I am a firm believer in delegating, and practice it as often as possible.
2. I am able to delegate a task or project, and feel comfortable that it will be taken care of.
3. I encourage my employees to participate more by delegating tasks whenever possible.

4. I set goals for projects and then look for people who can assist me in carrying out those tasks.
5. I am a firm believer in teamwork.
6. I reward employees who perform well, and don't hesitate to delegate tasks to them during future projects.
7. I am not a control freak.
8. I am a firm believer in "leading from behind."
9. I have read all of the latest information about delegation.
10. I encourage delegation as part of our corporate culture.

Well, how did you make out? Hopefully, you scored a perfect ten and are already a wizard at delegating tasks to others. However, if you answered "No" on three or more questions, then you need to brush up on your delegation skills.

Fortunately, delegation skills are skills that can be taught, although at first some small business managers have trouble putting them into practice. Delegation involves passing responsibility of one task to another person, so you need to have some level of confidence in the person you will be delegating to.

> Fortunately, delegation skills are skills that can be taught.

Five Myths about Delegation

Over the years a number of rumors, falsehoods, and myths have surfaced about the fine art of delegation. Here are the top five myths about delegation today:

Delegation will cost me more time—Most small business managers who have yet learned to delegate anything at all mistakenly think that if they delegate a task it will cost them more time to get the project completed. Maybe they had a bad experience at one time in their life when they did delegate. Maybe an employee was supposed to prepare a large section of a report, but when that employee turned it in, the manager found out that it wasn't exactly what he or she was looking for. And the manager uses that one incident as an excuse for being afraid to ever delegate again.

Embrace Failure

If you are worried about delegation because you're afraid someone will fail, then you need to learn how to embrace failure. If someone fails, at least they tried. Failure gives people a second chance; they know where they went wrong, and they have an opportunity to correct their course and sail on to success.

Delegation will result in mistakes being made—Hey, no one is perfect, and yes, employees will sometimes make mistakes. But that doesn't mean you should use a mistake an employee made as an excuse for never delegating again. Develop confidence in your employees by starting out delegating small tasks, and then give them more responsibility in the future.

Delegation will keep me out of the loop—Well, how far you are kept out of the loop depends entirely on you. When you delegate a task, you're not saying, "Hey, here you go, hope everything works out for both of us." No. You need to establish some ground rules for keeping the lines of communication open among everyone in the delegation loop.

Delegation means I'm giving up my authority—Again, this depends on you. Simply because you are delegating a task, it doesn't mean that you are giving up your authority. After all, you are still the manager or boss who is in charge of the entire project. When you delegate, you do surrender some aspect of authority, but not the entire scope of it.

Delegation means that people will think I have nothing to do—Are you a manager who is afraid to delegate simply because your employees will think you have nothing to do? Well then put that fear aside because if you are as smart as you have your employees believing that you are, it's not a valid one. Delegation involves teamwork, so make sure everyone on the team knows who is responsible for what task, and that everyone knows who is in charge of the project.

Do You Know How to Delegate?

The smart manager learns how to delegate and delegate well. But what does it take to delegate to today's employees? Here are some tips to help you learn how to delegate with style:

Know when it's time to delegate–You have to decide early on when you are planning a project when it's time to delegate a task or tasks to other employees. Don't delegate too early on in the project, or people will get bored and lose sight of the goal they are trying to accomplish.

Know what aspect of a project to delegate–Once you have decided that it's time to delegate, you have to know what aspect of the project you will be delegating, and to whom you will assign each task. Make a list of things that need to be accomplished, and then decide if there is someone more skilled in a particular area who can get the job done.

Know how to select qualified and capable people–When it's time to delegate a task for a project, don't just pick the next employee who happens to pass you in the hallway. Select capable and qualified people to carry out these important responsibilities, and the project will succeed more smoothly.

Make sure you are communicating your desires–In other words, make sure that the people you are delegating a task to fully understand what it is that you need them to do. Make sure your instructions are explicit, and that no further explanations are required.

Be ready to offer help and support if it is needed–There will be times during the life of a project that people will need your help and support, so be prepared to be there for them. It is extremely important that your employees know and understand that they can approach you if they are having a problem. Don't do the job for them, just advise them on how they can best accomplish it.

Be ready to give credit when a job has been successfully done–Make sure that you acknowledge a job well done when your employees come through for you. Send them a memo, shake their hands, buy them lunch, or any other

> It is extremely important that your employees know and understand that they can approach you if they are having a problem. Don't do the job for them, just advise them on how they can best accomplish it.

combination of creative methods, just make sure you do it. Employees thrive on praise, and it also sets a standard for other employees when they see their coworkers being treated fairly and with respect.

The Five Steps to Effective Delegation

Effective delegation allows you as a manager to achieve your goals through your employees. However, effective delegation will be one of the most difficult challenges you will face as a manager. It means more than simply walking up to an employee and verbally telling them what you want and then walking away.

> Effective delegation allows you as a manager to achieve your goals through your employees.

1. **Preparing to delegate**–Planning your strategies ahead of time will go a long way in ensuring the success of any project that involves delegation. Get your battle plan ready before you proceed, and things will run a lot smoother.
2. **Start the delegation process**–Once you have planned your strategies for the project, the next step is to start the delegation process. Don't put this important step off any longer than you have to. When the time is right, delegate.
3. **Monitor the delegation process**–Once the delegation process has been put into motion, it's your job to monitor the whole process. The amount of monitoring you will have to do will really depend on the complexity and scope of the project. You can monitor everyone's progress by asking for a regular status report, by holding weekly project update meetings, or even by simply staying in touch via e-mail.
4. **Evaluate what has been delegated**–You want to make sure that everything that was delegated ran as smoothly as possible. One way to achieve this goal is by evaluating every aspect of what was actually delegated. Get feedback from everyone that was involved in the project, and ask them how they felt everything went.
5. **Reward everyone who was involved**–This can be a very important step so you don't want to skip it. Make sure you reward everyone who was involved in some aspect of the

delegation process. Throw a party, hand out certificates, shake their hands, but do something—or the next time people will wonder if all of their work is really worthwhile to you or the success of your business.

The Benefits of Delegation

The benefits of delegation are actually threefold. It offers benefits for the manager, benefits for the team of employees who performed the tasks, and benefits for the business itself.

Benefits for the Manager

At the top of the list of benefits for the manager is that it allows you to achieve more in less time. Because you did not have to complete an entire project on your own, that project took less time to accomplish. And with more time on your hands, you are free to take care of other aspects of your small business.

Benefits for the Team of Employees Who Performed the Tasks

By simply being involved in the delegation process, employees have an opportunity to improve their job skills, which will allow them to eventually assume greater responsibility. It also encourages employees to have a better understanding of what the business is all about, and it may also increase the enthusiasm that they have for their jobs.

Benefits for the Business Itself

If both the manager and the team of employees benefit separately from a successful delegation experience, then it stands to reason that the business itself also benefits. The business suddenly becomes more efficient, and there is a sense of accomplishment among the employees who all worked together toward a common goal. This will help your small business to be able to stand out among the crowd and to shine to your customers.

> If both the manager and the team of employees benefit separately from a successful delegation experience, then it stands to reason that the business itself also benefits

Helping Employees Who Resist Delegation

Believe it or not, you will encounter some employees in your organization who are not receptive to the delegation process. For whatever reason, these employees will fight you tooth and nail to keep from being a part of a project that requires their participation in a delegated task. Following are the most common reasons why some employees resist delegation:

Lack of incentive or reason to participate—This is the top reason why many employees resist delegation. For them, they are not really certain of their incentive to be an active and successful participant. They may not feel that the job is worth any extra time or effort that they have to put into the project. It's your job, then, as a super manager and super delegator, to convince those employees that they do have a valid reason for being part of the team. You must convince them that their work is worthwhile, and will help contribute to the overall success of the project. Use whatever incentives you need to help employees overcome their resistance to being a part of this successful team.

Lack of adequate training—They may simply feel as if they lack the necessary training to get a job done. Remember, perception is reality, and if people think they can't do something, then they have convinced themselves that it will never happen. Ask yourself if the employees you are delegating a project to have had the proper training. If they have, reassure them that they will do okay. But if they haven't had the proper training, then it's up to you to make sure they receive it before you proceed any further on the project.

Desire to avoid responsibility—Let's face it, people will be people. If people can get out of being responsible for something, chances are that they will at least try. So it's your job to convince those employees that they are up to the challenge and that they are responsible enough to pull it off.

Fear–An employee who is afraid of a project certainly won't embrace it with open arms and give it her best effort. Find out exactly what it is the employee is afraid of, and help her to alleviate those fears. Once she becomes a valuable part of the project team, she will feel better about the project and about herself.

Lack of trust–If employees cannot trust the manager that is in charge of a project, they will resist any efforts on your behalf to get them more involved in any aspect of it.

Encourage Delegation at All Levels

If delegation is a new process in your small business, remember to start out slowly, and give everyone a chance to participate. By encouraging delegation at all levels of employment, you are encouraging and promoting growth—not only for your employees, but for you and your business as well.

When Not to Delegate

There will come a time in every manager's career when he or she will simply not be able to delegate. Sometimes it just doesn't matter how often and how much you work with an employee; some of them will just never be able to handle the responsibility you set out for them.

Factors to Keep in Mind to Help You Decide When Not to Delegate

If an employee is close to retirement–Sometimes people have already "retired" even though they haven't left the building just yet.

If an employee has made it clear he is not happy with his job, and will be seeking new employment–Clearly, these employees will not be in a position to handle a delegated task very well.

If an employee is going through a personal crisis– Sometimes a family situation needs to be taken care of first. Counsel the employee, and see what you can do to help her.

If an employee is a temporary or a contract person– Again, sometimes workers have to have some type of vested interest in your business before they can claim any type of ownership for a particular project.

Delegate From Behind

Probably the most difficult job you will face as a manager is to learn how to delegate from behind. But what exactly does that mean? Well, to put it in simpler terms: you must be willing to delegate and let go. That is difficult for many people to do, because there will always be that fear deep inside of them that a particular project will fail if they are not involved in every aspect of it.

The sooner you learn how to delegate from behind, and can stop worrying about a project, the better off you will be. You will gain peace of mind, you can move on to other projects and concentrate on running your business, and your employees will gain confidence in themselves because you have trusted them to carry the ball and know that they will succeed.

Come up with a few strategies that will help you learn to let go as you delegate. Start out slowly, and increase delegated responsibilities as time goes by. Get feedback as often as you feel comfortable; but don't end up nagging your employees to death about every little task that they are involved in. Otherwise, it could backfire and you will end up in a worse situation than when you first started.

Secrets of Successful Delegation

As your small business grows, there will be times when you will need to delegate a task or an entire project to someone else. Even though many small business managers are reluctant to delegate, there are

> You will gain peace of mind, you can move on to other projects and concentrate on running your business, and your employees will gain confidence in themselves.

some things you can do to help you become a more successful manager who excels at delegation.

Tips to Keep in Mind

- Make sure that your employees are ready for delegation. If an employee is new to your organization and you haven't yet judged his skill level or loyalty, hold off for a while before delegating a major task to him. Instead, take smaller steps, and monitor his progress along the way.
- Make sure that your employees have enough information to do the job. Before starting any new project, develop a checklist and see to it that everything on the list is taken care of.
- Have clearly defined goals in mind before delegating any tasks.
- Be certain to keep lines of communication open at all times. If an employee has a question or a problem, she needs to know she can contact you with her concern.
- Have a specific timeline for the project before the delegation process begins. Don't just say that you need to get it done as soon as possible. Instead, draw up a timeline and let everyone know what is due and on what date it is due.
- Be certain that everyone knows who is responsible. The worst thing in the world that can happen is that no one knows who is in charge or who is responsible for the project. Make sure that each team member knows who they report to.
- Make sure everyone knows that resources are available. Before a project begins, make sure that everyone involved knows what resources are available to help them complete their part of the job.

The art of delegation is only as difficult as you make it. Learn how to delegate successfully, and you will be doing your part to help your small business to succeed at all levels.

Watch and Learn

If you are new to the art of delegation, consider observing someone else who is successful at it before you venture out on your own. Watch, listen, and learn. Remember, not everyone was born with the skills to be a good delegator. But with practice, you will become more efficient and comfortable with the whole process.

Why Some Managers Just Can't Delegate

As with every rule in life, there will be some managers that just will never learn how to delegate. Some people are simply wired differently, and that's okay. So if you are a manager who has tried and tried over and over again to delegate, but it's simply not working out for you, that's okay.

Stop trying to delegate. You may simply be one of those personality types who will never embrace the art of delegation. If that is the case in your situation, relax. Do what you can yourself, but don't kill yourself and destroy your business in the process.

If you are having trouble delegating, why not put someone else in charge of the delegation process? Some people thrive on chaos; some people thrive on delegation. Find your balance, your middle ground, and things will work out best for everyone involved.

If you are having trouble delegating, why not put someone else in charge of the delegation process? Some people thrive on chaos; some people thrive on delegation.

For more information on this topic, visit our Web site at www.businesstown.com

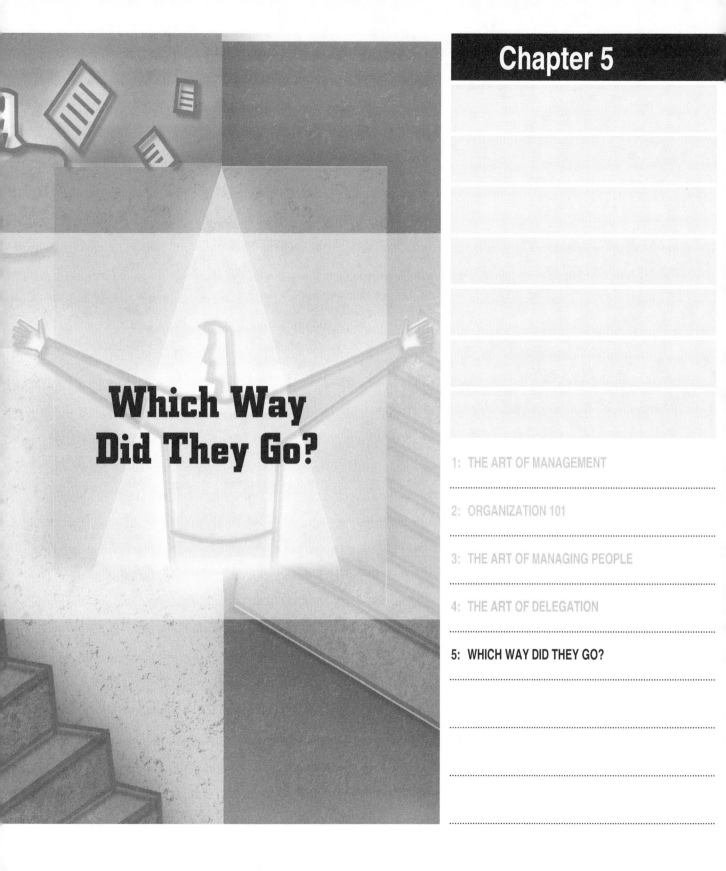

Which Way Did They Go?

I was attending a church retreat a few years ago and someone told this story:

It was lunch time in the downtown business district, and as I was getting ready to cross the street, I noticed a rowdy bunch of Boy Scouts running up the street toward me. They appeared to be laughing and having a good old time. Nothing seemed to be bothering them, and they looked as if they owned the world. I thought it was strange that they didn't appear to have an adult leader with them at the time.

When they reached the intersection where I was standing, they stopped and waited for the light to change. When the WALK sign appeared in large letters, they took off across the street and within a few seconds turned the corner and were out of my line of sight.

As I started to cross the street myself, I noticed an adult Boy Scout leader running toward me. He was clearly out of shape, and out of breath, but within a few seconds he was able to ask me if I had seen a group of Boy Scouts pass by this way.

I told him that I did. The scoutmaster seemed to get his second wind and promptly replied, "I'm their leader, which way did they go?"

> It's scary to think about the numbers of small business managers who scramble around each and every day saying the same thing, "I'm their leader, which way did they go?"

Which Way Did They Go?

"I'm their leader, which way did they go?" Scary thought, isn't it? It's bad enough to think about a scout leader losing a group of scouts on a busy city street in the downtown area at lunch time. But it's even scarier to think about the numbers of small business managers who scramble around each and every day saying the same thing, "I'm their leader, which way did they go?"

Stay in Control

Harry Truman once said this about the sign of a good leader: "I learned that a great leader is a man who has the ability to get other people to do what they don't want to do and like it."

That pretty much sums up what your philosophy should be when it comes to your style of management. You need to convince your employees that whatever job or task they are busy doing, they should embrace it and give it their best effort—even if they don't like doing it.

Great managers remove obstacles that get in people's way and keep them performing their job at their greatest level of excellence. But as Dwight D. Eisenhower once said, "You do not lead by hitting people over the head—that's assault, not leadership."

Test Your Management Skills

Answer "Yes" or "No" to the following:

1. I consider myself easy to get along with.
2. I let little interruptions interfere with my ability to manage.
3. I never get involved in office politics.
4. I think about goals, but never actually set any realistic ones.
5. I have never evaluated my own job performance.
6. I enjoy making presentations in front of people.
7. I have confidence in my ability to manage and lead people.
8. I don't like to write.
9. I try to be an organized person, but it seems I'm always too busy.
10. I have a set number of hours that I work each day, then I quit and go home.
11. I hate doing paperwork; most of it is a waste of my time.
12. I don't like change, especially in the workplace.
13. I can do several things at the same time.
14. I consider myself a good manager of money.
15. I consider myself computer literate.
16. I have a problem delegating.
17. I prefer to work alone.

Do You Know the Road?

How well do you know the employees you are responsible for? As a manager, it is imperative that you know the road that you expect them to travel. In other words, don't ask someone to walk in your shoes until you've made the journey yourself. Don't expect people to always know where they are supposed to go; it's your job to gently guide them towards the right road—the one that leads to success.

18. I hate to solve difficult puzzles.
19. I always have the right attitude.
20. I always look for the good in people and in situations.

Let's Look at Each Point Individually

Question 1–I consider myself easy to get along with. If you answered "Yes," then congratulations. If you answered "No," don't sweat it too much, because very few small business managers really consider themselves easy to get along with. If you have issues that are keeping you from getting along with your fellow employees, then identify those issues and deal with them before it's too late.

Question 2–I let little interruptions interfere with my ability to manage. If you answered "No," then congratulations. If you answered "Yes," you need to re-examine your time management skills and learn how to deal with unexpected interruptions–no matter how large or small they may be. It's a fact of life in the world of managers that interruptions will occur, and will occur more frequently than you want to think about. So take the time to learn how to deal with interruptions and move on with your schedule.

Question 3–I never get involved in office politics. If you answered "No," then congratulations. However, if you are one to keep out of office issues, then you need to take your head out from under the sand and get involved. It's a fact of life in the business world that office politics will take place on a daily basis. By ignoring the problems that occur and hoping that they will go away, you are allowing the problems to escalate and continue. Take a stand; become involved in whatever way you see fit.

Question 4–I think about goals, but never actually set any realistic ones. If you answered "No," and you do set

> If you have issues that are keeping you from getting along with your fellow employees, then identify those issues and deal with them before it's too late.

realistic ones, then congratulations. If you answered "Yes," then you have some work to do. As a successful small business manager, it is imperative that you have some sort of manageable goals to work toward. Remember the old saying, "If you fail to plan, you plan to fail."

Question 5—I never have evaluated my own job performance. If you answered "No," and you do evaluate your own job performance on a regular basis, then congratulations. However, if you have just been thinking you are doing just fine, then you have some work to do. How do you expect to ever evaluate your employees' performance if you never evaluate your own? If you want to be considered a super manager, then start leading by example, and give yourself your first performance evaluation. And remember, be honest; no cheating!

Question 6—I enjoy making presentations in front of people. If you answered "Yes," and you do enjoy making presentations in front of people, then congratulations. If not, then maybe you're in the wrong business. Every successful small business manager needs to feel comfortable making presentations in front of people. Especially when those people are your employees. If you come across as shaky and wishy-washy during a presentation to your employees, how do you expect them to respect you and follow you as their leader? Read a book, attend a workshop or whatever it takes to overcome your fear of making presentations in front of people.

Question 7—I have confidence in my ability to manage and lead people. If you answered "Yes," and have plenty of confidence that inspires people to follow you, then congratulations. If you answered "No," then you need to work on this issue immediately. Again, how can you expect your employees to respect you as a leader if you don't have the confidence it takes to be a good leader? If you are lacking confidence in your abilities, take some time to discover

> Every successful small business manager needs to feel comfortable making presentations in front of people. Especially when those people are your employees.

The longer you put off learning how to become organized, the harder your job as a manager will be. Seek help. Read a book, attend a workshop, hire someone to organize your life. But just do it.

what is blocking your confidence. Begin by having a "can do" frame of mind, and you're halfway there already.

Question 8–I don't like to write. If you answered "No," and you do like to write, then all is well. If you do hate writing, then you are in big trouble. In order to be an effective leader and manager, you need super communication skills, and part of those skills will require you to put your thoughts and orders in writing from time to time. You don't have to write a ten-page memo; but start by writing small ones, maybe just one or two paragraphs long. And those paragraphs don't have to be any longer than three or four sentences. Start brushing up on your writing skills today, and you will become a better leader and manager.

Question 9–I try to be an organized person, but it seems I'm always too busy. If you answered "No," then you are on the right track. If you answered "Yes," then get busy and get organized! Stop procrastinating and start organizing now! The longer you put off learning how to become organized, the harder your job as a manager will be. Seek help. Read a book, attend a workshop, hire someone to organize your life. But just do it.

Question 10–I have a set number of hours that I work each day, then I quit and go home. If you answered "Yes," then why do you think you want to be a manager? Being a successful manager and keeping to a set schedule may not always be something you can have. But that doesn't mean you have to be a slave to the business eighteen hours a day, seven days a week. But it does mean that you have to have some level of flexibility when it comes to your schedule, and getting your job done.

Question 11–I hate doing paperwork; most of it is a waste of time. If you answered "No," and you don't mind doing paperwork, then write yourself a memo of congratulations. Businesses thrive on paperwork, and while it is true that some paperwork can probably be eliminated, most of it is a necessary part of the business process. If you think your business is drowning in useless paperwork, then consider having a paperwork audit. Gather your employees and have them help you. Start by examining every piece of paper that it takes to get your business done every day. And if you can combine and streamline the process, go for it!

Question 12—I don't like change, especially in the workplace. If you answered "No," and you don't mind change, great. If you answered "Yes," and the idea of change in the workplace brings on a migraine headache, you've got some big problems. In business, change is constant. It's the only thing you can rely on happening, especially when you least expect it to. So get a grip, and come to terms with the changes that happen.

Question 13—I can do several things at the same time. If you answered "Yes," then congratulate yourself (while you are doing something else at the same time, too). But if you answered "No," then you need to work on your multitasking skills. You probably already have the necessary skills, and odds are you just never had a chance to put them into practice. Start out small, and try doing two tasks at the same time. For example, while you are eating lunch at your desk you can review a trade journal or look at some paperwork.

Question 14—I consider myself a good manager of money. If you answered "Yes," then give yourself a raise and a bonus! If not, then don't feel bad, because many small business managers have difficulty with money issues. Start by examining why you think you are having problems managing money. If it's a cash-flow problem, sit down with your accountant and review your business plan.

Question 15—I consider myself computer literate. If you answered "Yes," then congratulations. If you answered "No," then you have some important work to do. We are now in the twenty-first century, and every small business manager on the planet needs to have some computer

> Start by examining every piece of paper that it takes to get your business done every day. And if you can combine and streamline the process, go for it!

skills in order to succeed today. If your computer skills are nothing to brag about, then enroll in a computer course at your local community college today.

Question 16–I have a problem delegating. If you answered "No," and consider yourself a wizard of delegation, then congratulations. But if you answered "Yes," then you need to work on those delegation skills as soon as possible. (Make sure you read Chapter 4, on delegation.) The ideal manager has a staff that carries out all of the routine activities of the business. So if you are not delegating whenever you can, do whatever it takes to overcome this obstacle to your management success.

Question 17–I prefer to work alone. If you answered "No," and don't mind working with other people, then congratulations are in order. But if you answered "Yes," then you have some real people issues that you need to address before you attempt to manage any further. There's nothing wrong with wanting to work alone now and then. In fact, it's probably the only way that some managers can get caught up on some of their own work. But if you let that "alone" feeling carry over into your management style, you will begin to alienate your employees. And when that happens, you will fail as a leader and a manager.

Question 18–I hate to solve difficult puzzles. If you answered "No," and thrive on difficult puzzles, then congratulations are in order. But if you answered "Yes," then you've got to come to terms with your problem-solving skills. Now, it doesn't mean that you have to take time to learn how to assemble a 1,000-piece puzzle. But it does mean that you shouldn't be afraid to look at a difficult problem or issue, and not hesitate to come up with some creative solutions.

Question 19–I always have the right attitude. If you answered "Yes," and your attitude is always in check, then

> There's nothing wrong with wanting to work alone now and then. But if you let that "alone" feeling carry over into your management style, you will begin to alienate your employees.

you are in great shape. If "No," then you have a serious problem. Your attitude is your most priceless possession. It can make the difference between success and failure. With the right attitude, success is yours. With the wrong attitude, you're just asking to fail. Now which attitude would you prefer to have?

Question 20–I always look for the good in people and in situations. This can be a tricky question. If you answered "Yes," then that's okay. However, if you answered "No," then you are also okay. While there is nothing wrong with looking for the good in people and in situations, you need to be on your guard for people who have their own agenda. Don't be too harsh to judge people, but be on the lookout for warning signs that might indicate that an employee might be headed in the wrong direction. Balance is the key.

Why Managers Aren't Always Leaders and Why Leaders Aren't Always Managers

Just because you are a good manager doesn't mean that you are always a good leader. While the characteristics of a leader and manager are similar, they are also quite different.

A Manager Has Some Duties That Are Considered Sacred

- A manager needs to have a clear vision of where the organization is going and the ability to communicate that vision effectively to all those involved.
- A manager needs to define clearly the key objectives the organization must reach to fulfill its vision.
- A manager needs to make sure that all those in the organization know how doing their jobs will help reach the key objectives.

> A manager needs to make sure that all those in the organization know how doing their jobs will help reach the key objectives.

- A manager must learn how to appraise employees' performance honestly and fairly so they will know how their performance helped the organization reach its key objectives.
- A manager must be a source of good ideas and should inspire teamwork to carry out those ideas for the success of the organization.
- Managers know how to use their authority wisely. They learn as much as they possibly can about their employee's listening style, and adapt their management style accordingly.
- A manager knows how to give feedback, both positive and negative, without making the employee feel ill at ease.
- A manager knows how to calm an angry employee and take control of a bad situation.
- A manager can achieve balance by weighing the effort put into a task against the payoff for the organization.
- A manager is not afraid to admit when he or she has made a mistake, and will take the necessary steps to correct it.
- A manager knows how to encourage employees when they need encouragement.
- A manager will learn how to take control of a situation when it is called for.
- A manager knows what is going on in the organization.
- A manger is a master of time management.
- A manager can find an answer to any problem.

> A leader knows how to win over critics.

Here Are Some Things that Make a Leader

- A leader isn't afraid to lead, no matter what lies ahead.
- Leaders know that they must inspire people to follow them.
- A leader knows how to empower others to excel.
- A leader knows how to win over critics.
- A leader will carefully plan his or her next step before moving forward.
- A leader is an effective communicator.
- A leader is courteous to everyone on the team.

- A leader will wait twenty seconds before answering a question.
- A leader will embrace resistance.
- A leader will stay calm when chaos erupts.
- A leader won't hesitate to ask for help.
- A leader will never say, "It's not my job."
- A leader will have compassion.
- A leader will know when it's time to take a break.
- A leader will always want to succeed.

What's Your Communication Style?

As a successful small business manager and leader, you must realize that you need effective communication skills. You need to be able to communicate your wishes to the rest of the team in order for them to get the job done. But even though you may consider yourself to be a great communicator, you need to have the right communication style.

Research shows that managers spend about 80 percent of their time in some form of communication. That includes talking, listening, reading, and writing. Some managers think that communication means only one thing: giving orders to someone else.

Common Communication Obstacles Managers Face

- **Information overload**—Let's face it, in today's workplace climate it's not unusual to be swamped with telephone calls, voice mail messages, faxes, e-mails, and dozens of other communications you receive every day. With such a large volume of information being shared among workers in the business place today, it's easy to get caught up in the information overload. Solution: start by weeding out and delegating any tasks that will free up your time to do your job well.
- **Conflicting verbal and nonverbal messages**—Nonverbal communication will include your posture, your facial expression,

---

Communication Is the Key to Success

By now you must have realized that communication is the key to success in any relationship, whether it's business related or otherwise, which is why you need to adopt a communication style that works for you. If people relate to you and find it easy to follow your orders, then your communication style must be working. If they don't, find out what is wrong, and make the necessary corrections.

your mannerisms, and any other form of body language. It's a proven fact that when an employee receives a verbal message and a nonverbal message at the same time, they will usually listen to the nonverbal one. Say what you mean, but don't act like you don't mean it.

- **The "selective listening" trap**–When you have selective listening, you only hear what you want to hear. You don't hear what is actually taking place, and when that happens, problems are sure to surface.
- **Avoid ambiguity**–In other words, make sure your instructions and messages are crystal clear and understood by everyone involved. If you need something completed by a certain deadline, then give that person a deadline. Don't say, "do this as soon as possible," when you really mean to say, "I need this job finished by noon tomorrow." Say what you mean, and mean what you say.

> Miscommunication has been one of the biggest reasons for failure among small business managers. Make sure your instructions are crystal clear.

Make Sure Your Communications Are Received

Many employees may appear to be listening to your instructions, but make sure they feel comfortable enough to ask questions if they are confused or don't understand what it is that you really want them to do. Miscommunication has been one of the biggest reasons for failure among small business managers. Don't get caught up in the "he said, she said" trap. Instead, make sure your instructions are crystal clear.

Ask yourself these questions whenever you give someone an order:

- Are my instructions being presented in easy to understand terms?
- Am I sure that whoever is receiving my communications is actually qualified to handle this task?
- Am I prepared to give feedback, both positive and negative, when it's called for?
- Am I communicating the importance of this task?
- Am I listening to this employee's response to my instructions?

By communicating effectively, you are ensuring that your wishes and orders will be carried out to the best of everyone's ability.

Can You Inspire?

Are you one of those managers who inspire their employees by just walking into the room? Or are you one of those managers who is still trying to figure out how to be an inspiration? Here are some ways you can inspire your employees and become a super manager at the same time:

Model your work team after a flock of geese–You've probably heard the story about flocks of geese, and how they work together toward a common goal. In case you haven't, here's a shortened version: Each member of the flock is responsible for getting itself to wherever the flock is going. Each member looks to itself, not the leader, to determine what to do. Every member knows the direction of the flock. Sharing the common direction makes assuming the leadership role easier. Every member is willing to assume leadership when the flock needs it. When the lead goose gets tired, a more energetic goose from the back of the pack assumes the leadership position. Members look after each other, helping all members achieve the goal. If a wounded goose goes down, two geese follow it and protect and feed it until it either recovers or dies.

Let your team set their own schedules–Once employees have demonstrated that they are consistent contributors, let them set their own schedules.

Make sure you offer praise when it is called for–And be sure to do so in front of their coworkers.

Give your team the tools they need to complete the task at hand–If your employees can't get the job done because they lack the proper tools, who's really at fault? Make sure

Be a True Inspiration

Employees will know if you are just patronizing them, or if you really are sincere. So if you want to win their trust and expect them to give 110 percent, be a true inspiration to them. Be the leader who inspires her troops on to a victory each and every time they venture out into battle.

the proper equipment is available before dishing out that next assignment.

Offer some type of an incentive—Sometimes it might be worth your while to offer some type of an incentive to inspire a team to finish a project before their deadline. The reward can be financial, or it can be in the form of additional time off, use of company vehicles, or whatever you think will work in your particular situation.

Leading from Behind

What type of a leader are you? Are you one of those leaders who acts like a sheep dog, and constantly barks and guides your flock to where your destination is? Or are you like the Boy Scout leader in the beginning of this chapter, still trying to figure out where everyone went?

In order to be an effective leader, you must learn how to lead from behind. In other words, you must be willing to do everything in your power to inspire and empower your employees to excel. And you must do so from behind them, not in front of them.

Don't think of your small business management technique as Custer's last stand. You don't have to lead the charge, holding your sword up high in the air as you lead everyone into battle.

Instead, learn to lead your team from behind the scenes. Give them the tools and the instructions that they need to do their job, and let them do it. It doesn't mean that you are giving up complete control to the team. Instead, it means you are a great leader, and know how to inspire others to do their very best.

Be Available

If you want your employees to see you as a great manager and leader, then be available for them. Don't lock yourself in your office and expect everyone to get the job done without your support. Successful managers make themselves available to their employees to help them get their jobs done. It doesn't mean you have to do the work for them, but just be there. Be available.

For more information on this topic, visit our Web site at www.businesstown.com

Small Business: Start-ups, Family Business, and More

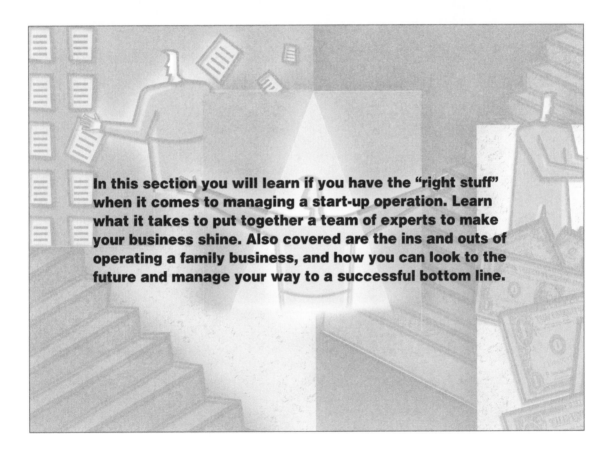

In this section you will learn if you have the "right stuff" when it comes to managing a start-up operation. Learn what it takes to put together a team of experts to make your business shine. Also covered are the ins and outs of operating a family business, and how you can look to the future and manage your way to a successful bottom line.

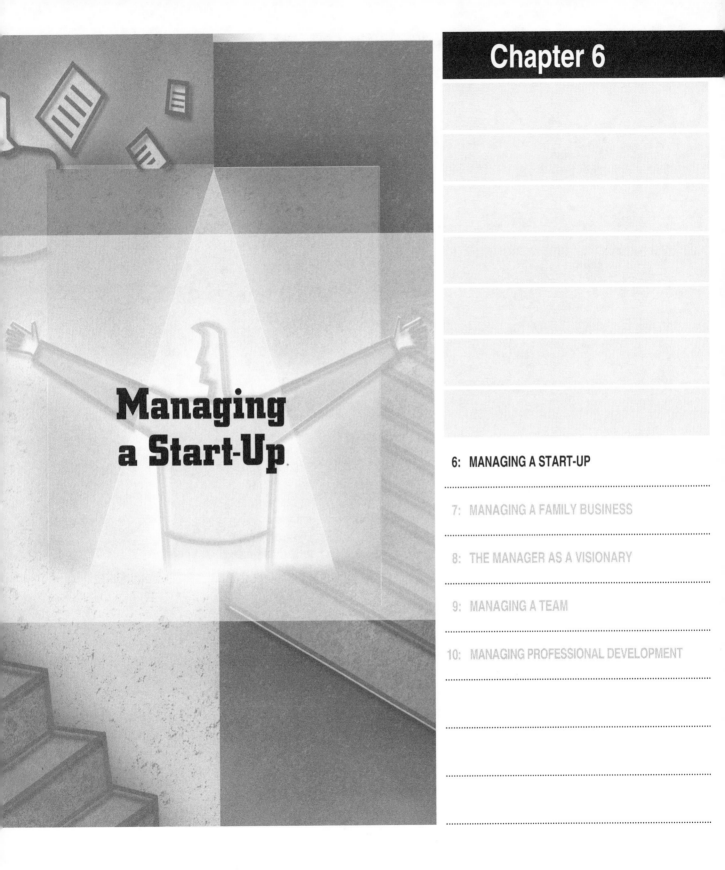

Chapter 6

Managing a Start-Up

Use the Web

Use the many resources that are available on the Internet to help you locate information and ideas that will help your small business succeed. There are literally millions of pages that have all sorts of business information available for your use. Schedule some time during your workweek to surf the Web and look for information that you can use.

There are some areas in which your small business may need outside help in order to succeed. For example, if you do not have the expertise to handle your own payroll needs at the present time, then it's advisable to use an outside organization that specializes in payroll services. The same rule applies to legal services, accounting services, and virtually anything else you need help with—a wise manager knows when it's time to seek outside help.

Do You Have What It Takes to Manage a Start-Up Operation?

Take our quiz and find out. Answer "Yes" or "No" to the following questions:

1. Do you believe that your business will succeed?
2. Are you prepared to do whatever it takes to make your business a success?
3. Have you passed on your passion for your business to your employees and associates?
4. Are you willing to work for little or no salary during your start-up phase?
5. Do you have a five-year business plan in place?
6. Have you taken the time to discover who your competition really is?
7. Do you have a marketing plan in place?
8. Do you have a public relations plan in place?
9. Do you have a sales plan in place?
10. Are you prepared to handle customer complaints?

Unless you answered "Yes" to all of these questions, you are not quite ready yet to manage a start-up operation. So if you answered "No" to some, get busy and make those corrections.

Why Most Start-Ups Need a Little TLC

If you have created a new venture, you know by now that you must use a little TLC to help move it along toward a successful outcome. Here are the top reasons why most start-ups need that extra dose of Tender Loving Care:

- Most new businesses are created by people with little or no experience in managing a business.
- Most new businesses have limited cash flow.
- Most new businesses do not know who their competition really is.
- Most new businesses do not put enough effort into marketing.
- Most new businesses give up when things get really tough.

The Right Stuff:
Finding the Right Employees for Your Start-Up

Okay, you've made the decision to start a new business, and now you're ready to hire some employees to help make your business a success. But before you waste your time by placing a few "help wanted" ads, keep these tips in mind that will help you find just the right employees for your new venture:

Look for word-of-mouth referrals. There's nothing like a word-of-mouth referral, is there? Whether your neighbor talks about his or her experience with a new car, or a coworker talks about a new restaurant that you should try, word of mouth rules! The same holds true when looking for new employees. Ask around. Who can recommend someone to you, and why?

Try a recruitment agency. While these tend to be costly, they have done a lot of the legwork for you. The screening process, initial interviews, etc., will all be handled for you.

Hold your own job fair. But don't make it look like the same job fairs that everyone else puts on. Instead, make yours different. Make it a carnival-like atmosphere, and advertise that you are looking for employees who are ready

> Try a recruitment agency. While these tend to be costly, they have done a lot of the legwork for you.

to "live life on the edge," because that's what working for a start-up can be!

Post a Web site. This simple and inexpensive means of recruiting the right people can be the answer you are looking for. More and more people are looking to the Internet to find new places of employment, so why not join the crowd?

Look for employees who are ready to go above and beyond the call of duty to help your small business become a success. Look for employees with good work ethics, and ones who strive for success.

Office Stationery for Your Start-Up

Buying and selling office stationery has become a big business in this country. The savvy business owner knows that their stationery tells the world something about their business. From business cards to letterhead, everything you hand out or mail out can help your business succeed. But you can be overwhelmed by the choices of office stationery on the market today. However, with a little careful planning you can learn how to determine what your office stationery needs really are.

The first thing you need to do is to assess your needs. When is the last time you took an inventory of the office supplies that you really use in your business place? If you're like most business owners, you've probably been too busy to think about your office stationery needs on a daily basis.

The Most Common Types of Stationery a Small Business Uses

- **Brochures**—From a simple tri-fold to a glossy four-color, thirty-two-page piece, brochures are an important aspect of any business.
- **Letterhead**—Your letterhead should present a professional look.

> When is the last time you took an inventory of the office supplies that you really use in your business place?

- **Business cards**—These days, they come in all shapes, sizes, and colors, and carry additional information, such as e-mail and Web page addresses.
- **Envelopes**—From the standard letter size to the giant 9" × 12" size, even your envelope says a lot about your business. After all, it's the first thing everyone sees when you mail them something.
- **Invoices**—Invoices are now available in various forms, from multiple copy types to perforated types. Again, your invoice is representing you, so make sure it is a first class piece.
- **Checks**—While many businesses purchase their checks from their bank, you can also buy a wide variety of checks from office supply stores and mail order companies.

Depending on the type of business you are operating, you may have additional office stationery needs, such as customer surveys, requests for information, and other pieces. Take a look at each piece of office stationery to determine when you last had it updated and also to see if it includes all of the necessary contact information. For example, on your letterhead, are all of your telephone, fax, and message center numbers listed correctly? And are the e-mail and Web page addresses still current? When employees come and go, e-mail addresses usually change, and you don't want a customer trying to send an important e-mail to your business, only to find it returned to them as "undeliverable." What sort of an impression would that give about your small business?

Don't forget to ask for input from the employees who use the various forms every day in their job, because they might be aware of changes that you may inadvertently overlook.

Seek Advice from Your Employees

Don't forget to ask for input from the employees who use the various forms every day in their job, because they might be aware of changes that you may inadvertently overlook. Once you have an inventory of the office stationery your small business needs to operate, keep an adequate supply on hand at all times. There's nothing worse than running out of a form or letterhead when you are in a hurry.

If you decide to purchase your office stationery from an outside company, you have your choice of office superstores, such as Staples and Office Max, or many mail-order companies, or even locally owned and operated ones. Check with your local Chamber of Commerce to see what office stationery suppliers are on their recommended vendor list.

But with so many choices, just how can you be certain you are making the right decision? And are you getting good prices and good quality? Should you purchase everything from one supplier? Some business owners prefer to order from several places, while others prefer to use the same one to supply all of their stationery needs.

Finding the Right Stationery Supply Company

- Ask about delivery service. Is it free? Or is there a fee involved?
- Ask about their return policy. Can you get a refund, or is a store credit the only option that is available?
- Ask about special orders. How fast can they process them? And will they rush an order overnight without extra charges?
- Ask about discounts and special sales. How often does the merchandise you normally purchase go on sale? How often do they run specials?
- Ask about items that are back ordered. How soon will they get that item in?
- Ask about hours. Are they open on weekends and holidays? And do they open early and close late during the work week?
- Ask how long they have been in business. If you are thinking about buying from a new company, ask if they have been around long enough to have any other satisfied customers.
- Ask about references. What other businesses do they work with?
- Ask for referrals from business associates. Where do your business associates purchase their office stationery? There's nothing like a word-of-mouth recommendation from a satisfied customer.

Because of the number of office superstores, discount catalog businesses, and now even online Web sites that sell everything from

If you are thinking about buying from a new company, ask if they have been around long enough to have any other satisfied customers.

A to Z, you will have a field day when it comes time to compare prices and terms. Many companies will claim to offer the lowest prices in town. So the "buyer beware" rule applies here, too. A little time and effort spent in doing some research will pay off in big dividends when it comes time to getting the best price and quality that you are looking for.

Tips for Finding the Best Prices

- Compare prices carefully. One place may advertise letterhead at a much lower price than somewhere else because they are using the lightest weight paper available. It's a good idea to create a chart so that you can compare prices and quality.
- Ask about their return policy. If you're buying from a catalog supplier or an online Web site, ask about how you can ship unwanted items back to them.
- Make sure you inquire about guarantees, especially if they advertise that they will meet or beat a competitor's price.
- Ask them about volume discounts. How much will you be able to save if you place a larger than usual order with their company?

Be careful if you decide to purchase from a catalog supplier or a new Web site. Be certain that you know who it is you are dealing with. Never place an order unless you have checked to ensure that their business is a legitimate operation. As a small business owner, you have the right to expect the best prices, quality, and service for all of your office stationery needs.

Outsourcing Payroll

Payroll plays an important part in the life of your small business. Employees expect to be paid on time, and don't want to see any mistakes in their paychecks. And the government expects that your payroll taxes will be paid on time, and they will provide a stiff penalty if you pay them late.

Keep Updating Your Inventory

If your small business uses a lot of office supplies, then consider updating your inventory at least twice a year. As your business grows, so will your office stationery needs. So make sure whoever is responsible for purchasing office supplies is using an up-to-date checklist of items that everyone needs.

Many small businesses still process their own payroll checks because they believe that it's cheaper to do it themselves instead of contracting with an outside payroll firm. But when you factor in all of the costs of processing it yourself, you may be surprised to discover that it's actually costing you more money than you need to spend.

> Many small businesses still process their own payroll checks. But when you factor in all of the costs of processing it yourself, you may be surprised to discover that it's actually costing you more money than you need to spend.

What's Needed to Do Payroll In-House

- Computer equipment
- Accounting and payroll software
- Accounting personnel
- Training
- Business forms (checks, tax reporting forms, W-2s, etc.)

Some businesses are quite comfortable with handling their own payroll needs. For larger companies this can enable them to save money and be more flexible in their payroll system. However, for smaller operations handling payroll can either be expensive, due to having a full-time employee dedicating a large portion of his or her effort to the task, or a major nuisance in terms of needing to get hefty amounts of paperwork completed every other week.

Some Advantages of Outsourcing Payroll

- Paychecks are delivered on time. No longer does a small business owner have to worry when the payroll clerk or accountant is out sick or on maternity leave. Outside payroll companies always deliver checks on time, every time.
- W-2s are delivered on time. Again, no more late nights in the office, trying to figure out how to issue the W-2s to your employees before the deadline gets here.
- Quarterly taxes are paid on time. No more worries about getting hit with penalties and fines if your quarterly payroll taxes are filed and delivered late.
- You receive payroll reports and management reports you can read and understand.

If your payroll is different each time period, due to changes in the number of hours that your employees work, then outsourcing your payroll makes good sense. It can provide you with the peace of mind that you need, knowing that everyone will be paid on time, and paid the correct amount as well. But if on the other hand, you are quite comfortable with handling your payroll needs in-house, go ahead and continue with what you are doing. As long as you feel it's working for you, that's great.

But if you are ready to outsource your payroll needs, just how do you go about finding just the right company that suits all of your needs? Obviously, you will want to work with a local company that is near your business, and one that has an excellent reputation for customer service. Ask some of your business associates who they are using, and why they are pleased with them.

If your payroll is different each time period, due to changes in the number of hours that your employees work, then outsourcing your payroll makes good sense.

Before Signing a Contract with a Payroll Company

- Ask the payroll company just how long they have been in business.
- Request a detailed list of services included in your basic fee. (You don't want to be surprised with an extra bill for services you thought were part of your package.) Some typical basic services include issuing payroll checks, Section 125 plans, benefit statements, and others.
- Ask the payroll company for samples of their checks, tax reports, and other management reports they will be issuing.
- Ask to see samples of the forms your employees will have to fill out in order to be paid.
- Ask them how you will need to transmit the payroll data to them. Some payroll companies prefer to have the hours phoned in to them, while others may want the information faxed or even transmitted over the Internet.
- Ask if you will have your own customer service rep, or if you will be dealing with different people each time you call.
- Ask how quickly a payroll check can be reissued if you discover a mistake or need to correct an amount before a check is issued to one of your employees.

- Ask them how they check for accuracy, and what they do in case of an error on their end.
- Find out exactly what tax filings they handle. For example, in addition to federal and state taxes, do they handle local tax filings as well?
- Ask them how they keep up on the latest changes in the tax code and laws.
- Ask when funds need to be deposited from your business to cover the payroll checks and payments that are made.
- Ask about their security and confidentiality policy. In other words, how do they keep your employees' payroll and other confidential information safe and secure?
- Ask them how new their computer equipment and systems are, and what type of backup and retrieval system they have in place. It is extremely important that you feel comfortable with the payroll company you have selected. They need to earn your respect, and provide you with everything you have contracted with them for.

Other Things to Know Concerning Payroll Companies

- How often will you be billed? Monthly, biweekly, or other?
- What are you getting for your money? Do you have several different packages from which to choose? Or do they price every service separately?
- If a mistake is made as a result of an error on your end, how much do they charge to reissue a new payroll check?
- If a mistake is made as a result of an error on their end, do they offer a credit on your next invoice?
- What type of guarantee comes with your contract? Do they promise never to make a mistake, or be late filing a tax payment?
- Do you have a free trial period?
- Is there a limit on the number of changes you can make in one payroll period?
- How long are their rates guaranteed?

> Ask about their security and confidentiality policy. In other words, how do they keep your employees' payroll and other confidential information safe and secure?

- How often do they raise their rates?
- Are payroll checks and tax payments drawn against your business checking account, or one of their accounts?
- When are funds transferred into the payroll or tax account?
- When comparing prices between different payroll companies, make sure you are comparing the same services in order to make an educated decision.
- Ask if there will be any additional charges if you have your payroll delivered to multiple locations. Some payroll companies will deliver only to one site, then will charge an additional fee for making deliveries to other sites.

Find out as much information as you possibly can about the prices and terms of any payroll services company before signing a contract with them. If there is something you don't understand about its pricing structure or what you are getting for your money, don't be afraid to ask questions. Have them clarify what you are paying for, and what you can expect for your money.

Because a payroll company will be providing a very important service to your small business, it is extremely important that you deal only with a reputable firm. With so many accounting and payroll software programs for sale these days, virtually anyone can obtain a business license and set up shop as a payroll company.

> Some payroll companies will deliver only to one site, then will charge an additional fee for making deliveries to other sites.

Deciding Factors in Choosing a Payroll Company

- Check to see if they have had any complaints filed against them. Contact your local Better Business Bureau or Chamber of Commerce for that information.
- Ask for at least three references from other businesses that are similar in size to your own. And make sure you take the time to contact those references.
- Are they flexible and willing to meet any special needs your company may have?
- Do they admit to making mistakes when processing payroll checks or tax payments in the past?

Payroll Issues
Are Important

Whether you prepare your own payroll, or hire an outside firm to handle it, remember that payroll issues are important to your employees. Simple things like making sure a raise has been entered on the correct date is important to employee morale, so pay attention to payroll issues.

- Have they been in business for at least three years?
- Are they willing to go that extra mile and provide your small business with everything you need?

When you make the decision to outsource your payroll, do so with confidence and take your time to find just the right company that suits all of your needs. A little time and effort invested beforehand will pay off in the long run. And once your payroll needs are taken care of, you can concentrate on doing what you do best: managing your small business.

Business Machines

Business machines are a vital part of every small business. From the fax machine and calculator all the way up to the most complex computer system and photocopier, business machines help keep the wheels of commerce turning.

If you have never taken an inventory of the different types of business machines your company uses on a daily basis, you need to pencil in some time to do so. Every small business needs a complete inventory of its equipment for insurance and tax purposes. So when you have your list ready, examine it carefully. What have you discovered? That you own too many business machines? Or not enough business machines? Are you one of those management types who insists on buying all of the latest gadgets that are on sale? Or is your secretary still typing your letters on an old Royal typewriter?

Take the time to evaluate the condition of each of those business machines that you own. How long have you been using them? How old are they? If your copier is running smoothly and no one is complaining, then chances are it's okay and doesn't need to be replaced.

Assess your business machine needs very carefully. Keep up with the latest changes in technology that might affect your inventory of business machines. If you don't read trade journals, attend business or trade shows, or even notice articles in the daily newspaper about new business machines or improvements in existing ones, you will have a difficult time trying to keep up with what's new. If you don't have time to monitor what's new in the field of business machines, then delegate that task to a trusted employee who does have time. In addition to the trade shows, trade journals, and newspaper articles, there is plenty of information about the latest technology in business machines on various Web sites. A quick search on any number of search engines will reveal plenty of sites to visit for additional information and help.

Your employees are also an important source of information concerning business machines. Ask them if they are happy with their current equipment, and if they aren't, ask them what they would like to use instead. Listen carefully to their feedback, because they are the ones who are using those business machines on a daily basis.

When you are ready to purchase some new business machines, you will find that prices vary from vendor to vendor. But don't just compare prices, either. Make sure you compare warranties, service contracts, delivery and setup, and other factors as well.

Tips to Help You Buy New Business Machines

- Check with your local Chamber of Commerce, Better Business Bureau, or other association to see if they have a list of preferred vendors from whom to purchase equipment.
- Ask your business associates who they purchase equipment from and if they have been satisfied with what they have. Word-of-mouth recommendations are usually pretty good sources of information.
- Ask a potential vendor for a price list so that you can compare prices and shop around. Avoid using a vendor who won't quote you a final price until you sign for a service contract as well.
- When you are comparing prices among vendors, make sure you are comparing similar types of equipment. For example, an inkjet printer will no doubt cost less than a laser printer, so don't compare the two as if they were the same piece of equipment.
- Find a salesperson or business machine consultant that you are comfortable dealing with. Remember too, however, that

> Don't just compare prices, either. Make sure you compare warranties, service contracts, delivery and setup, and other factors as well.

most salespeople are working on commission, so it's their job to sell you as much as they can. Find a salesperson you can trust and like working with.

- Ask about delivery and setup. Will the vendor you choose deliver your new equipment and set them up for free? Or is there a charge involved? And how soon can they deliver? You don't want to be sitting around, waiting for equipment to arrive, only to have it not show up on time.

- Ask how long the company has been in business. While ordering business machines from a new vendor is okay, you want to make sure they have been around long enough that you feel comfortable dealing with them.

- Ask about service contracts. What is included in the standard contract? Are parts and labor included, or are there any "hidden" costs that will pop up later? And what are their terms for extended service contracts?

- Ask about their customer service options. Do they have someone to assist you 24 hours a day, seven days a week, including holidays?

- Ask about the advantages of buying versus leasing. Do they have any special programs where you can lease some business machines now, and then trade up a few years later when new models become available?

- Compare prices carefully. If one vendor is advertising the same piece of equipment at a much lower price than another one is, investigate why. Read all of the fine print. And make sure if you are buying reconditioned or used equipment, that you know about it when you are making your purchase.

- Ask about guarantees. What is included? And will they meet or beat any similar ad from one of their competitors?

- Ask about emergency deliveries. If you are in the middle of a rush project, and a piece of equipment dies on you, will they come through with a replacement within a few hours?

- Ask about special discounts for volume purchases and repeat customers. Will they work with you to give you a preferred price that you are comfortable with?

Compare prices carefully. If one vendor is advertising the same piece of equipment at a much lower price than another one is, investigate why.

Don't rush out and purchase the first computer, fax machine, or laser printer that you come across. Take your time and learn about what your small business really needs to use, and do whatever it takes to help you get the most bang for your buck.

Remember that the "buyer beware" rule applies to business machines as well as to anything else you need to purchase. If an advertised price looks too good to be true, chances are it probably is. Always look for quality when it comes to any business machines that you need to purchase. There are plenty of cheap models on the market today, but you don't want to have to keep buying equipment every few months because they are already worn out.

Find a company that listens carefully to your small business needs, and find a company you feel comfortable dealing with. Work with someone who has a "can do" attitude and that shows genuine interest in helping you select what you need.

Keep Up with the Latest Equipment

Are you keeping up with the latest business machines that are available? If you haven't taken the time to visit an office supply store lately, it's probably time to do so. New technology has resulted in some really neat gizmos and gadgets that will help your employees do their jobs. If you don't have time to get to the office supply store, delegate, or have them send you their latest catalog.

Why Most Start-Ups Fail

It's a known fact that most new businesses fail within the first two years of opening their doors. (Many are lucky if they are still open after six months!) The top ten reasons why most start-ups fail include:

1. The business is operated by inexperienced managers.
2. Cash flow issues cannot be controlled.
3. The business fails to identify who its competition really is.
4. The business fails to identify who its customers really are.
5. The business has no five-year plan.
6. In the case of a family-owned business, too many relatives are working there.
7. The business has no internal controls, especially when it comes to spending.
8. The business isn't sure where to put its advertising dollars and efforts.
9. Decisions are put off until it's too late.
10. Not everyone in the business has embraced the business as their way of life.

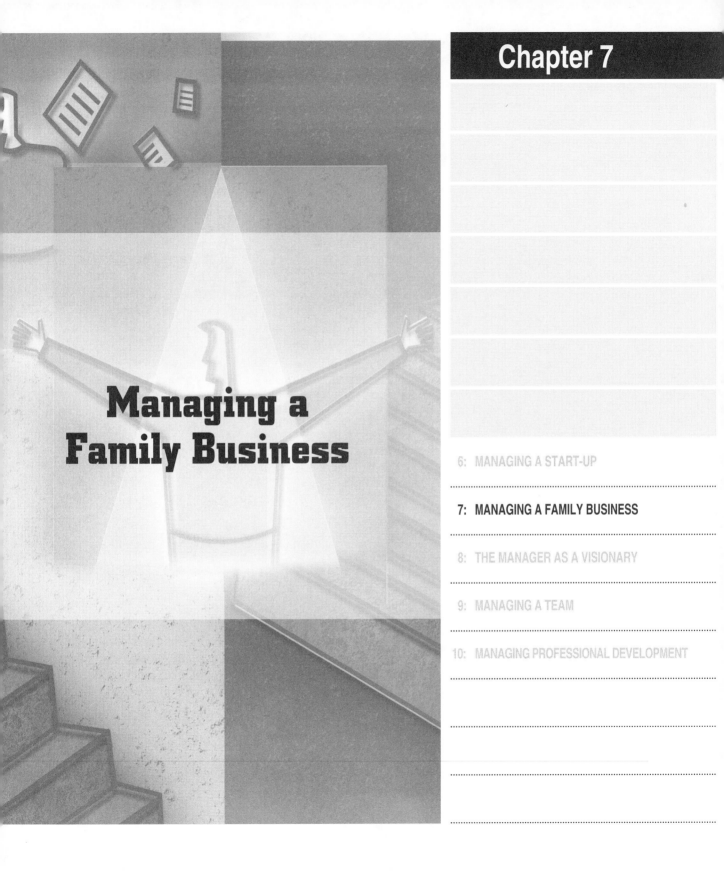

Managing a Family Business

Chapter 7

Do You Have What It Takes to Manage a Family Business?

Answer "Yes" or "No" to the following questions:

1. Are you the type of person who can keep business and family affairs separate?
2. Are you prepared to work with your spouse or other family members up to 18 hours a day?
3. Do you play favorites when it comes to family members and their activities in your business?
4. Will you let emotions, instead of good business sense, rule your family business?
5. Are you prepared to do everything possible to keep your family business afloat? (Including laying off your mother-in-law?)
6. I love every member of my family who works in our family business.
7. I trust every member of my family who works in our family business.
8. I require family members to gain experience elsewhere before I will hire them.
9. I reward family members who go above and beyond to get their job done.
10. I am as happy as a clam running a family-owned and -operated business.

Let's see how you scored:

1. If you said "Yes" to this question, then congratulations are in order, because this is the one area that most family members fail miserably at. It is extremely difficult to keep business and family affairs separate; but you must do so, otherwise, you're in for a heap of trouble. If you said "No," you might want to rethink how you treat your affairs.
2. If you said "Yes" to this question, then give yourself a trophy, because you certainly deserve it. Working with your

> Are you prepared to do everything possible to keep your family business afloat? (Including laying off your mother-in-law?)

spouse and or other family members up to 18 hours can be taxing, to say the very least. But that's what it takes sometimes, and even more. But if you said "No," then you're in for some big trouble on the home front, my friend.

3. If you said "No" to this question, then "you da man!" Because it's certainly not easy not playing favorites to your relatives over "regular" people who work for you. But if you said "Yes" to this question, then you must realize by now that it's not working out this way, now is it?

4. If you said "No" to this question, then you are a man (or woman) of steel. Because that's what it takes sometimes, my friend. It takes a heart of steel, not a heart of gold, to rule a family business. If you said "Yes" to this question, then you have no doubt encountered many problems by now, haven't you? And until you start ruling with your business sense, instead of your family emotions, things will continue their downward spiral.

5. If you said "Yes" to this question, then you truly are a smart family business owner. (But could you really lay off your own mother-in-law?) You know sometimes that really tough decisions have to be made, and you must be prepared to do whatever is necessary to keep your family business afloat. If you said "No" to this question, then maybe you need to rethink why you are running a family business in the first place.

6. If you said "Yes" to this question, are you really being honest? If you love every family member who works in your family business *most* of the time, that's still okay. But if you said "No" to this question, you might want to take a long hard look at the relationship that you *do* have with those family members that you do work with. It may be time for a pow-wow, and a time to bury the hatchet.

7. If you said "Yes" to this question, contact the media right away. Because you are probably the only person on the planet to say "Yes" to that question. Trusting family members not to embezzle, steal, or just plain "goof off" is a big

> It takes a heart of steel, not a heart of gold, to rule a family business.

deal. And if you said "No" to this question, who don't you trust, and why not?

8. If you said "Yes" to this question, then you have a pretty good head for business, my friend. Too many small business owners and managers end up hiring family members before they have gained experience elsewhere. And that can have tragic results. If you said "No" to this question, then you have experienced first hand what those tragic results can really be, haven't you?

9. If you said "Yes" to this question, I hope it means you are also rewarding nonfamily members when it comes to performance. Family or not, if someone is going "above and beyond" the call of duty, let the rewards equal the effort. If you said "No" to this question, you're probably wondering why none of your family members ever stick around and work very long for you.

10. If you said "Yes" to this question, then you have obviously mastered the fine art of running a family-owned and -operated small business. Congratulations are certainly in order, my friend! But if you said "No," when is the last time you sat down and had a real heart-to-heart conversation with yourself—to find out what part of running the family business you're not happy with?

Why Most Family Businesses Fail

"A family business is exceptionally difficult because individuals within a family interact with each other on an emotional level," said Michael J. Zanoni, who operates Ground Zero Marketing Communications in New Jersey. "Business needs to be conducted in a non-emotional fashion, but sometimes family members allow their personal feelings to cloud their judgment and adversely influence their behavior during business interactions."

More than 90 percent of U.S. businesses are owned and managed by members of a single family, but many of those family businesses end up in failure.

> More than 90 percent of U.S. businesses are owned and managed by members of a single family, but many of those family businesses end up in failure.

Some Advice for Those Running Family-Owned Businesses

Robert Scott, professor of management at the Gabelli School of Business at Roger Williams University in Bristol, Rhode Island, says that the average life expectancy of family businesses is roughly twenty-five years. "It makes management succession within a family-owned and operated business a very difficult issue," he said.

Require that family members gain full-time experience elsewhere before they work full-time for the family business. "Part-time or summer work in the family business may motivate teenage family members, but full-time employment without at least two to five years' college experience elsewhere is usually a mistake," says Scott. "Let the younger generation prove themselves to someone else. Let them taste success without wondering whether they earned it, and let them taste failure without their family standing by."

When younger family members work full-time, give them responsibility and the freedom to make mistakes. "Placing younger family members in 'safe' jobs, where they cannot fail or do much damage, is short-sighted and virtually guarantees their eventual failure as well as damage to the family business," he says. "Many successful succession programs involve allowing key young family members to create and launch a new product line, service, marketing strategy, or business model."

> Require that family members gain full-time experience elsewhere before they work full-time for the family business.

Keep Family Members Separate Within the Business

Avoid management responsibility overlap among family members. "Much discord in family-owned businesses arises when family members second-guess their relatives and resent taking suggestions or orders from them," says Scott. "A clear separation of responsibilities and authority goes a long way toward reducing tension and promoting harmony in the family and the business."

Establish a board of directors made up of approximately 40 percent outside members. "Perhaps the most important step an owner can take to improve management of a family-owned business is to add competent outside members to the board," he says. "Such directors bring experience and objectivity to the table and provide strength to make the difficult business decisions that involve family members."

Minimize the overlap between the business and the family that owns it. "Family homes and events should not serve as extensions of the workplace," he says. "With rare exceptions, home-based business should be moved out of the home as soon as finances permit."

Plan Ahead

Begin succession planning early and make a written commitment. "This is the single most important element in succession planning," says Scott. "The younger generation's full-time employment should be viewed as an experiment that may or may not lead to a career commitment. But from the beginning, everyone involved should understand that the trial period is not indefinite," he says. "When the younger generation reaches age thirty, the senior generation is usually into their fifties—a good time to make a specific written commitment to the future. If the older generation is uncomfortable with or unwilling to make such a commitment, the younger generation can interpret this hesitancy as a signal to seek employment elsewhere or start a new business."

"In family business as elsewhere, the best people leave when unfairly held back," says Scott. "If the older generation fails to commit to a succession plan and the younger generation fails to leave, the business is probably in decline."

> "If the older generation fails to commit to a succession plan and the younger generation fails to leave, the business is probably in decline."

Unique Aspects of a Family-Owned Business

Kevin Haggarty, vice president and senior consultant for Farr Associates in High Point, North Carolina, has extensive experience dealing with family-owned businesses. He says that there are some issues that are unique to family businesses, including:

- You are a family business owner experiencing difficulty transferring managerial responsibility to another family member.

- You see a split forming between family and nonfamily members of your management team and you want to ensure things don't become worse.
- You are already seeing evidence of damage to your organization's bottom line caused by a rift between family and nonfamily managers.
- You perceive that others in your company have a real lack of confidence in family managers running the business, and you need to instill confidence in both camps and their abilities.
- You're faced with the difficult decision and task of transferring leadership power to an "outsider."
- You are experiencing trouble working with family members, but the continued success of the company requires you work together.
- You are in the process of transferring ownership or wealth to other family members, but are faced with perceptions of "promises not kept" regarding both money and titles.
- You are trying to change your company's culture from a "mom-and-pop shop" to a progressive organization in the face of mounting competition.

Haggarty says that managers of family-operated small businesses need to achieve certain objectives, including:

- **Alignment among family members**—Get everyone working on the same team.
- **Alignment among family and nonfamily managers**—You must bridge the "us against them" gap and attitude.
- **A workable succession plan**—If you don't plan now, how do you expect the future to go?
- **Winning through successive generations**—Put your plans down on paper, and work through any possible problem areas.
- **Ways to manage nonaligned family members**—Strategize and brainstorm ways to make this work.
- **Exit strategies for disenchanted family members**—Why make people stick around when they'd rather be doing something else?

Keep the Peace

If conflict is a problem among family members at a family business, chaos will surely result. Remember, a family business is made up of family members, and family members won't always get along (remember those holiday dinners?). So it's your job to keep the peace at all times. Nip a problem in the bud before it has a chance to get worse.

Creating "Win-Win" Situations in Your Family-Owned Business

In any type of family-owned and -operated small business, you will need to create a working environment that is positive, upbeat, and one that moves forward. In other words, you need to create a win-win situation whenever possible.

But just how do you create a "win-win" situation? Here are some tips to help you achieve that goal:

Create company goals and objectives—Without goals and objectives, how do you expect to move your business forward? Once you have identified those goals and objectives, share them with everyone, and work together until they are fulfilled.

Accept the fact that mistakes will be made—Ever wonder why John F. Kennedy hit his highest level of popularity after he flubbed the Bay of Pigs? It's because he showed the world he was human, and that he wasn't afraid to admit when he made a mistake. And he took responsibility for his actions. That won him plenty of respect and admiration, two things that every small business should be overflowing with. Accept the fact that mistakes will sometimes be made; they're not the end of the world, so get over them.

Find out what motivates your employees—What do you think motivates your employees to do their best? Money? Health Insurance? A parking space with their name on it? Well, the first step in finding out what motivates your employees is to simply *ask*. It doesn't take a rocket scientist to determine what makes your workers tick, but too many small business owners think they will never be able to figure it out. You'll be surprised at their answers; but make sure you act on them, too!

Learn to conquer fear—There is no room for fear in the workplace, so learn to conquer yours. If you walk around all day worrying that some crisis is going to hit you in the head when you're not looking, your employees will pick up on

> What do you think motivates your employees to do their best? Well, the first step in finding out what motivates your employees is to simply ask.

that. So learn to deal with and conquer your fears, no matter how large or small they appear to be.

Involve your employees in the decision making process– In a study of workers at small businesses, it was revealed that 25 percent of workers said they were capable of doing 50 percent more work, but that they were never given the chance. How about you? Are you allowing your employees to live up to their potential? Are you involving them in any important decision making these days? If not, you don't know what you're missing out on.

Treat your employees fairly–Employees want to be treated equally and fairly, so is it too much to ask for you to do so? Employees who feel they are being treated fairly are more productive workers than ones who feel they are being discriminated against.

Keep your employees informed–Hold meetings on a regular basis, and vary the locations where you hold those meetings. Wanna bet that some employees use their meeting time to mentally make a grocery list or some other personal task? So stop holding boring meetings, and start holding fun and exciting ones. Take everyone to a local fast-food restaurant, or the zoo, or some other creative place that will keep them attentive.

Praise them whenever you possibly can–These days, employees are always on the lookout for a "well done" and a high-five from their superior. So don't disappoint them; when is the last time you praised an employee for a job well done?

Everyone Is a Winner

People want to win; it's human nature. People love to compete, and can get really discouraged if they fail. In business it's no different. So create an atmosphere in your small business where everyone is a winner. Encourage open communication and creative solutions to problems. Praise employees for a job well done, and if someone does fail, encourage their effort that was made, and offer to help them correct their mistake.

Managing Family Members Can Be Tricky

One of the reasons family businesses fail is because it can be so difficult to separate a family environment from a business environment. It is especially difficult in such situations where emotions can get in the way.

Ten Ways to Manage Family Members and Your Small Business for Failure

> Don't worry about family members who abuse their power. After all, that's what family is all about, isn't it?

1. Promote a family member just because they are family. Don't worry about if they are qualified, just make sure to move them on up to the top because, after all, they are family, aren't they?

2. Let family members get away with murder. Well, not quite murder, but things that are just as bad. Like letting them come to work late all the time and not saying anything to them. But if a nonfamily member is late, well, remember to read them the riot act and threaten to fire them.

3. Don't worry about family members who abuse their power. After all, that's what family is all about, isn't it?

4. Let family members sit back and relax all day, while those nonfamily members do all of the work. After all, it's their tough luck if none of their relatives can give them a cushy job, isn't it?

5. Let family members have access to as much cash as they want, as often as they need it. Hey, it's only money, right? And when it runs out, watch who is the first one running out the door.

6. Give family members extra benefits. If you want to pay their whole health insurance bill, while only paying a portion of nonfamily members, don't worry about those federal laws. Who really enforces them, anyway?

7. Let family members take business trips, and make sure they always fly first class. But for other employees, well, coach is good enough for them. And expense reports? For family members? Hey, we're family, remember? But those other guys, well, they better make sure they have receipts for everything!

8. Create an "us against them" corporate culture. After all, who wouldn't want to work at a business where family members and nonfamily members fight like cats and dogs?

9. Don't make any type of plans for transferring ownership to younger family members. Hey, when they're ready, they'll just show up and ask for the keys, right?

10. Don't hold family members accountable. If they make a mistake, so what? And if they do make a mistake, why not shift the blame on a nonfamily member?

Conflict Resolution in the Family Business

Another area in which it is sometimes extremely difficult to manage is conflict. But when conflict does rear its ugly head, it must be dealt with. And you must learn to deal with it immediately, before it has a chance to escalate and get worse. Unresolved conflict among owners, managers, and employees can sometimes destroy a business. In some businesses, especially ones where many members of the same family are employed, it can be deadly. Shouting matches may be the norm; but what kind of an atmosphere are you creating (or endorsing, if you choose to do nothing about it)?

But things can be corrected. Family businesses can be taught to have healthy family relationships and balanced perspectives. And once everyone is on the same page and working together toward the same goal, your business will move forward and succeed. Here are some tips to help you keep conflict from getting out of control:

Accept the fact that conflict does exist—No business, whether it is filled with family members or not, can ever be totally conflict-free. Pretending that everyone is always getting along is not a good way to manage your small business. You're just asking for trouble, my friend.

Learn how to manage the conflict that does exist—Some companies use conflict as a way to keep people sharp. For example, suppose two people disagree on what should be done about how a product is marketed. Instead of handing out boxing gloves, give them forty-eight hours and tell them they will have their chance to plead their

> No business, whether it is filled with family members or not, can ever be totally conflict-free.

Treat Everyone Fairly

Whether all of your employees are family members or not, you need to treat everyone fairly. Hold everyone accountable for their actions, family members or not. When people feel as if everyone is being treated the same, harmony will result. And a small business that has an atmosphere of harmony among its employees has a very good chance of success.

case in front of the whole department or management team. Encourage them to research and come up with statistics, facts, and other info that will help them prove their case.

Ask family members for ways to handle conflict resolution—Sometimes the best solutions will come from the people who are involved in the situations in the first place. When conflict surfaces, ask the parties to take a "time out," and to come up with at least three creative solutions to the problem.

Keep conflict under control—Make sure your policy and procedures manual deals with conflict issues, and how to handle them. Lay out specific guidelines that will produce positive changes and results.

Questions to Ask Yourself

It doesn't matter how much experience you have as a manager, when it comes to running a family-owned and -operated small business, the rules are different. Family members sometimes feel as if they are exempt from the rules, and therefore you will find many opportunities for chaos to rule. Here is a checklist to help you survive as a manager of a family business:

"Am I using my time on high-priority tasks?" As a manager, you have the responsibility of the entire operation resting on the many decisions that you will be forced to make each and every day. But how are you spending your time? Are you using your time strictly for high-priority tasks? Or are you having to hold the hand of different family members, stroking them, and telling them how much they are loved and needed? While there is nothing wrong with encouraging employees, you shouldn't be spending all of your time on those tasks.

"Am I setting goals and objectives?" Do you write down your business goals and objectives, and review them on a regular basis? If not, you should be. Once your goals and objectives are laid out for everyone to see, it will be easier to get everyone working towards the same common goal.

"Do I provide incentives for everyone?" In other words, how do you motivate your employees (whether they are family members or not)? People really do want to do a good job, whether you think they do or not. But why not provide some type of incentives or rewards as a means to encourage them to do their best? Incentive pay, bonuses, time off with pay, and so on. Sit down and brainstorm some creative ways you can develop some incentive plans.

"Am I encouraging open communication?" Is your small business one that encourages open communication among all its employees (not just family members)? Or do you operate on a "need to know basis" only? Communication is the key to success in any small business operation, especially one that is filled with different family members. Develop a communications plan, and make sure you review it periodically to see that it is still working.

Looking into the Future of Your Family Business

Jill Lubin, founder and CEO of Promising Promotion, a communications and public relations agency in Novato, California, says that family businesses, like other businesses, need to commit to marketing every day in order to be successful.

"First of all, make sure you have good people helping you," she said. "To make your business succeed, make sure you are passionate about what you are doing. Create an 'oooh . . . aaah factor,' something that makes people stop and listen to who you are and what you do for your business. Seed the ground for publicity from the very beginning. Do your gardening from the moment you open your business, and never stop promoting your businesses," she said.

"Market a minimum of two hours per day. Put your butt in the seat and make phone calls and do not stop. You must commit to marketing every day, no matter how successful you are," she said.

> Do you operate on a "need to know basis" only? Communication is the key to success in any small business operation.

Marketing Is a High Priority

Whether your family business succeeds or not depends partly on your marketing efforts. Statistics show that small businesses that devote a substantial time to marketing have a higher success rate than ones that do not market that frequently. The choice is yours; market frequently and help your chances of succeeding, or market sporadically, and help your chances of failing.

One of the most significant challenges you will face is how to keep the future of your family business intact. While family harmony is an important factor, you shouldn't allow it to be the basis for how you make all of your executive decisions. As with any small business, common sense should be the rule of the day. Without common sense, you might as well kiss the future of your small business goodbye. Clean out your desk and leave now, because if that's the way you are running your family business, it's only a matter of time before you will be hanging out the "closed" sign.

Family businesses can be challenging, to say the least. But once you learn the fine art of managing a family business and get over all of the hurdles that you will discover, everything else will fall into place, and you will move your business forward, towards the success it, and you, certainly deserve.

For more information on this topic, visit our Web site at www.businesstown.com

Chapter 8

The Manager as a Visionary

What does the future have in store for small businesses in America? The future has always been a fascinating subject. Books have been written about it. Movies have been made about it. And while some of those books and movies have been right on target, many have proved to be just what they really are: a simple work of fiction.

But smart business owners realize that while the future is an uncertain entity, there are some predictions about the economic pathway of tomorrow that can be utilized in planning and preparing for the customers of tomorrow. Change is one constant that every small business owner and manager needs to keep in the back of their mind.

How Far Can You Really See?

As a small business owner, you need to have a reliable crystal ball with you at all times, because you will constantly need to know what the future has in store for you and your small business. But since crystal balls, reliable ones anyway, haven't been invented yet, you will have to start relying on something else: that little voice inside of your head.

You know the one. It's that little voice that says, "Call home, someone needs you," and you call home and find out that there has been a minor emergency and someone needs to speak to you. Or maybe the little voice is telling you, "Maybe I should hold off buying a new computer until next month and maybe I'll get a better price," and then before you know it, next month rolls around and bingo, computer prices have dropped nearly 30 percent. That's the inner voice we're talking about.

Trust Your Instincts

That inner voice is going to help you see into the future of your small business. And that inner voice is going to guide you to make the right decisions that will help you reap the rewards of a successful company.

> That inner voice is going to help you see into the future of your small business. And that inner voice is going to guide you to make the right decisions that will help you reap the rewards of a successful company.

As we enter the twenty-first century, the rules will be changing for small business owners. It will no longer be acceptable to do business "like we did in the old days." Instead, the new century will see the balance of power between consumers and retailers shifting. Fierce competition, combined with increased sophistication of consumers, means that small businesses are no longer in control as much as they used to be.

Consumers Rule

The power has shifted over to the consumer side of things, and the consumer is going to be more demanding than ever before. As the world grows increasingly wired, Web sites are popping up with consumer horror stories. These new consumers don't pull any punches when it comes to voicing a complaint about a product, service, or a company.

Consumers of tomorrow have arrived, and only the strongest small business managers will survive their conquest. Gone are the days when a company could produce a product, put it on the store shelves, and expect the consumer to purchase it. Small businesses that respond to these new consumers will thrive and succeed. Those that don't heed their call will be left on the side of the road, wondering just what went wrong.

Keep in Touch

One way to keep in touch with industry trends is to subscribe to trade journals that service your type of business. Those trade journals can provide up-to-date information concerning the movers and shakers of the industry, as well as providing forecasts and economic indicators. Contact the reference librarian and ask for a list of trade publications that are available, or do a search yourself on the Internet.

Why the Whole Picture Is Important to the Success of Your Business

You have just read some information about future trends, and hopefully you are formulating a plan of action to deal with the upcoming changes in the way consumers do business. But it's important to emphasize that you shouldn't get caught up in one or two segments, because looking at the whole picture is very important to the success of your small business.

It doesn't matter what product or service you are now offering—if you don't see the big picture as well as the individual segments, you're headed for deep trouble.

Tips to Help You Consider the Whole Picture

- Be aware of the business climate in your neck of the woods
- Know who your competitors are
- Know who your customers are
- Get to understand what your customers are looking for
- Have a clear plan of action in place
- Set goals for your business and review them often
- Take time to learn who your employees are
- Treat your employees with respect and loyalty
- Establish accurate controls
- Identify the key factors needed for your business to succeed
- Assess your business's strengths and weaknesses
- Focus on strategic thinking, not just on planning

> Does everyone in your company share the same vision?

Why Everyone Needs to Share the Same Vision

Remember the story of the Three Little Pigs? While they might have thought they each shared the same vision—to build a house to protect them from the big bad wolf—only one of them really had the correct vision. That one little pig who built his house out of brick knew what it would take to keep the wolf away from the inside of his home.

How about you? Does everyone in your company share the same vision? The next time you have a chance, assemble your staff in a conference room for an informal meeting. Shut the door, and tell them that what they are about to hear and say will not affect their standing at the company at all.

Quiz Your Employees

It would be helpful to provide refreshments, and maybe open with an ice breaker, but then quickly get down to the heart of the meeting. You have called everyone together to give them a quiz. And the quiz answers need to be given openly, honestly, and without judgments. Pass out the "quiz," on which you have typed the following questions:

1. When was our business founded?
2. Who founded our business?
3. What products or services do we sell?
4. What is the company's mission statement? (Assuming you have one.)
5. What is our reason for being in business?
6. Where do you think our strengths lie?
7. What do you think our weaknesses are?
8. Do you think our business has a future?
9. Are you willing to commit to that future?
10. How do you think we are doing with customer service relations?

Discuss the Responses Openly

Those ten questions will give you plenty of information for discussion. Hopefully, everyone will be able to complete the quiz in about twenty minutes or less. You might also hand out the questions ahead of time, so people have a chance to type up their answers. That way, they can remain anonymous, without fear of getting into trouble for what they say.

Those ten questions are the basics of what makes your company tick—what makes your company live and breathe each and every day. So evaluate the answers carefully, and if there are some areas that are weak, and people aren't sure what the answers are, start holding a series of training sessions. There's no better way to get everyone to know your mission statement and goals.

It is very important that everyone in your business share the vision. Share the dream, and learn how to make those dreams come true. If you don't, those dreams will quickly turn into nightmares.

The Future Is Closer Than You Think

Is the future ever really here? People are always talking about the future as if it holds some magic answer to all of our cares and woes. But just exactly when does the future ever arrive? As a small business owner and manager, it's your job to think about and plan for

New Employee Orientation

When new employees are hired, they are usually overloaded with information about the company: employee handbook, rules and regulations, safety information, etc. But that's the perfect opportunity to pass out an index card that contains your company's mission statement, and why you are in business. The index card can be tucked inside of a briefcase, purse, or placed on a bulletin board near their workspace. That way they will have a constant reminder of why they, and you, are there.

the future. The future success or failure of your business depends on how you plan for it.

When you think about all of the advances in technology over the past decade, it's amazing to consider the results. You can now check the weather anywhere in the world on the Internet. You can check traffic conditions anywhere in the world on the Internet, and you can find telephone numbers, street addresses, maps, and just about anything you are looking for on the Internet.

So, now that the Internet has made its way into society, is it safe to say that the future has arrived? No, not really. What makes the future special and so exciting is the "unknown." That's right; people are always hoping that the future will hold the magic answer to all of their cares and woes. It's what makes the world go round. It's what makes us tick; it give us something to look forward to.

Do You Know What Your Competitor Is Doing?

Do you know what your competitor is up to? Or a better question might be, do you know who your competitor really is? Too many small business owners don't spend enough time thinking about their competitors until it is too late. There are many advantages to learning what your competitor is up to, including the following:

- It helps you to plan your next strategic move
- You can see how consumers are reacting to their plans
- You can see what strengths and weakness they may have
- It gives you a chance to compare prices

Ways to Monitor What the Competition Is Doing

- Subscribe to and read industry trade publications. You might see an ad or read an article about your competitor.
- Whenever possible, purchase your competitor's products and assess their quality and features. How do they stack up against your own merchandise?

In Plain Sight

Some companies hire mystery shoppers to see how their own stores are doing when it comes to customer service, accuracy, efficiency, and other issues. But have you ever considered using someone to check up on your competition? Chances are your competition as already checked out your operations and you didn't even know it was happening. There's no better way to see what the competition is up to than to visit them in person and see what's going on.

- Subscribe to a firm like Dun & Bradstreet, which provides credit data and other types of information.
- Use the Internet to see what your competitor's Web site looks like. What features are they offering via the Web? Make sure you use this information to stay competitive.
- Visit your local library and see what information is available about your competition. Look for articles, books, brochures, etc., and study them carefully.
- Visit trade shows and stop by your competitor's booth and see what they have on display. Don't forget to pick up any literature that they may have available.
- Survey your own customers to see how familiar they are with your competition.
- Visit your competitor's location. Stop by their store or place of business and see firsthand what they are up to. If you live in a small town and are afraid you will be recognized, hire a mystery shopper to do the work for you.

When Setting Prices

When it comes time to setting prices for your products or services, keep in mind the prices that your competition is offering. If two products/services are identical in quality, then you know that a wise consumer will most likely go with the less expensive brand. So if your product is of the same caliber (or even slightly better), you'd better come up with some strategic ideas to steer those customers to your front door. Consider a coupon, a percentage off sale, or some other type of gimmick that will entice buyers to come to you.

For more information on this topic, visit our Web site at www.businesstown.com

Chapter 9

Managing a Team

How to Build Your Very Own Dream Team

In the sports world coaches and owners are lucky enough to be able to build and create the type of team they feel will lead them to a championship season. They carefully watch players on their own teams and other teams, and look for opportunities to recruit, train, and trade. Players know they must put forth their best efforts, or they may find themselves on the trading block—or on their way to an early retirement.

Managers of small businesses might be envious of those coaches and owners, but in reality, they too have the same opportunities to create their very own dream team. It consists of that group of employees who will go above and beyond the call of duty to make that small business succeed—and leave the competition at the starting gate.

It's not as hard as you might think, and it's a lot less expensive than shelling out millions of dollars for a star player, too. But you do have to use some common sense when it comes time to hiring the right employees for the right position. When the economy is going strong, the competition for good workers is really fierce, so do your homework.

Know What You Are Hiring For

Before you actually hire someone, create a killer job description. And don't include lines like "miscellaneous duties as required." If you don't know what you want this employee to do, then maybe it's not time to hire someone. Look for examples of job descriptions in employment books, on the Internet, and other places. Then spend some creative time and develop your own ones.

Create a series of questions that you will ask every candidate who applies for the job. Make them as short or as long as they need to be. Again, you can use some employment guides to draft some examples, but use your own common sense and create questions that really give you a sense of where the candidate is coming from, and how you think they will really perform if hired for the job.

Don't ask questions that require "Yes" or "No" answers. Use open-ended questions because they encourage people to talk about previous work experience. Instead of asking, "Do you consider yourself

> Before you actually hire someone, create a killer job description. And don't include lines like "miscellaneous duties as required."

a creative person?" which could lead to a simple "Yes" answer, try asking, "Can you give me a few examples of how you were creative in another position?"

Make the Applicant Comfortable

Ask everyone you interview to be honest. That might sound easier than it really is, but most people will want to impress you and land the job that they might be tempted to "tell a little white lie." Explain to them that honesty is the best policy, and that you won't hold anything against them if they are honest. Then ask them to describe a recent failure and success, and how they handled both situations.

Hold interviews in neutral territory. Ever hear about the "white coat syndrome?" It's when people who are having their blood pressure taken by someone in a white lab coat tend to have higher blood pressure simply because they are reacting to the medical professional and their uniform. Well, the same thing can happen during the interview process. Think back to all of those times your palms were sweating and your stomach was in knots when you were being interviewed. So try holding the interview on neutral territory. Be creative. Take the person on a walking tour and ask a few questions. It just might be the difference between hiring the right person and the wrong person.

Be a good listener. If the candidates are going to that much trouble to answer your questions, then listen to their answers. Really listen. And take notes. If they say something in their answer that will lead to another question, or that you feel needs an explanation, then follow up. Don't just rely on a list or "canned" questions, otherwise, after a few weeks or months you really won't care or listen to anyone's answers.

Respect the candidates. They are doing you a favor by coming out and putting themselves through the grinder, without ever knowing if they will be hired or not. So give them the respect that they deserve. If you treat your employment candidates poorly, you are probably treating your employees the same way, which might explain your high turnover rate.

> Respect the candidates. They are doing you a favor by coming out and putting themselves through the grinder, without ever knowing if they will be hired or not.

Think Before You Hire

Before you offer someone a position with your business, think carefully. Make sure you have asked every question you can think of. Be sure they understand what the job will consist of, and that they are enthusiastic about performing that job. There's nothing worse than hiring someone for the wrong job. You're better off letting that job go unfilled instead of putting the wrong person in the position.

Is Everyone on the Same Page?

Being a small business manager can create some special challenges for some people. If you have years of experience in creating a dream team and managing that dream team to a winning season, then congratulations. But more often than not, small business managers need help in this area. They need to make sure that everyone is working toward the same goal—the success of the small business.

Who to Hire?

Decide that you will hire only the best people for the job. Even in a tight labor market, you might be tempted to hire someone "because they have a pulse." But resist that temptation, no matter how enticing it looks. You will probably live to regret it, and may have even already made that mistake. Seek out the best and the brightest workers; they are the ones who will lead the charge to victory.

Don't rule out hiring older workers. Older workers bring experience to the table that you won't find in that bright young college graduate. They usually have excellent work ethics and habits, and tend to want to do a better job than their younger counterparts.

How to Hire New Employees and Keep Them

When you advertise for a position, don't skimp on costs. If your local newspaper is gouging local employers with high ad costs because they are the only paper in town, consider alternatives. Trade associations, Chambers of Commerce, tourism bureaus, etc., are all excellent alternatives to consider placing help wanted ads. Most of them have their own publications, and their rates are probably much cheaper than the local newspaper, anyway. Brainstorm other creative ways to get the word out; if you are looking for creative people (writers, artists, etc.), consider putting a notice on a bulletin board at the local bookstore or art gallery. Take your message to their location.

Create a fun workplace that will keep people happy and challenged at the same time. No one wants to come into a work environment that is boring and lifeless. So create an atmosphere that screams, "Isn't this a cool place to work?" If you're at a loss as to how to create such an environment, here's an important tip: Ask your employees what it would take to turn their workplace into the ideal job site.

Managing Older Employees

Managing older employees is not as difficult as it may sound, but too many small business managers miss the boat completely when they try and figure out what makes these older workers tick. You need people skills like never before if you have older workers on your payroll. Older employees are a special breed, and once you learn how to meet their needs, then your needs will be met at the same time. Remember, it takes two to tango!

Tips for Managing Older Employees

- Concentrate on their strengths, rather than their weaknesses. When you discover what tasks they excel in, make sure you assign them the ones they are good at.
- Understand their abilities and potential. Just because a worker is getting up there in years doesn't mean they don't have any worthwhile abilities or potential left.
- Make sure you listen to what they are saying. Hey, they've been on the planet a little longer than you, and chances are, they know more than a few things that you don't.
- Ask them what they feel they are good at accomplishing. And make assignments accordingly. Help find their place at work, and you'll be surprised at the results.
- Older employees seem to enjoy an "open door" policy, so make sure yours is open. Allow them ample opportunity to have their say, but without dominating your valuable management time.
- Make sure they understand the business goals and objectives. And if they don't, take your time and explain it to them. A well-informed employee, no matter how young or old, is a productive employee.

> Older employees seem to enjoy an "open door" policy, so make sure yours is open. Allow them ample opportunity to have their say, but without dominating your valuable management time.

The Graying of America

Is your business prepared for the future? In the next few years, the graying of America will result in more people over the age of 60 being in the work force. Older employees can be an asset to your business; just make sure you know how to manage them and encourage them to do their very best.

- Be sensitive to dietary needs of older employees in your snack machines and cafeteria. Don't just offer soft drinks and Twinkies; make sure you have healthy options available.
- Remember that you are supervising a person who has feelings, and is also a valuable member of your team. Treat them with the respect that they so greatly deserve.
- Treat them fairly and sensitively. Remember that they might be someone's grandmother or grandfather; how would you want an employer treating yours?
- Make sure you keep your older workers involved and busy. But don't just give them busy work for the sake of something to do while they ride out the clock waiting for their retirement party. Research has proven that a person who stays active and uses their critical thinking skills even in their golden years fare better than those people who don't.
- Keep them informed about what's going on in their department and in the business in general. Don't keep them in the dark just because they are older and you think that they probably don't care about what's going on.
- Understand and acknowledge the years they have put in on the job. They have probably made some very valuable contributions to the success of your business.

Managing older employees means you must have the right attitude about the task at hand. If you see them as a valuable part of the team, then they will respond accordingly. But if you just see them as "the old people who should have retired by now," then you're in for a heap of trouble, my friend.

Managing Younger Employees

Remember what it was like when you started in your first job years ago? If you're like most people, you were probably ready to kick butt first and take names later. Sound familiar? Of course it does; because that's what today's younger employees are trying to do.

And when you think that you didn't act that way when you were in your twenties and thirties, then you're only fooling yourself.

Whether you refer to your younger workers as the "kids," "gen X-ers," or any other fancy label, remember that they are just people who are just starting out in their career, and they will need your help and guidance along the way.

Tips for Managing Younger Employees

- Let them have their freedom as much as possible. If possible, allow them to have flex time and give them the option and ability to manage their own schedule.
- Give them a work environment in which they will excel. Provide the best computer equipment and other techno-gadgets your business can afford. If you're not sure what they need or want, ask them, and involve them in the purchasing process.
- Let them have an opportunity to shine. Don't think just because they are young that they won't have any good ideas. Let them have an opportunity to show you what they can do. Give them a chance to excel.
- Make sure they have a boss who understands their corporate culture. Younger workers sometimes need a boss who is sensitive to their needs and their methods of working, so don't give them a boss from hell. You'll both live to regret that decision, trust me.
- Let them make their own rules—to a certain extent, anyway. We all know that younger workers sometimes rebel at authority, so make sure you allow them a chance to make their own rules. As long as they produce the desired results, does it really matter how and why they do so?
- Let them have their creature comforts. Stock a refrigerator with soft drinks, juice, and the finest bottled water money can buy. And don't forget to include some healthy and not-so-healthy snacks while you're at it.
- Encourage younger employees to create a workspace that is comfortable for them. It might mean allowing them to

> We all know that younger workers sometimes rebel at authority, so make sure you allow them a chance to make their own rules.

arrange their desks and chairs in a way that works for them. If they like listening to music all day while they work, let them. Again, as long as they are producing the desired results, why rock the boat?

- Allow younger employees to come up with a time management schedule that works for them. Don't try and figure out why they want to keep crazy hours; you never will.
- Make sure you allow them to have "down time" when they need it. Maybe even a stroll in the park, or a quick trip to the mall (the Gap is always having a sale, you know). Give them the opportunity to do something that will let them feel like they can accomplish something non-work-related when they need to.
- If the corporate culture will allow it, consider job sharing, flexible hours, or even telecommuting. Again, if the job gets done, do you really care how?
- Make sure you offer child care, if your younger employees have children. If your younger employees need to work any type of overtime, it will be beneficial for you to let them have the peace of mind that their children are nearby and being cared for.
- Seek their input on both big and small business decisions. Let them know that their input is important, and that you do value their opinion and discussion on all matters.
- Make sure you offer feedback to younger workers. And if you must criticize, do it with kid gloves. (Remember how it was when you were younger?)
- Create a training schedule that includes every young worker. Give them as many opportunities as possible to grow and to learn. You will be glad you did when they start becoming some of your top producers of ideas and work.
- Encourage younger employees to "think outside of the box" and to seek creative, multiple solutions to problems and projects.

When you provide an environment that is conducive to productivity for younger workers, you will be pleasantly surprised at what they will begin producing. Most younger workers are results

> Create a training schedule that includes every young worker. Give them as many opportunities as possible to grow and to learn.

oriented, and they look forward to accomplishing a task and saying, "Hey, look what we did!"

Benefits of Working with Younger Employees Include:

- You will begin to see loyalty emerge from these young people. And these days loyalty can be an important value for any small business.
- You will soon realize that they are not that difficult to work with, once you understand how to care and feed them.
- You will be challenged to come up with creative ways to motivate them. And that thought process will help you in other aspects of your small business.
- You will be rewarded with a plethora of new ideas and enthusiasm. It seems like younger workers never run out of ideas these days, so why not take advantage of their creativity and energy?

Managing Creative Employees

Of all the types of employees on the planet, creative ones can be the most challenging. If you have managed creative employees in the past, then you know what I'm talking about. And if you haven't, then my friend, you are in for a real treat!

Tips for Effectively Managing a Creative Team

- Give them some space. Creative people are different by nature. They need their space to be, well, creative. So make sure you give it to them. Creative people are not like assembly line workers, where you have to worry that if one person goofs off the whole line is affected. Instead, creative people need space, some breathing room, some time to think and create. They need time to come up with those great ideas that are making so much money for your small business. So don't over-manage or over-supervise them.

Encourage New Talent

Younger employees sometimes have a difficult job to do. Not the actual job they are performing, but the fact that they are young, and most often have to "prove" themselves to the rest of the work force (especially if that work force is a lot older). Encourage younger employees to risk a little, and not to be afraid to be the best employee they possibly can be. Sometimes younger employees just need a little encouragement to shine. And when they shine, your business succeeds.

- Let them create their own environment. By nature, creative people are stimulated by visual objects, so by all means let your creative team decorate their office, workspace, or entire building with things that inspire them. Movie posters, lava lamps, basketball hoop, jukebox, whatever they want, let them put it there. Once they start cranking out those award-winning ideas, you'll be glad that you did.
- Give them the resources they need. If they need a library filled with creative books, magazines, and trade journals, then put one in. Or if you're on a tight budget, allow them time to go to the library. Creative people need creative resources for inspiration, and to compare and evaluate what's already been created. In the ideal world, you have enough money in your budget to build an extensive library (over time) that will keep your creative team jumping for joy.
- Give them access to training when it's available. Just because they are creative and dress (and think) differently doesn't mean that they wouldn't benefit from a workshop or seminar on some latest creative ideas or techniques. Budget something for training for your creative team, or that team will soon be looking elsewhere for employment.
- Let them be their own leaders. This is the area that is most difficult for many small business managers. They are not used to "letting go" and letting the creative team be in charge of themselves. But remember, creative people "think outside of the box," and need time to develop those crazy ideas—without worrying if some stuffed shirt supervisor is going to stop by and demand to see their time sheets. Let them lead themselves—and you—to success.

The traditional method of supervising employees does not work with creative people. So when you drop in their office and see them browsing through books and magazines, or playing with toys, don't panic. It means they really are hard at work.

> Small business managers are not used to "letting go" and letting the creative team be in charge of themselves. Creative people "think outside of the box," and need time to develop those crazy ideas.

Goals Everyone Can Agree On

Okay, you've gone to all the time and trouble of hiring the greatest team on the planet, and have learned how to manage older, younger, and even creative types of employees. Now it's time to create goals that everyone can agree on.

This is where your average small business owner drops the ball. Think of it as the championship game: there are only a few seconds before the game ends, and you have an opportunity to score one more time. And that final score will lead your team to victory—to the championship you have been dreaming about and working towards all year. But something happens, and you decide to toss the ball aside—on purpose. The crowd gasps in horror; every member of your team looks like they can't understand what just took place. And when you lose the big game, you want to blame everyone else for what took place.

Well, that is exactly what happens in the real business world, especially in some small businesses. For some reason, that same small business owner or manager who took time carefully building the perfect team decides that "okay, now that we're altogether, this is how it will work." And that, my friend, is the quickest way to business failure on the planet.

Include Your Team in the Goal-Setting Process

Ask everyone's input. This is an area that is difficult for many small business owners and managers. But if you don't ask for input, then your output will certainly reflect your lack of care and concern. Gather everyone together, and tell them it is up to them to come up with a winning plan they feel comfortable with. And watch what happens.

Ask everyone how they can meet those goals. It's one thing to come up with a list of goals that you want to accomplish, but you need to go one step further and ask for a plan, a road map, of how you will get there.

Put everything down in writing. And revise when necessary. Don't just record your goals, and then stuff them in a drawer. Study them, and change them when you need to.

Visual Stimulation

Creative people are visually stimulated, so make sure you are providing an environment that is conducive to creativity. Let your creative employees bring in their own "trinkets and trophies" and decorate their workspace so that they can use their creative gifts.

Develop a winning strategy that's just right for you and your team. Remember you are the coach, and it's up to you to create a winning strategy for your team. Lead from behind, and offer guidance and advice when it is needed.

Keep Looking to the Future

Dream big dreams. Don't let anyone or anything get in your way. Did you know that Walt Disney was once told that he lacked creativity? Can you imagine how the person who told him that must feel now that Disneyland and Disney World are the most popular vacation spots in America?

Focus on the end results. Don't get caught up in the nuts and bolts of the journey along the way. If your goal is to increase the fourth quarter's earnings, then come up with a winning plan and strategy and go forth with them. Focus on the end results.

Reward everyone when goals are met. Take everyone to an amusement park; buy them lunch at the fanciest restaurant in town. But do something to reward the team that has taken your business to a successful level. At a loss as to what to reward them with? Ask them for a list of possible rewards.

Don't dwell on mistakes and failures. Yes, sometimes mistakes will be made along the journey. And plans will fail. But don't spend so much time licking your wounds and feeling sorry for yourself that your competition races by when you are not looking. Get right back up into the saddle, and continue the ride.

It doesn't take a rocket scientist to assemble a team and manage them to success. It only takes a savvy small business owner. So get busy, assemble your team, and guide them toward a common goal that will keep everyone smiling and happy.

> Dream big dreams. Don't let anyone or anything get in your way. Did you know that Walt Disney was once told that he lacked creativity?

For more information on this topic, visit our Web site at www.businesstown.com

Chapter 10

Managing Professional Development

Professional development doesn't happen by accident. It takes careful planning and common sense, along with a killer "can-do" attitude, for it to work. If you don't spend time and energy investing in your employees and your business, well, soon you won't have to worry about even having a business.

A Company Has to Grow from Within

Steve O'Leary, president of the T&O Group, a public relations company in California, believes that the key to small business management begins and ends with the management of the people you work with. "They make or break any company, in particular, a small company that wants to grow. How do you get them to see the big picture? How do you get them to buy into all the things that need to be done? The key to managing people is motivating them and giving them a structure to succeed within. In my opinion, the motivation comes in the form of sharing information and profits," he said.

"In a service business like ours where people are your biggest expense and your biggest asset, it's crucial they know what their role is in terms of the time that it takes to complete a project. If they take twice as long to complete a project based on what was originally budgeted, there goes the profit. So by sharing the information on how much time it takes, it helps them to understand why it's important to stay on track or hurt the company's profitability. By allowing them to share in the profits, their own pockets benefit from good time management," he said.

> "The key to managing people is motivating them and giving them a structure to succeed within. In my opinion, the motivation comes in the form of sharing information and profits."

Managing "Talent Time"

"To assist us in this managing of our 'Talent Time' we've created a system for reviewing our time expenses on a monthly basis. We come together in what we call financial 'huddles.' The information distributed in the huddle tells the 'business partners' (i.e. how we refer to ourselves, not employer and employee) how we are doing in terms of monthly profitability.

"If our goals are met in terms of profitability, then at the end of each quarter and then again at the end of the year, we reward all the business partners with monetary checks. This past year in terms of bonuses, what were given out were almost 18 percent of salaries that each 'biz partner' receives," O'Leary said.

Improve Communications

To assist this sharing of information and management of time, the T&O Group is organized into teams rather than departments. "This helps to break down politics and improve the communication between fellow biz partners. Each team is constructed around a set of clients making the team client-centric rather than department-centric. Teams cut down on the frequency of mistaken communication, and eliminate the solo mentality that can exist with one department blaming the other department. Teams also build teamwork amongst the team members and create some good-natured competition between teams.

"Our financial rewards program, PIP (Partners in Profit), is also designed around the teams to reinforce the time management and profitability of the team. The end result is the management of a small company through a series of smaller teams who have access to detailed information on how their team is performing and has the motivation to improve their own delivery of work to achieve a better financial reward," O'Leary said.

> "Teams cut down on the frequency of mistaken communication, and eliminate the solo mentality that can exist with one department blaming the other department."

Why Everyone Needs a Mentor

Think back to your early years—when you just graduated from college, or landed your first big break, and got that really cool job. Did you look up to someone? Was there someone who "showed you the ropes?" Probably there was.

In every occupation, everyone needs a mentor. A good mentor is like a guide that is there to show you the way; to show you what you need to do to succeed in business, and in life. So don't think that by having a mentor that you are showing a sign of weakness. In fact, just the opposite holds true; if you have a mentor, it shows that you are smart enough to realize that mentoring is an important part of your training process. Mentors can help make a difference in everyone's life, including yours.

Is Networking Still Alive?

Whatever happened to networking? Is it still alive? Well, the answer is "yes!" Networking is alive, but only the smart managers are still using this invaluable tool to become a success. Once you realize the benefits of networking, it's easy to embrace the concept.

Benefits of Networking

Attend a Chamber of Commerce luncheon or business card swap and make some new friends.

- You create a lifeline that can help you in your time of need. If you network with other people in your industry, you can share ideas and frustrations with them. Sometimes just talking about a situation will be beneficial.
- You keep up with what's going on. Sometimes managers of small businesses get so bogged down with the day-to-day operations that they fail to keep up with the latest happenings in their industry. Attend a Chamber of Commerce luncheon or business card swap and make some new friends.
- You can create a resource list of experts whom you can call on when needed.
- You can use networking opportunities to find out information you are searching for.

Are You a Good Mentor? Take Our Quiz

1. I am a firm believer in the mentoring process.
2. I understand that my business will succeed by using mentors.
3. I know where I can locate a good mentor at any time of the day or night.
4. I understand the A to Z of the mentoring process.
5. I always jump at the chance to be a mentor.
6. I encourage my employees to embrace mentors with open arms.
7. I want my business to succeed, and will use mentors if I need to.
8. I often wonder why other small businesses don't take advantage of mentors.

9. I remember a mentor who helped me in the past.
10. I encourage my employees to be mentors if they have an opportunity.

Hopefully you said "Yes" to all ten statements. But if you didn't, that's okay, because mentoring is still a relatively little known and used commodity in small businesses.

Do you have what it takes to be a mentor? Many small business owners and managers owe their success to a mentor who crossed paths with them sometime in their past working life. So why not pay it forward, and help someone you come into contact with?

How to Be a Great Mentor

Be open and honest. Don't just tell someone you are mentoring that they are doing a great job if in fact they are not. By being open and honest, you are opening the doors of communication that will ultimately help them and you become a better manager. They may be shocked to hear that you are not their "yes" person, and that you are prepared to offer constructive criticism, but it will benefit them in the long run. People may resist your honesty at first, but stick with it, and soon they will see the error of their ways.

Realize that being a mentor takes time. So be prepared to stick around until the job is completed. It would be nice to pencil in on your daily planner "mentor today; allow one hour and the job will be done!" But it doesn't happen that way. A good mentoring process takes time, effort, and energy. So be prepared to offer everything you have until the job is done.

Build a bridge of trust between you and the person you are mentoring. Once that bridge has been completed, it will be easier to work together toward a common goal. If you can't completely trust each other, then the process won't work, no matter how many hours, days, weeks, months, or years you devote to the project. So start trusting each other today.

Use the tools you need to be a good mentor. To be a good mentor, use the resources that are available. If it's equipment, buy

Mentoring Means Success

Ever wonder what successful people have in common? Mentors. That's right. Somewhere along their career path, successful people had a mentor to show them the ropes. So encourage mentoring in your small business, and watch as successful people begin to surface.

it, borrow it, or find a place that has it and ask if you can stop by. If it's materials, such as publications, then find what you need. Invest some money, or if money is tight, look for a good library that subscribes to the publications that you need. Without the proper tools, the job can never be completed the right way.

Recognize that this is an experience that will change both of you. It doesn't matter how many times you have mentored someone, the experience will always be different and unique each and every time. You both will grow and learn new things about the business that you are involved in. Mentoring doesn't have to be that hard. So if you haven't mentored anyone lately, why not pencil something in real soon (just be sure to allow ample time)?

Training Is the Key to Success

To meet the demands required of businesses in today's highly competitive market, companies are finding it necessary to provide ongoing training to their employees. In the past, the training offered by most businesses was driven by regulation, customer service requirements, and safety compliance issues. However, businesses are now providing training as a means of increasing worker productivity and performance and improving worker retention.

U.S. companies—small and large—are increasing their investment in training. The typical private-sector business with fifty or more employees spends approximately $500 per employee on training. Most training money is allocated to trainers' wages and salaries with outside training companies, tuition reimbursements, and training facilities making up the rest.

Although large companies are more apt to provide training than smaller companies, size is becoming less of a predictor of training than complexity of the environment, degree of market competition, and the internal makeup of the company. Companies involved in total quality management practices, technology change, and organizational restructuring, for example, are more apt to provide employee training as they are focused on high performance as a strategy for survival.

> U.S. companies—small and large—are increasing their investment in training. The typical private-sector business with fifty or more employees spends approximately $500 per employee on training.

The American Society for Training and Development's State of the Industry Report highlights the influence of technology on industry training needs. Although small businesses have been slow to adopt new technologies, the increasingly technological nature of the workplace is prompting them to increase their spending in this regard. A *Computer Reseller News* Technical Training Survey conducted in 1999 revealed that 92 percent of small and midsize companies plan to offer technical training to their employees this year, making it the single most important area for training growth.

As small business operations become more computerized and telecommunication activities increase, it is expected that these trends will continue.

Training Employees Without Paying a Fortune

There are several different ways you can provide training for your employees. Depending on your type of business, available resources, and company environment you may want to try some or all of the following examples.

On-the-job training

There are approximately 6.3 million small businesses in the United States, 6 million of which have fewer than fifty employees. Most often, training in these companies is offered in-house and performed on an informal, sometimes random, basis. It is typically provided during a worker's pre-employment period or on the job. Experienced and skilled workers are paired with newly hired ones to explain the operational processes of the company and answer questions related to job roles. Mentors and coworkers provide much of this type of in-house training.

Seminars and speakers

Another form of informal in-house training offered by small businesses involves the use of volunteers who are recruited from the local Chamber of Commerce, colleges and vocational schools, and professional associations to offer skill training seminars free of charge. Brown bag lunches offer a forum in which general information can be conveyed, discussed, and shared. These inexpensive training methods

Take Time for Training

Training is where many small businesses fail miserably. They make all sorts of excuses: "Our business is too small to worry about training," or "We're too busy for training." If you want to fail, then don't bother with any type of training. If you want to succeed, schedule and budget time and money for adequate training for everyone at your company.

offer opportunities for one-on-one interactions, affording employees the personal touch and coaching that motivates learning.

Classroom instruction

Although most small businesses that have fewer than 100 employees provide little formal training, this is not true of all small businesses. An increasing number of growing businesses are starting their own universities—ongoing skill enhancement programs that draw on both internal and external resources to train new employees and keep veteran ones current with a rapidly changing business environment. The prime delivery method for most in-house training, however, continues to be classroom instruction.

One-on-one training

In-house training departments are less the norm in small companies than in large ones because of limited training budgets. However, individual trainers in small companies can have a great impact on employee learning and skill development as they can more readily target employees' development needs, cultivate relationships, and engage in one-on-one communication.

Training partnerships

Partnering with other businesses and securing support from suppliers are other ways in which small businesses are supporting their training functions. For example, noncompeting small businesses are combining their resources to leverage their training options. They are finding that collectively they can provide enough employees to take advantage of a single class offering, share costs of consultant seminars, and provide their employees with other types of formal skill training that they individually could not offer.

Vendor training

Some formal training for small business employees is provided by suppliers, for example, from such vendors as Intel and 3Com. Value-added resellers who sell Intel and 3Com computers to small companies see small businesses as their largest emerging market.

> Partnering with other businesses and securing support from suppliers are other ways in which small businesses are supporting their training functions.

Outsourcing Your Training Needs

Several small business have opted to pay for their training needs. While this can be pricey, it does save the company a bundle in terms of time and resources.

Training companies

Approximately one-third of all small businesses use external sources for their training. Sources of external training include training companies and professional trainers, including those from professional associations, who tend to provide customized programs targeted to a company's specific needs, e.g., conflict management, sexual harassment, and other management skill areas.

Educational institutions

Educational institutions generally provide more generic training developed to meet the needs of the industries and businesses they serve. For example, Guilford Technical Community College in North Carolina has developed a model training division to serve the local area's private sector. Its Business and Industry Services division and Small Business Assistance Center have developed training courses in both the soft skill and hard skill categories. In Ohio, two-year colleges and the vocational and adult education system are providing formal education and training programs for business and industry employees in such areas as statistical processes.

Learning technologies

Because small companies either lack technology specialists or time for them to train other employees, many small businesses are outsourcing technology training as a way to ensure that it is conducted company wide. Gaining in popularity are training programs offered over the World Wide Web or on CD-ROMs. These programs are cheaper than in-house classroom training and afford flexibility of time, space, and access.

> Approximately one-third of all small businesses use external sources for their training.

Obstacles in Training

Trainers in small businesses face time, space, and staff restrictions because of the limited funding for their efforts. Other factors that influence the type and quantity of training provided in small businesses include no recognition of the need for more or better skills, and attitudes and beliefs that training is not necessary and a waste of time.

Make it Work for Your Business

Small businesses can enhance employee training by adopting mentoring, coaching, and peer review practices. Company job manuals, packaged curricula, and worksheets can be supplemented by CD-ROMs, and videotapes, audiotapes, and other media to expand training options and capabilities. Other training practices that small companies can use to gear toward high performance include the use of job rotation, quality circles, and problem-solving team practices.

Although small companies may have limited training budgets, they can get the most out of their training dollars by assessing their training needs most important to the company's operation and employee growth. Companies should also investigate creative training options, such as outsourcing, distance learning, using volunteers as trainers, and linking to external providers such as equipment vendors, private consultants, industry associations, and technical/community colleges.

Training support for special populations is sometimes available through company or foundation grants. For example, AT&T, through its Supplier Diversity Program, is contributing $1.2 million to provide financial assistance and training to high-tech minority-owned companies that are in need of capital for expansion and training.

Innovative compensation practices, such as stock ownership plans, employee profit-sharing, and team-based or individual incentives are some of the motivational strategies that have effectively prompted employees in small as well as large companies to seek and continue training.

The Biggest Obstacle

Unfortunately one of the biggest obstacles to implementing any type of training program may come from one of your brightest employees. They may feel as if "they know everything," and don't see how they will benefit from training. You need to address that attitude as soon as it surfaces; otherwise, that mode of thinking may spread to other employees in your company.

Top Ten Ways to Encourage Mentoring in Your Business

1. Hold quarterly meetings that focus on mentoring.
2. Publish a newsletter that includes information about mentoring.
3. Make mentoring a part of the job description.
4. Offer incentives and rewards for those employees who become mentors.
5. Host a workshop to teach employees the ABCs of mentoring.
6. Be a good example, and be a mentor yourself.
7. Provide tools for mentors to use.
8. Remind employees that mentoring benefits both parties involved in the process.
9. Stress that mentoring doesn't have to take a lot of time.
10. Include information about mentoring in your employee handbook.

Solicit Employee Input

If you're not sure how to implement a training program at your company, or don't know what workshops your employees would benefit from, simply ask them. People who do their jobs day in and day out will have a better understanding of their job, and what training might be beneficial to you.

For more information on this topic, visit our Web site at www.businesstown.com

The Manager's Role in Marketing

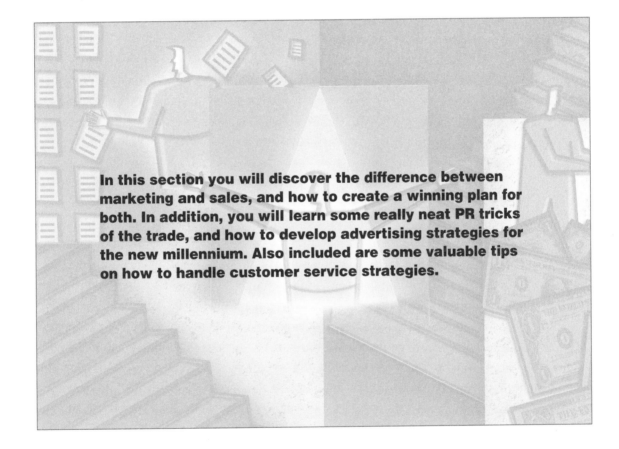

In this section you will discover the difference between marketing and sales, and how to create a winning plan for both. In addition, you will learn some really neat PR tricks of the trade, and how to develop advertising strategies for the new millennium. Also included are some valuable tips on how to handle customer service strategies.

Chapter 11

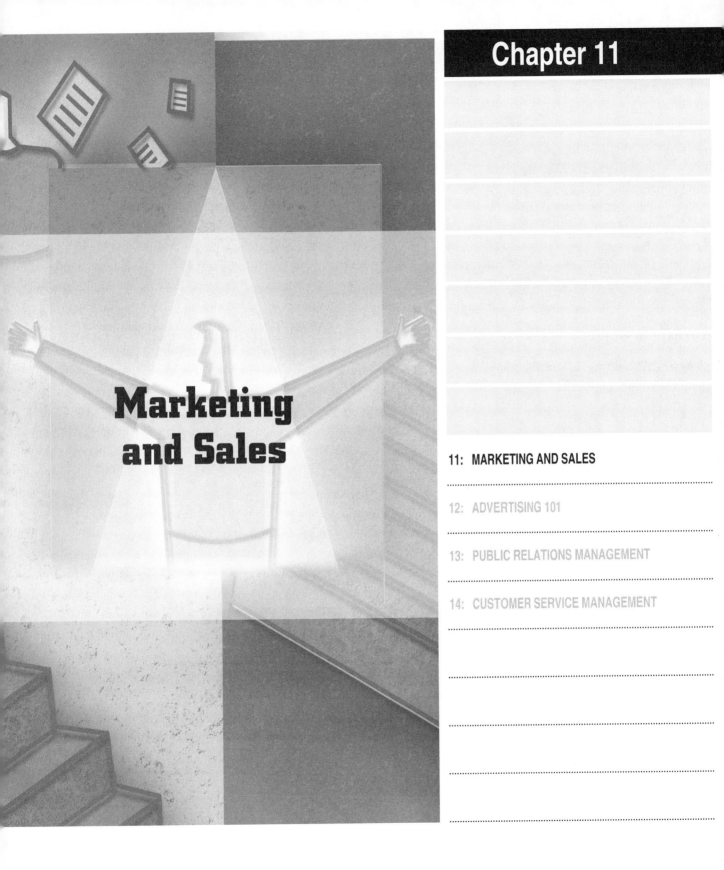

Marketing and Sales

Many small business owners and managers think that marketing and sales are the same thing. While they are closely related (sort of like kissing cousins), they are as different as night and day.

Don't fall into the trap of confusing marketing with sales. Marketing is a system by which you create a sales plan. It's not really that difficult once you understand the definition of marketing and the definition of sales.

Marketing

The marketing folks have an important job (just like the salespeople do). It's up to them to discover what your customers want, and help you create a plan that will get the goods and services they want into their hands.

The Marketing Process Has Three Basic Components

While at times it may seem as if marketing is a series of unrelated activities, marketing requires a successful relationship among everyone in your business. Once you and everyone else understands this, the marketing process will be easier to plan and implement.

Marketing is a managed set of activities. Successful small business owners take responsibility for creating a marketing department that can carry out those activities until they are successful.

Marketing must always be based upon the needs and desires of your customers. Without them, there would be no business at all. So it's up to the marketing department to discover what your customers want, and to produce a product or service that is tailor made for the customers.

Marketing also involves promoting the product or service, and spreading the word about why customers should buy or use it.

Get the Word Out

Joan Steward, who is also known as "The Publicity Hound," is a speaker, trainer, and expert in media relations and promotions. She knows the value of getting media attention for small businesses. "If you're just starting your business, send a news release to local newspapers, magazines, and trade publications that serve your industry. They can be about new product lines or additional services, classes or workshops you are conducting, new contracts, contests, surveys, or a charitable contribution you are making," she said.

Steward also believes that every small business owner and manager should get to know reporters in their hometown. "Be helpful to reporters and prove to them that they need a source like you. Let them know who you are and how you can help them. That might include letting them know about emerging trends in your industry, explaining your industry's complicated lingo or just inviting them to call on you when they need anything. Once you have positioned yourself as a valuable source, they might decide to write about you," she said.

She really thinks that it is important to look for photo opportunities. "Newspapers, magazines, trade publications, and newsletters are always looking for interesting photos that aren't necessarily accompanied by a story. For example, a florist who is creating special floral centerpieces using very unusual flowers a day or two before Mother's Day should call the local newspaper as the centerpieces are being created. It could make a gorgeous color photo. Call the publication and ask for the photo editor or the assignment editor," Steward said.

> Steward believes that every small business owner and manager should get to know reporters in their hometown.

Put the Word Out on Your Business by Writing about It Yourself

Another area that is open are letters to the editor. Steward believes that more small business owners and managers should write them whenever they have an opportunity to do so. "Editors always welcome timely, compelling, controversial letters. Be on the lookout for every opportunity to write one. Think of clever ways to weave into the letter what you do, how you can help people, and your areas of expertise," she said.

She is also a big fan of having business owners become experts by writing how-to articles. "Whether you're telling people how to grow gargantuan tomatoes or how to stay out of trouble with the IRS, 'how to' articles are an excellent way to call attention to your talents and establish yourself as an expert. Call your local newspaper, pitch your idea to an editor, then ask for the length limit and deadline," she said.

Additional Ideas for Getting the Word Out about Your Product or Service

- If you are a member of your local Chamber of Commerce, call and offer to be an ambassador. Chambers often need people to represent them at ribbon-cuttings, check-passings, ground-breakings and other events that are often covered by smaller newspapers. This will give you the chance to appear in the local paper over and over again.
- Give free classes or demonstrations. If you cut hair, offer to demonstrate how people can cut their children's hair. Chances are that many of the parents won't want to bother doing it themselves. Once they see how well you do it, they'll bring their kids to you.
- Offer to be a guest on a local radio talk show. The more controversial or helpful your topic, the better.
- Write a newsletter that you distribute free to customers. Don't forget to send copies to the media. Reporters often peruse these for story ideas.

> Write a newsletter that you distribute free to customers. Don't forget to send copies to the media.

Sales

If marketing is getting the word out about your product or service, then sales must be the actual activity that takes place. In other words, selling is the act of enticing or persuading the customer to buy something you are selling. Sounds pretty simple, doesn't it? While it may sound simple and you might think that anyone can do sales, don't think it's ever that easy (if you're still skeptical, try spending a week in the sales department and you'll see what I mean).

A Good Sales Force Should Have Certain Characteristics

- The ability to communicate effectively with people at all different levels. There will be times when they need to charm the receptionist to get in to see the decision maker, and other times they will be dealing directly with people at the upper end of the management food chain. So make sure their communication skills are top notch.

- The ability to get along with all types of people. They will be meeting and dealing with people from all walks of life, so your salespeople should be trained to get along with everyone they meet.
- The ability to show concern about the problems of their prospects. They need to be able to show them "I feel your pain," and at the same time be prepared to offer them a solution to their problem.
- The ability to always have a positive mental attitude. There is no room in the sales force for people who are whiners and complainers. If you do hire whiners or complainers, they won't last long, because they will be too busy complaining about everything to be able to sell anything for you.
- The ability to have common sense in all aspects of what they are doing. You don't need a loose cannon out there shooting up the town and making trouble for your business. Hire a salesperson who has a good head on his or her shoulders and who exhibits common sense.
- The ability to be humble when necessary. While many salespeople truly are "super sales" types, the ability to be humble can be an asset when the situation calls for a little humility.
- The ability to see good in people they meet. You don't need a sales force who is so cynical that they'll never make any sales for your business. While it is true that there are bad sides to a lot of people, look for a sales force that is able to see the good in the people that they meet.
- The ability to be self-sufficient. You want a sales force that could find their way off of a desert island with only a safety pin. The sales world is probably the last known frontier, so you want your sales force to be prepared to do battle and survive.
- The ability to show enthusiasm. To sell successfully, your sales force must not only believe in the product or service they are representing, they must be enthusiastic about it as well. And make sure that the enthusiasm is genuine, so that they don't come across as phony to your prospect.

The Perfect Match

Are the people in your sales department right for the job? When is the last time you evaluated their performance? If it has been awhile, it's time to do some serious soul searching. Sometimes salespeople can get burned out, or lose their perspective, their edge. If that is happening to your sales force, it's time to circle the wagons and come up with a plan. It may be time to bring in some fresh troops, and retire the ones that have been faithful in the past.

- The ability to use their imagination. There will be times when your sales force will need to draw upon their imagination to make the sale. They will be creative and come up with ideas at the drop of a hat. Do what you can to encourage and foster creativity and imagination in your sales team.

Creating a Marketing Plan That Will Succeed

Your marketing plan is an important document, one that will make the difference between the success and the failure of your small business. Before you develop a marketing plan, make sure you hire the best people on the planet to help you do so. Keep these tips in mind when you do finally create your marketing plan:

> Your marketing plan is an important document, one that will make the difference between the success and the failure of your small business.

- Make sure that you keep your marketing plan as simple as possible. Just because it is an important document doesn't mean that it has to be as complicated to read, understand, and implement. By keeping it simple, you won't get bogged down by so many details and lose sight of the reason you created it in the first place.
- Make sure that you do put your marketing plan in writing. Just because you need to keep it simple doesn't mean that you don't have to put it in writing. Write it down, and review it often; update it when necessary.
- Make sure you have someone review the first few drafts. Yes, that's right, the first few drafts. (You didn't think you could get away with writing only one draft now, did you?)
- Make sure you draft a marketing plan that has some degree of flexibility. But don't make your marketing plan so flexible that it's too difficult to implement.
- Makes sure you review your marketing plans on a regular basis. Depending on the nature of your small business, you might want to review your marketing plan on a quarterly basis, or even on a monthly basis.
- Make sure you take your marketing plan very seriously. It can make the difference between the success and the failure of your small business, so treat your marketing plan accordingly.

A Typical Marketing Plan Is Made Up of Six Basic Components

- The mission statement (also referred to as the purpose statement by some businesses)
- Your target audience
- The explanation of the benefits of your service or product
- How you are positioned in the market
- What marketing steps you will take (also referred to as your action plan)
- The marketing budget

Analysis of the Components of a Typical Marketing Plan

The mission statement—This statement doesn't really have to be a complicated piece of work. If you operate a tire store, then your mission statement for your marketing plan might be as simple as: "Our goal is to sell as many tires as possible in the tri-state area." Period. End of sentence; now that doesn't look too hard to write down, now does it?

Your target audience—If you can't identify your target audience for your product or service in one or two sentences, then you need to rethink why you are in business. Using the tire store example again, your marketing plan might read: "Our target audience includes anyone who owns an automobile and needs to buy or replace worn-out tires."

The explanation of the benefits of your service or product— If you think you are marketing a product or service, that's not entirely correct. What you are really marketing are the *benefits* of your product or service to the consumer, the end-user. Ask yourself this important question: What is the true benefit to the consumer if they buy whatever it is I am selling? If you are running that tire store, the benefit

Compile Sample Marketing Plans

Before you put your signature on your company's marketing plan, make sure you have taken the time to evaluate other marketing plans to see how yours stacks up. There are dozens of good books that have sample marketing plans, as well as hundreds of Web sites. Spend some time reading and evaluating those other marketing plans before you execute yours. You may just find something that you hadn't thought of before.

to the consumer would be "having peace of mind because they know they will be operating their automobile with a brand new tire."

How are you positioned in the market–Your positioning is your identity in the marketplace. In other words, it's how you want the world to view your product or service. Your positioning will have an impact on all components of your sales and marketing efforts. This is one area where many small businesses fall short. They don't bother with the positioning; but it is important, so work on it.

What marketing steps you will take (your action plan)– Here's where we separate the men from the boys. Where will your action plan take you? Have you taken the time to draft an action plan and marketing steps that will take you to the success you have always dreamed of? Some examples of an action plan or marketing steps include: sending out press releases, direct mail campaign, free samples, premiums, trade shows, and more.

The marketing budget–This is another scary section of the marketing plan that many small business owners and managers fall short in. Don't just pick a figure out of a hat; sit down and plan, plan, plan. And then plan some more. If you don't budget enough for your overall marketing plan, then you are just setting yourself up for failure, my friend.

> If you don't budget enough for your overall marketing plan, then you are just setting yourself up for failure.

Creating a Sales Plan That Will Succeed

Having trouble coming up with an award-winning sales plan that will knock your socks off? Try creating a sales pitch that is unique for your individual product or service. Make sure everyone will walk away saying "oooh" and "aaahh" about whatever it is you are trying to sell. Challenge yourself and your entire sales department to craft a winning sales pitch and implement it as soon as possible.

Be sure to set goals for your sales department. Without goals, you're dead in the water. With the right sales goals, and a plan to implement them, the sky is the limit. Set sales goals, and review them frequently. Always try to build on your past sales and maintain constant growth.

Define your sales territory, but be sure not to limit yourself. If you think your business is limited by your local geographic region, think again. In today's high-speed communications world, you are limited only by your own sales and marketing efforts. So when you are busy defining your sales territory, keep that in mind.

Managing Your Sales Staff

Do you know how to manage your sales staff? Or do you just give them a catalog, a few product samples, and send them along on their merry way? If you are not managing your sales staff very effectively, your bottom line will soon reflect your lack of leadership in that area. By not taking control and directing and guiding them, you will be losing a great deal of potential business, and probably end up with a high turnover in your sales force. Why? Well, believe it or not, most salespeople, while they prefer to act independently, also look to management for some type of leadership, guidance, and advice.

An effective and successful sales force doesn't happen by accident. A successful sales force definitely doesn't happen overnight.

Establish Goals and Keep Everything in Writing

Set clearly defined goals. Without a goal, your sales force won't have a clue as to what to do. Of course, they probably will go out and make a few sales, but everyone, including your sales force, needs clearly defined goals and a plan as to how to work those goals.

Develop a policy and procedures manual. You need to have a written, documented plan in place before you send your salespeople out the door. Every company is different, and every policy and procedures manual will be different. So don't make them have to reinvent the wheel every time they meet with a potential client.

Encourage them to keep good records. Sure, your sales force is very busy, but unless they take a few minutes every day and record what has taken place, you may never know what has transpired.

> Most salespeople, while they prefer to act independently, also look to management for some type of leadership, guidance, and advice.

There are plenty of software programs on the market today that will help even the busiest salespeople keep records and evaluate their performance.

There are plenty of software programs on the market today that will help even the busiest salespeople keep records and evaluate their performance. And if all else fails, paper records will work, too.

Shower Your Sales Staff with Attention

Offer training as often as you can schedule and afford it. Too many small business owners and managers think they need to train their salespeople only one time. Like any other worker, salespeople will benefit from additional training and information about the product or service they are trying to sell.

Create incentives and motivational factors. You need to stay competitive and offer incentives to your sales force that will rival anything a competitor might not have thought of yet. Whether it's a trip, a cruise, a new car, something, anything; just make sure you offer something to those people who perform an outstanding job for you and your small business.

Hold sales meetings. And hold them at least once a week, unless your sales force is out on the road and are too far away to make it back for a meeting. And make your sales meetings fun; brainstorm ways to make them interesting and challenging. It's a great way to keep everyone up to date on what's taking place, too.

Ten Reasons Why Managers Don't Understand Marketing and Sales

1. They think that marketing and sales are the same thing.
2. They think that one person can do the marketing and the sales.
3. They never fully understand why the marketing department and the sales department need their own budgets.
4. They think that a marketing person can fill in for a salesperson if they are out sick.
5. They think that a salesperson can fill in for a marketing person if they are out sick.
6. They don't understand why salespeople need incentives.

7. They don't understand why marketing people are a little different, just because they are creative (and good at what they do).
8. They don't understand why salespeople have to talk so much.
9. They think they can have a marketing department without having a sales department.
10. They think they can have a sales department without having a marketing department.

What's Your Marketing and Sales IQ?
Take Our Quiz

1. Sales and marketing are the same thing.
2. As long as sales are up, I don't have to worry about marketing.
3. As long as marketing is fine, I don't have to worry about sales.
4. Sales staff shouldn't require training.
5. Sales staff can be weak on their people skills.
6. Marketing people can work without goals.
7. Marketing people shouldn't worry about what the competition is doing.
8. As a small business owner, I don't have to worry about sales and marketing.
9. Sales and marketing can be handled by the same person.
10. Sales and marketing plans should never be reviewed and updated.

Hopefully the answers were pretty obvious. In order to have a perfect Sales and Marketing IQ, you must have answered "No" to each of the ten statements. Try thinking about why the answer is "No," and what you can do to help your sales and marketing efforts out in your company.

Be Supportive

How well do you support your sales staff? After all, they are the ones out in the field, doing battle for you and your company. So make sure you are providing the support that they really need. Before you send them out, ask them what they need. A salesperson who is fully armed and prepared is ready to do battle with the world.

For more information on this topic, visit our Web site at www.businesstown.com

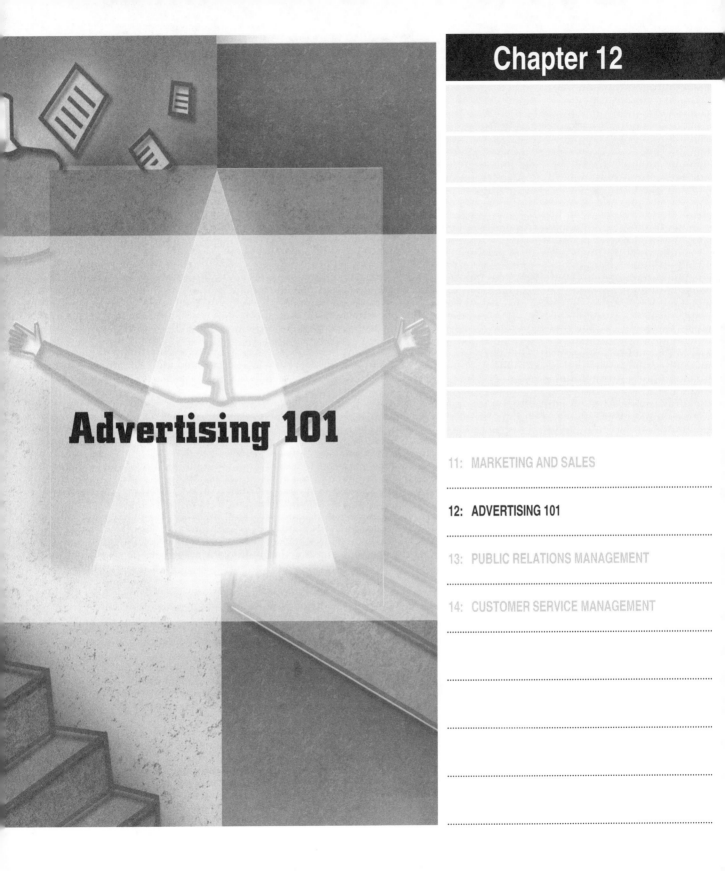

Advertising 101

Chapter 12

Most small business owners and managers think they know all they need to about advertising. After all, what could be so difficult about placing a few ads and watching thousands of new customers flock to their business? Advertising can't be that difficult, can it? It's not exactly rocket science, now is it?

Well, my friend, if you agree with that philosophy about advertising, then be prepared to start wasting your hard-earned money and get nothing in return. You see, the fine art of advertising is as difficult as rocket science, if not more complicated. It is certainly less predictable.

In the old days, a small business owner could place a display ad in their local newspaper, and sure enough, when people read the newspaper and saw the advertisement, they would drop everything and flock to that business to make a purchase they just couldn't live without. But that was fifty years ago, when things were quieter and not so complicated. Today, if you place a display ad in the local newspaper without spending time preparing your strategy, then you are setting yourself up for failure and doom.

> The fine art of advertising is as difficult as rocket science, if not more complicated. It is certainly less predictable.

Advertising Strategies in the New Millennium

Almost every business needs advertising, otherwise, they would not be able to stay in business. But have you ever given any thought to what type of advertising is just right for your particular business? Have you ever sat down and taken the time necessary to learn the basics of advertising? Have you ever put together an advertising plan, and budgeted enough money to make that advertising plan succeed? If you haven't, don't feel bad, because most small business owners would barely get a passing grade when it comes to knowing the ABCs of advertising.

But don't agonize over it any longer. The basics of advertising aren't that difficult to learn, and I am prepared to present them to you. Learn how you can create an advertising strategy and take your business to the next level of success.

Newspaper Advertising

This is probably the type of advertising that most small business owners and managers are familiar with. After all, everyone reads the newspaper each day, right? Well, almost everyone. Let's start with some basic questions to ask yourself before you decide if newspaper advertising is right for you.

What is your planned response? In other words, what exactly is it that you want the readers of your newspaper ad to do? Is your ad purely an "informational piece" that's just announcing the dates of some special sales? Or does it include a coupon where your potential customers can save money by clipping the coupon out of the newspaper and bringing it into your business?

Who are you trying to target? In other words, who are you trying to reach with your newspaper ad? You need to identify the characteristics of those customers you are trying to reach. What is their age, sex, income, lifestyle, culture, and geographic location? These are important factors to consider when you are ready to place a newspaper ad.

What type of positioning are you looking for? In other words, how do you want your ad positioned? Good advertising leaves a clear impression on the mind of the reader. Make it easy for them to remember you. The style or look of your ads and your products or services you advertise are key elements that position you in the minds of your customers, and potential customers.

What type of frequency should you get? Does your customer think of you first when they are ready to buy? Advertising on a regular basis can build strong awareness. Things to consider are your business goals, business cycles, economic trends, and what your competition is doing.

Customer Response

When is the last time you surveyed your customers to see how effective your advertising has been? Your customers can give you the feedback you need to continue with a successful advertising campaign, or to create a new one if it is needed. Consider offering an incentive or reward for your customers who take time to fill out your survey. It can be a discount coupon, or a free gift. But get that customer feedback; it is an important part of your advertising and marketing strategy.

When should you place your ads? Newspapers can be especially effective when your customer is ready to buy. They are also great ways for customers to compare prices, products, and coupons before they make a decision to buy. So, timing can be everything when it comes to placing newspaper ads. Make sure you are advertising at the right place, and at the right time.

Newspaper Ads Should Attract Attention

Newspaper ads can be an effective way to drive customers to your business. But there are a few rules to remember when it comes to creating the actual newspaper ad. Your newspaper ad should attract attention. This may sound obvious to most people, but many small business owners and managers don't give it a second thought. Think about your own experience when you read the newspaper: what ads do you stop and read?

The ad needs to be appealing to the reader. Again, this may sound like common sense, but the next time you're reading the newspaper try and look for some ads that really look out of place, and you'll know what we're talking about. Your newspaper ad should jump up and down on the page and scream, "Read me, I can save you money!" or something similar.

Your newspaper ad should communicate your business to the customer. In other words, it should let the reader know why they should chose your business over your competitor. (Important tip: Start clipping newspaper ads that have attracted your attention and put them in a file. When you are ready to design and place your own newspaper ad, you'll have some good examples to use as models.)

Your newspaper ad should motivate the reader to buy. This is really the main goal of any newspaper ad: to motivate the reader to look at the ad, and want to respond by making a purchase, either now, or at some time in the near future. So think about your own experience as a consumer. What newspaper ads motivated you to buy a product or service? Then design your ad accordingly.

Start clipping newspaper ads that have attracted your attention and put them in a file. When you are ready to design and place your own newspaper ad, you'll have some good examples to use as models.

Print Ads Have Only Seconds to Catch a Potential Customer's Eye

Sometimes a customer will only scan the newspaper page, and that means your ad has only a few seconds to do its job. So, will the ad you're thinking about using do the trick? In other words, would it pass the five-second rule? Would readers be able to glance at your ad and within five seconds realize that they want to look at it more closely?

Because your ad may have only precious seconds to do its job properly, it's very important that the headlines in your ad work. Advertising experts may disagree on many things, but one common belief they have is that on average, five times as many people read the headlines of ads than the ads themselves. The best headlines that convince newspaper readers to read the entire ad are ones that promise the reader a benefit. In other words, it must convince them that they will save money, live longer, lose weight, be happier, etc., by reading your ad.

> Would readers be able to glance at your ad and within five seconds realize that they want to look at it more closely?

Example Headlines from a Current Newspaper:

- 10 percent off
- 20 percent off
- 50 percent off
- Don't think, just go
- Good for you
- Now is an excellent time to lock in guaranteed interest rates
- Different year, same solution
- Clean up and save big
- Imagine your destination
- Remarkable
- Super
- Peace of mind
- Proven results
- New
- Now
- Guaranteed
- Win

Experiment with Placement

Don't always rely on the newspaper salesperson to let you know where they think your ad will draw the most response. Experiment by placing your ad in different sections. For example, if you're trying to target males, then the sports pages would be a logical place in which to run an ad. However, men also read the business sections, and even the comics. So the next time you're putting together a newspaper ad campaign, don't just run the same ad in the same place day after day, or week after week. Readers won't even realize it's there.

- Save
- Safety first
- Discover this
- Golden opportunity
- Free

Contact your local newspaper's advertising department and set up an appointment to discuss the best advertising strategy that's just right for your small business. They have trained professionals on staff who are waiting to help you. But don't go in to a meeting unprepared. Think about what your goals are for wanting to place a newspaper ad beforehand. Bring in samples of ads that you have clipped out of the newspaper that you thought were really creative and fun. Newspaper advertising works, but you still have to do your part in the planning process.

Radio Advertising

Newspapers are an excellent way for your small business to offer blanket advertising coverage to a particular geographic region, but radio permits advertisers to appeal to specific audiences over large geographic areas. By choosing just the right radio station, program, and time for your ad, your small business can reach virtually any target market. Radio can be a very effective means of advertising, and an excellent way to drive new customers to your front door.

Advantages of Radio Advertising

- **Universal infiltration**—Homes, cars, fitness centers, workplaces, waiting rooms, street corners, you name it—often these places will have a radio playing, which means radio ads receive a tremendous amount of exposure in your target market. According to the Radio Advertising Bureau, radio reaches nearly 80 percent of all people each day and 95 percent each week.

- **Market segmentation**—Advertising on the radio is efficient because you can choose stations that are directed toward a specific market within a broad geographic region. Radio stations design their formats to appeal to specific types of audiences. And you have the luxury of picking and choosing the radio station that is just right for your target audience.
- **Immediate access**—When you decide to place a radio ad, it's possible to have your ad on the airways sometimes within a few hours of when it is written and recorded. Ads can be changed quickly to accommodate your particular needs.
- **Familiarity**—With everyone being used to listening to radio ads, you don't have to worry if someone will forget to read the sports section and maybe miss your ad that day. Whenever the radio is turned on, the customers and potential customers are literally a "captive" audience. But it's up to you to make sure your radio ads are creative, funny, witty, and something that people remember and talk about to their friends and coworkers.

Consider the Station When Placing the Ad

As a small business owner, you can reach just the right demographic makeup of your customers and prospective customers. Radio stations have a variety of formats in today's market, including:

- Country
- Pop
- Rap
- Middle of the road
- Easy listening
- Rock
- Modern rock
- Oldies
- Rhythm and blues
- Talk

It's up to you to make sure your radio ads are creative, funny, witty, and something that people remember.

Making a Radio Ad

Before you set up a time to speak with an advertising rep from a radio station where you'd like to buy airtime for your advertisements, listen to some radio ads yourself. And when you listen, do so with a tape recorder and hit the record button when you hear a radio ad that you really like. Do this over a period of several days and find at least a half dozen radio ads that you think were creative and that you'd like to use as models for your own advertisements.

Most radio stations have professional copywriters on their staff who will take care of writing the radio spots. Some small business owners, however, also like to write their own ads and have them edited and rewritten to fit the format of a thirty- or sixty-second spot.

Guidelines to Follow in Making a Radio Ad

Make sure that you mention your business name often. This is an important rule in writing radio ad copy. You want to make sure listeners can identify the business that is running the spot. If they've just tuned in or were distracted when your ad first started running, they need to be able to hear your business name at least three times.

Take care to make sure the listeners receive some sort of benefit from hearing your ad. In other words, you need to tell them something that will benefit them. Tell them they will save money, or that the new, hard to get toy that everyone is looking for around the holidays is now available at your place of business.

Explore the full range of what radio can offer. With radio, you can do practically any sound effect you can think of. Use a combination of music, sound effects, cartoon voices, etc.—whatever you can think of that will make people stop and listen to your radio ad.

Keep your radio copy short and sweet. Don't use big words or hard to understand words when writing your radio copy. Keep the copy short, sweet, and to the point. Remember, you only have thirty or sixty seconds to convey your message. Take advantage of every word you use.

The ad should convey a sense of urgency. Not necessarily a life or death kind of urgency, but the ad needs to draw people in fast.

> Make sure the listeners receive some sort of benefit from hearing your ad. Tell them they will save money, or that the new, hard to get toy that everyone is looking for around the holidays is now available.

Take advantage of radio ads by including words such as "now" and "today only" and others that let the listeners know they have to respond as urgently as possible. If this isn't accomplished, a listener might like the product or service you are offering, but feel as if it can wait a few weeks. By then, that same person has listened to thousands of other radio ads, not to mention looking at print and television ads, meaning your ad is quite forgotten.

You should also make sure to use humor whenever possible. Research shows that people respond to humorous radio ads, so work something funny into your copy. But make sure it's really funny, and stay away from offensive or degrading humor and jokes.

Television Advertising

Many small business owners may feel that advertising on television is something that they cannot afford. Everyone has heard about the six figures that businesses pay for a spot during the Super Bowl. While it certainly is true that advertising on national television may be out of your price range, there are advantages to placing your ad on local stations, especially cable ones. In fact, in some markets, it's possible to place a thirty-second spot on a local cable television station for as little as $500.

Benefits of Television Advertising

With television advertising, you get a much broader coverage area. With today's television ads, you get extensive geographic coverage of a fairly large region, and nearly every home has a television. Advertising experts estimate that the average television is on for nearly eight hours everyday, which makes it possible to reach many potential customers using this medium. And the top 200 cable channels now draw about 50 percent of television viewers.

Television also offers a visual advantage. Newspaper ads can show pictures of your merchandise. Radio ads can describe your merchandise. But television can actually show your product being used by people. Many small businesses are taking advantage of television by producing their own infomercials, thirty-minute television

Humorous Ads and Radio

The next time you hear a funny ad on the radio, think about what made you laugh. Chances are, it was something that you could identify with. And odds are that funny ad and the product it was selling will stay in your head for some time. That's why humorous ads on the radio are so successful. People love a good laugh, and even tell their friends, family, and coworkers about what they just heard. You couldn't ask for a better word-of-mouth referral. So start drafting your next funny radio ad today.

programs featuring the benefits to a consumer if they purchase or use your product.

You have flexibility to offer a variety of spots. It has been said that advertising on television is the next best thing to having your own personal salesperson sitting in your living room with you. You can design your television ads to be thirty, forty-five, or sixty seconds in length, or offer a variety of each. Many small businesses experiment to see what types and what length television commercials work best for them.

Don't Go Overboard

Before you jump into television advertising, take some time and check out the competition. See what other businesses are advertising on television, and ask yourself if you think their ads are effective and worth the money they spent on having them produced. And think about who it is you are trying to reach through your television advertisements. Contact your local television stations and set up an appointment to speak with them about potential ads. While it is true they are the experts in knowing what works and what doesn't work in terms of advertising on television, remember, too, that they are also in the business of making money by selling advertising space on their shows. So while they may suggest to you that your television ad needs to run for at least two or three months in order to be effective, carefully weigh that cost against what it would cost to run newspaper or radio ads. Talk with other small businesses and see what kind of experience they have had with television advertising. But remember, just because one business had a good experience by advertising on television, the same rule might not apply to your own small business. So, just like anything else in life, it's buyer beware. Be careful what you buy, or think you are buying in terms of television advertising.

If you do decide to spend money on a television ad, remember that in addition to buying airtime to show the advertisement, you will also have to pay production costs to have it created. So make sure you compare prices carefully. You want the best television ad your money can buy.

Before you jump into television advertising, take some time and check out the competition. See what other businesses are advertising on television, and ask yourself if you think their ads are effective.

Guidelines for Crafting a Creative Television Ad

Keep to one basic idea–Your ad should focus on a single, important benefit to the consumer. Explain to them why they should buy a product or service from your business.

Keep your ads simple–Unless you have an unlimited supply of advertising dollars, stay away from expensive special effects and other gadgets, that, while may be fun to watch, may be too expensive for your wallet. But that doesn't mean you can't take advantage of colors, motions, sounds, and other basics.

Make your ad effective from the second it begins–If viewers are halfway through your ad and they still don't know what it is you are selling, or worse yet, who you are, then you are in big trouble. From the second your television commercial begins, put the focus on your business and your product. And be sure to mention your store's name, location, and telephone number if it is relevant to the ad.

Network with other small business owners who have used television advertising and see how they made out. Ask them if they thought the return on their investment was worth their time and effort.

> If viewers are halfway through your ad and they still don't know what it is you are selling, or worse yet, who you are, then you are in big trouble.

Web Advertising

Still considered the "new kid on the block" when it comes to advertising, using the World Wide Web to promote your product or service can be an effective and lucrative way to reach your target audience. By using the Internet, your small business can reach the demographic profiles of the young, educated, and wealthy, while at the same time exposing your business to growing numbers of customers outside the United States. Through the use of your own Web page, you can showcase your products and services for less than $100 a month, and still make your site one that makes use of photos, colorful graphics, creative images, and text that can literally dance across the screen.

The Internet's explosive growth makes it a unique and appealing tool for many small business owners. People are logging on to the Web more and more each day, and some studies have shown that 25 million Americans consider the Internet something they cannot live without. Because you have the capability to use sound, color, video, and visual appeal, the Web offers pretty much the same advantages as you would find with a television ad, but at a fraction of the cost.

Use the Web as an Advertising Vehicle for Your Small Business

Make your site appealing to view. Your Web site should be pleasing to the eyes of the visitors who stop by there. Don't use harsh colors or colors that are too bright as background graphics. Use a variety of photos and graphics, if your site calls for them.

Make your site easy to navigate. How many times have you gone to a Web site and gotten lost? And what was your immediate reaction? If you're like most people, you probably hit the back button, or typed in another Web address. No one wants to get lost in a maze of Web pages. Keep your site's design simple and easy for your customers to navigate around in.

Avoid Web pages that are slow to load. Your site should not make viewers have to wait for more than a few seconds for your home page to load onto their screen. Research proves that if a Web site takes too long to load, viewers will find a new site to explore. Don't let the home page of your Web site fall into the slower than molasses category, or you'll be losing customers and their spending power.

Update and change your site's content often. Visitors who return to your Web site will quickly get bored and leave unless they have something new to view. Take the necessary steps to revise the content on your site at least once, if not twice a week. If you offer consumer tips or other information, make sure you hire a freelance writer to supply you with fresh articles to post as frequently as your budget will allow.

> Update and change your site's content often.

Generate Interest *and* Revenue from Your Web Advertising

Don't beat around the bush. Use your Web site to sell a product, a service, or a combination of both. But don't waste valuable time and Web pages by creating pages that don't try to sell something. Visit other small business Web sites that you consider successfully done, and see how they are handling the sales end of the picture.

Offer your visitors something of value. Visitors to your site won't waste very much time trying to determine if your Web site is of any value to them. Let them know from the time they land on your home page what you have to offer them. Have links clearly marked that help take them to different areas of your Web site, and make sure you have a "help" button that will really help them.

Make sure you accept credit cards or debit cards. Studies have shown that customers are interested in making purchases online using debit or credit cards. Make sure you offer them this feature, and make sure that their information is safe and secure from hackers and thieves. There is special software to handle credit and debit card transactions.

Offer your visitors a way to request information. The smart business owners who have Web sites are taking the time to respond to visitors' request for additional information. Remember, these are live customers and prospects that have contacted you, so don't make them wait for a response back from you. Treat them with respect and give them the information they are searching for, and you will be doing your part to help increase your customer base.

The Web can be a valuable advertising tool. Make sure you take advantage of it, and everything it has to offer you.

> Don't beat around the bush. Use your Web site to sell a product, a service, or a combination of both

Direct Mail

Direct mail is another popular method for small business owners to do their advertising. Using letters, postcards, catalogs, coupons, brochures, card decks, and other print-related methods, direct mail has its rewards. In today's marketplace, direct mail is used to pretty much sell everything on the planet from A to Z.

Advantages of Direct Mail

Selecting your target audience–By using direct mail, you can target a specific audience to receive your advertising message. Are you looking for consumers who purchased a washing machine in the last six months? Or are you looking for consumers who purchased a new car in the last two years? All of that data is available, and you can obtain mailing lists and labels to target your direct-mail campaign to your new prospects.

Holding your reader's attention–By using direct mail, your ad doesn't have to compete with other ads on a newspaper page. Believe it or not, people really do enjoy getting mail, and if your ad brings information about a product or service they are interested in, then you have hooked a possible customer.

Getting rapid response from your customers–In most cases, direct-mail advertisements produce results in a fairly short time frame. Small business owners should know whether a direct mail campaign has been successful or needs to be reworked.

Using different strategies–Because you have the ability to control your own mailing lists (and any mailing lists that you might rent), you can use different strategies to see what works best. For example, you can send one group a flyer with a coupon, and see how many people respond. And you can compare that with another group who gets the same coupon but without the flyer.

> Because you have the ability to control your own mailing lists (and any mailing lists that you might rent), you can use different strategies to see what works best.

Drawbacks of Direct Mail

Despite the ideal advantages of direct-mail campaigns, they sometimes do have their drawbacks, however. For example, you may end up spending your hard-earned money to rent a mailing list that may be inaccurate or incomplete. The Direct Marketing Association estimates that 60 percent of the success of direct marketing is based on the quality of the mailing list. So when you rent a mailing list, make sure you are renting one from a reputable dealer. Contact other small business owners in your area and see what mailing list companies they have used and if they have been pleased with the results of their own direct-mail marketing campaign.

Direct-mail campaigns sometimes are not very popular with consumers, too. The average family receives about ten pieces of direct mail each week, and unfortunately, they classify it as "junk mail," and most of it will land in the trash can without even being opened.

To get consumers to open your envelope is a big challenge. Direct-marketing experts agree that getting someone to open your mailing piece is half the battle. Then, once they have opened it and are scanning the contents, they have a few seconds before they decide to read it more in depth, or toss it away.

> Sixty percent of the success of direct marketing is based on the quality of the mailing list.

Direct-Mail Strategies

When I worked as a fundraising consultant about ten years ago, I created a direct-mail campaign for several nonprofit organizations in Delaware and Maryland, which were very successful for everyone who used them. I called it the "No Go, No Show" fundraising event. The agencies would design an invitation to a New Year's Eve party that wasn't really going to take place. It looked just like a wedding invitation or any other party invitation. On the front cover was a cute cartoon (usually drawn by a volunteer who had artistic talent), and inside was the copy. It listed all sorts of clever reasons why the person who had just received the invitation should stay at home on New Year's Eve, and send an invitation. The mailing also included a brief mission statement and facts about the nonprofit agency, in case the person wasn't familiar with the work they were doing in the local community.

Two strategies were the key to the success of this campaign. One was that each invitation had a personal note written inside from a friend or relative of the person who received it. For example, some people would write "Aunt Mary, I just wanted to let you know about the great work the ABC agency is doing, and hope you will consider lending your support this year, love, your nephew, Stanley." This way, when Aunt Mary read the direct-mail piece, it had a personal connection, something that would keep her from immediately tossing it into the trash can.

The other strategy that worked really well was the design of the envelope. In short, there was nothing to it. Literally. It was simply a blank, white envelope. And to send these special invitations out to everyone, each agency held a List Party. Because the agencies didn't want their special invitations to be lost in the shuffle of all of the holiday mail season, we decided to physically drop them into the mail on the morning of the Wednesday before Thanksgiving. That way, most people would start receiving them on the Friday after Thanksgiving, and throughout the Thanksgiving weekend. When people came to the List Party, we had holiday decorations in the room, and holiday music playing on the CD player. We also had plenty of food. Then everyone would sit down and break out their own mailing list. Yes, that's right. They brought their own mailing list. It contained friends, family members, coworkers, their doctor, dentist, and other professionals, and anyone else they could think of that included people they knew. Some people had lists of friends they had attended college with, and others even had their dry cleaner and other businesses they frequented on the list.

Then, people would take their time and hand address each invitation. And a first-class stamp was used, instead of a bulk-mail stamp or postage tape. The point was to make the invitation look like either a wedding invitation, or perhaps even the first Christmas card that would be arriving over the Thanksgiving holiday weekend.

And it worked. When people received the personalized, hand-written plain white envelope with the first-class stamp, it always became the piece of mail they opened first that day. And because it also contained a personal note from someone they were connected with, in 93 percent of the cases, it resulted in a donation being made to that particular nonprofit agency. In this case, the strategy and careful planning paid off and was a very successful direct-mail campaign.

> When people received the personalized, hand-written plain white envelope with the first-class stamp, it always became the piece of mail they opened first that day.

All Options Should Be Considered and Scrutinized

So what type of direct-mail piece should you consider using for your small business? There is so much conflicting advice floating around out there that it's no wonder people get confused. But unfortunately, that confusion often leads to large sums of money being spent to create a campaign that's doomed to fail even before the direct-mail pieces are dropped into the mailbox.

Many small businesses often consider using a letter as a means of communicating with existing and potential customers. But what kind of a letter should you write? What are the rules of direct mail? Well, it's a good thing that you asked, because the only direct-mail rule you need to know is: *there are no rules!* Let me clarify that statement. There are no rules that apply to two different businesses at the same time. A quick visit to your library or local bookstore to find some books on how to write direct-mail pieces will result in all sort of tips "all guaranteed to produce successful results." Some books will tell you to write short letters, and others will say no, write long letters. Some books will say to include some type of a premium as an incentive, while others will say it's a waste to include a premium. Still other books will say to use a fancy envelope, and other books will say no, use a plain envelope.

With so much conflicting advice on the market today, it's no wonder that small businesses have trouble producing the best direct-mail piece that is just right for their particular business. Remember, trying to figure out what works in direct mail is an inexact science at best. Consultants, experts, professional copywriters, and others all have different—and sometimes conflicting—ideas about what works when it comes to creating a direct-mail marketing piece.

Start collecting samples of direct-mail pieces that have touched your heart and made you want to buy something or make a donation. Put them into a file, and then one day when you are ready to come up with your perfect direct-mail marketing campaign, you will at least have some examples of what you consider to be very good appeals.

> Make sure that your readers know and understand what the most important benefit to them will be either in a big headline or the opening paragraph.

Additional Guidelines for Creating Direct-Mail Ads

- Make sure that your readers know and understand what the most important benefit to them will be either in a big headline or the opening paragraph.

> Studies have shown that people will sometimes skip portions of a direct-mail letter, but will be drawn to the PS. Use that PS as a way to make them want to read the rest of the letter.

- Make sure that you use a postscript (PS) at the end. Studies have shown that people will sometimes skip portions of a direct-mail letter, but will be drawn to the PS. Use that PS as a way to make them want to read the rest of the letter.
- Repeat your offer or notice about a special sale at least two or three times. Just like a radio commercial where people need to hear the name of your business several times, readers need to read the info a few times.
- Write your letter in a friendly, easy to read conversational tone.
- Use eye-catching words such as: free, save, now, profit, improve, etc.
- Make sure you use short paragraphs. Your letter can be long, but break up the paragraphs so the reader's eye doesn't panic at the thought of reading long paragraphs.
- Include a way for the reader to respond—either with a coupon they have to bring into your business, or a postcard they return for further information, etc.
- Use testimonials if possible.
- Make sure you address your letter to a person by name, and not by "occupant." Most "occupant" letters never even get opened.

Transit Advertising

This type of advertising includes advertising signs that are used inside and outside some of the 80,000 public transportation vehicles throughout the country's urban areas. The number of vehicles is likely to increase in the years to come as additional public transportation agencies are created. You've seen ads on the side of buses, inside of buses, on the tops of taxi cabs, and other things.

The Advantages of Using Transit Advertising

- **Wide coverage**—Because those buses, taxi cabs, and other public transportation vehicles are constantly on the move, they cover a large geographic area. This means that a greater number of people will be exposed to your advertisement.

- **Repeat exposure**—These types of ads offer the small business owner a way to get their message repeated over and over throughout the day.
- **Low cost**—Most small business owners with even the most limited of advertising budget will be able to afford some type of transit advertising.

Transit advertising can be worthwhile for many small businesses, especially those with a limited advertising budget.

Outdoor Advertising

For many decades consumers have been exposed to billboards and other outdoor advertising mediums. While it does offer limited geographic coverage, if your ad appears in a high-traffic area thousands of commuters per hour can see your ad. Many small businesses supplement other advertising methods with an outdoor ad.

Benefits of Outdoor Advertising

- **The ads grab the commuter's attention**—Special effects, such as 3-D, fiber optics, and other creative methods are now being used on many outdoor advertising billboards. Gone are the days when a billboard consisted of just a picture and a few words of copy. These days, anything is possible.
- **The ads give the small business owner high exposure—** Studies have shown that an average billboard reaches an adult consumer approximately thirty times each month. And since commuters tend to travel the same route to and from their workplace, billboards can be an effective way to get your message across in a short but repetitive manner.
- **The ads are usually very cost effective**—When priced at a cost per thousand customers reached, billboards can be very cost effective.

> Studies have shown that an average billboard reaches an adult consumer approximately thirty times each month.

Make an appointment with your local billboard company to discuss the many options that are available. Before you agree on a package, think about any creative billboards that you have seen recently and come up with a similar design and artwork. Keep in mind, however, that because billboards are stationary and the consumer viewing it is moving, you have only a few seconds to capture their attention.

Tips for Creating an Ideal Outdoor Billboard Ad

> Don't use very many words. People need to be able to read your message literally within seconds, so don't put up more words than are absolutely necessary.

Use short words in the copy—and don't use very many words. People need to be able to read your message literally within seconds, so don't put up more words than are absolutely necessary. When you're driving around over the next few days, make a note of what some other outdoor ads are doing in terms of the length of the words that are being used to sell a product or service.

Make sure artwork and illustrations are large enough—They should be able to be seen and recognized at a great distance. You don't want people driving by and not being able to figure out what it is you are trying to say or sell to them.

Use a font that is easy to read—Don't pick a gothic font or other hard to read font, otherwise, no one will be able to read your message in the few seconds they have when they are passing your billboard.

Ask for a billboard on the right side of the highway—Marketing studies have proven that billboards on the right side of the road draw higher recall scores from consumers than billboards located on the left side of the highway.

Directories

Another medium used by many small business owners to promote their companies is directories. Directories can be an important and inexpensive means to reach customers and potential customers. They can include telephone books, industrial guides, buyer's guides, catalogs, and yearbooks that feature ads from local businesses.

Before purchasing an ad to place in a directory, do your homework and determine if that particular directory will be seen by your target audience. If not, then pass it on by.

It Starts with a Careful Plan

As with anything else in life and in business, advertising starts with a carefully crafted plan of action. As a small business owner, it is your responsibility to brainstorm and think about what advertising is going to give you the most return on your dollars that you are spending.

Steps for Creating a Great Advertising Plan

1. Do your homework. Get to know the target audience that you are trying to reach. Figure out what your competitors are doing in terms of advertising. Are they using newspaper and radio ads? If so, why? And are their ads very successful? Understand the current trends in your local market. Keep on top of the latest in consumer studies and statistics that apply to your product or service.
2. Plan to position your product or service. You need to position your product or service clearly in the mind of the consumer, whether they are currently a customer, or merely a prospective customer. Who is your product for? What does it do? Know its features and benefits inside and out and understand clearly why your target market can't live without it.
3. Be ready to identify a need. And when you identify a consumer's need, be prepared to tell the customer how your product or service can fill that need.
4. Learn how to grab the reader's attention. Come up with copy and artwork that is so creative that it attracts readers and says, "Hey, you!"

> Get to know the target audience that you are trying to reach.

5. Be ready to create a lasting image or brand. When it's time to buy your product or service, you want consumers to think of you. If they do that, then your advertising is doing its job. Branding is the key to capturing your share of the market.

Secrets of Successful Advertising Campaigns

It's no secret why some advertising campaigns succeed and others fall flat. The winners do everything right. They plan, they study, they brainstorm, and then they create the perfect ad and find just the right medium in which to present that ad to their customers and prospective customers.

Many small businesses envy the success of Ben & Jerry's Ice Cream, and the sales they have produced. But remember, too, that Ben and Jerry started out as a simple, small business. In Burlington, Vermont, entrepreneurs Ben Cohen and Jerry Greenfield created their ice cream business with a difference. They weren't afraid of wild and wacky promotions, and they made up their minds early on in the life of their business that just about anything goes when it comes to advertising.

Creative Ways for Producing a Successful Advertising Campaign

- Make sure you offer special promotions. Come up with your own wacky, creative ideas and offer special promotions to your customers. People are attracted to the promotions that are different and unusual, so come up with a Christmas in July sale, or something similar.
- Make sure you give away samples. Every consumer loves to get something free, so don't forget to include some type of give-away in your promotional package.
- Hold some type of contest. Consumers like to get involved, too, so don't forget to come up with some type of creative contest for them to enter.
- Create a special event that people will remember and talk about. Come up with a wacky idea for a special event that will

> Many small businesses envy the success of Ben & Jerry's Ice Cream, and the sales they have produced. But remember, too, that Ben and Jerry started out as a simple, small business.

have the whole town talking about what you did. Word of mouth can create lots of excitement that can translate into increased sales and a boost to your bottom line.

- Come up with an advertising campaign that you believe in. If you don't believe in your own ad campaign, how can you expect consumers to do so? Put everything you have into the planning and execution of your ads and success will be yours.

Who Is Your Target Audience?

Believe it or not, this is one area that many small business owners fail miserably in. If you ask them who their target audience is, they just hesitate and mumble, because they are not really sure themselves. To help identify who your target audience is, ask yourself these questions:

- Who are the customers who use my product or service now?
- Where do they live and shop?
- Who do I think is my ideal customer?
- What is the demographic makeup of my prospective customers?
- When do my customers buy?
- When would I like them to buy?
- Am I fulfilling a need for my customers?
- Am I taking advantage of customer surveys to see what they want?
- Am I responding to my customer's ever changing needs and wants?

Know Your Audience

Just how well do you know the people that buy your product or service? Many small companies think they don't have to worry about getting to know their audience. Your customers are the lifeblood of your business. If you don't get to know them, and respond to their needs and wants, they will soon take their business elsewhere.

Ten Ways to Get Free Advertising in Your Community

1. Provide a sample. For example, if you have a landscaping company, offer to landscape an area near a busy intersection. You can then post a sign, "Landscaping courtesy of XYZ Nurseries." Thousands of people each day will pass by and see a sample of your work.

2. Write a letter to the editor. Comment on an issue, and sign it as the business owner. (It's a proven fact that more and more people are now reading the "letters to the editor" section of the newspaper than ever before.)

3. Write articles for local Web sites. If you have a small business that provides printing services, then consider writing an article for a local Web site. Look at your local Chamber of Commerce and see if they have a Web site; odds are, they will be looking for articles.

4. Sponsor a Readathon or some other type of special event at a school. Your business name, logo, and other information will be sent home to hundreds (or thousands) of students and their families. They are potential customers!

5. Sponsor a local sports team (little league, bowling, etc.). Your logo and business name will be put on uniforms, signs, and other venues, thereby exposing your business to literally thousands of potential new customers each week.

6. Offer your services as a speaker. Many community groups (Lions Club, Chamber of Commerce, etc.) are always looking for a speaker for their next luncheon or special event. When you become their next speaker, you are exposing your business as well.

7. Hold a "free" event at your business. Customers like "free," so anything you can provide will surely bring in people to your business. For example, you might provide free haircuts, free pet grooming, free auto inspection, etc.

8. Ask a local restaurant to sponsor an entrée and name it after your business.

9. Swap ads with noncompetitors. In other words, find a business that will run one of your ads in their publication, and do the same for them.

10. Provide bookmarks with information about your business and have the library and local bookstores give them away.

> Swap ads with noncompetitors. In other words, find a business that will run one of your ads in their publication, and do the same for them.

For more information on this topic, visit our Web site at www.businesstown.com

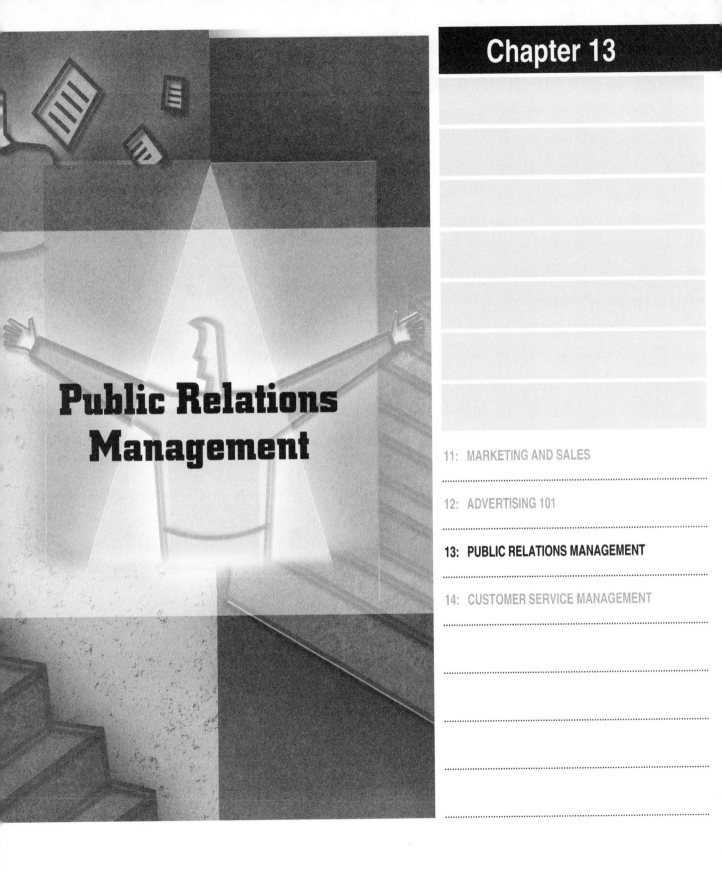

Public Relations Management

What Is Public Relations and Why Should You Care?

Public relations is kind of like the weather. Everybody is always talking about it, but nobody really ever does anything about it. But what really is public relations, and why should you, as a successful business owner even care about it?

What Public Relations Is Not

- **Advertising**—Many small business owners equate public relations with advertising. Advertising is advertising, and public relations is public relations. They may be similar, but they are definitely not the same. As a business owner, you can place ads in the newspaper, on the radio and TV, and dozens of other venues. That's advertising. You pay for advertising, and these days, it can cost you some really big bucks.
- **Marketing**—Again, for some reason, many small business owners equate public relations with marketing. Marketing is marketing, and public relations is, as mentioned before, public relations. They, too, are related, and can work together; but they are definitely not the same. You can have a marketing plan, and that's marketing. In other words, marketing involves influencing the behavior of potential customers to have them purchase whatever it is you are selling.
- **Publicity**—Here we go again. Just because public relations and publicity begin with the same letter, many small business owners think they are one and the same. But they are not. You can get publicity for your business, but you will need a public relations plan. It may sound confusing, but once you learn the basics of public relations management, it will become crystal clear to you.
- **Selling**—Why would anyone think that selling and public relations are the same? Who knows? But far too many small

You can get publicity for your business, but you will need a public relations plan.

business owners think they can sell their product or service and ignore the public relations aspect of selling. The modern approach to selling is not to sell to the customers, but rather to help them buy. That's why selling is selling, and public relations is public relations. And in this case, they definitely need each other.

What Public Relations Is

All right, now that you know what public relations isn't, it's time to find out what exactly it is. The dictionary defines public relations as "the business of inducing the public to have understanding for and goodwill toward a person, firm, or institution." In other words, public relations happens when the public views your business in a positive tone. But what should you bother with public relations? After all, you are a very busy small business owner who must have more important things to do than worry about public relations.

If you think like that, you couldn't be more wrong about the subject. Public relations should be at the top of your "to do" list each and every day. Because if you don't keep a good handle on your public relations, disaster is right around the corner.

Public relations can include press releases, press conferences, special events or any other methods used to gain public recognition of an event or organization. (For the record, publicity includes advertisements, fliers, and news articles that appear either in print media, such as newspapers, trade journals, etc., or in broadcast media, such as radio, television, etc.)

Your public relations plan should include the best ways to generate positive publicity about your business. Have you ever wondered why some businesses seem to get all of the media's attention? The answer is simple: those business owners have learned the fine art of working with the media, instead of working against them. And their rewards are seen by the general public every time their business name or product is given positive recognition in the newspaper, on the television or radio, or any other number of venues.

> Public relations should be at the top of your "to do" list each and every day.

So make sure you learn as much as you possibly can about creating a public relations plan that is just right for your small business. If you don't have any real experience in this area, don't panic. There are plenty of books, workshops, seminars, etc., that can give you the basics and teach you Public Relations 101. Or you can network with other small businesses through trade associations and groups like the Chamber of Commerce or Jaycees. Do whatever it takes to come up with a good, solid public relations plan.

Network with other small businesses through trade associations and groups like the Chamber of Commerce or Jaycees.

Top Ten Reasons Why Most Managers Fail at Public Relations

Despite the information that is available, many managers still have difficulty grasping the concept of what makes up a good public relations plan. In fact, many of them fail on a daily basis when it comes to public relations. Here are the top ten reasons why most managers fail at public relations:

1. They never take the time necessary to build a working relationship with the local media.
2. They don't bother networking with other business owners.
3. They fail to budget any time or money for public relations activities.
4. They don't worry about negative publicity, and the impact it can have on their business—and their bottom line.
5. They never offer their services as a speaker for local groups, associations, and the like.
6. They don't know what a media list is, or how to obtain one.
7. They don't sponsor major events or contribute time, resources, or money to local charitable organizations.
8. They don't plan ahead to see what public relations activities are taking place in their city and state.
9. They never publish a newsletter for their customers and potential customers.
10. They fail to keep their present customers happy and coming back for more.

Public Relations Can Be Taught in Ten Easy Lessons

Let's take another look at the list. By examining each one in a little more depth and detail, you will see how public relations can be taught in ten easy lessons.

1. Build a working relationship with the local media. (We'll cover more about this in a few minutes.) Find out who the reporters and editors are that cover your business. For example, if you have a retail shop, call your local newspaper and ask for the name of the reporter who is responsible for writing about the retail scene in your community.
2. Network with other small business owners. When is the last time you took time to attend a Chamber of Commerce networking function? If you think you are too busy to take time to attend these types of events, you are sadly mistaken. There is power in networking. Take advantage of it today and sign up for something real soon.
3. Make sure you budget time and money for public relations activities. It doesn't mean that you have to spend thousands of dollars every month on big special events—or spend all of your time shaking hands and creating good will. But by spending a little time and effort creating a budget for your time and money, it will pay off in big dividends when customers start talking to their friends about your business and the service you provide. Remember, you can't put a price on good, solid word-of-mouth public relations and publicity.
4. Take care of any negative publicity before it happens. Have a contingency plan ready to put into action if something goes wrong. Remember, a story or event doesn't actually have to be true. But if the public and the media perceive something to be wrong, in their eyes it is wrong.
5. Offer your services as a speaker to local community groups. By putting yourself in the spotlight at their next function, you have a captive audience and have the opportunity to turn everyone who is within listening range into a potential

> Take care of any negative publicity before it happens. Have a contingency plan ready to put into action if something goes wrong.

customer. Some service organizations that are always looking for public speakers include:

American Legion
Lions Club
Rotary Club
Kiwanis Club
Chambers of Commerce
Elks Lodge
Masons
YMCA/YWCA
PTA Organizations
VFW Chapters

6. Learn about media lists: what they are used for, how to obtain one, and how to make the best use of them. (We'll talk more about this soon.)

7. Make sure you become a pillar in the community by becoming a sponsor at the next Walkathon or other special event that is taking place. And in addition to sponsoring money, you can also donate prizes of merchandise, gift certificates, and other goodies from your business.

8. Plan ahead to see what public activities are taking place in your community and town. Contact your local Chamber of Commerce or department of tourism bureau at the state. They routinely publish a calendar of events, some as far as a year in advance. Review it several times a year to see what potential events might be good for your business to get involved with.

9. Consider publishing a newsletter for your customers and potential customers. It doesn't have to be anything fancy, or cost an arm and a leg to publish. Just something that can show your customers (and prospects) what is taking place at your business. You might even let local community groups publish public service announcements as another goodwill gesture. Remember, the more the public sees and reads about your business, the better off you will be.

10. Keep your customer happy, and keep them coming back for more. What have you done for your customers lately? Have you done anything to give them a reason to smile and say, "What a great experience I had at that store!"? Do you hold customer appreciation days, and roll out the red carpet? Remember, when people feel special, they'll tell their friends. And you can't beat that word-of-mouth public relations.

Working with the Media

One of the most important decisions a small business manager must make is to work with the media. Too many small business owners, however, fail in this department. Ask yourself these questions to see how well you know the media in your community:

- Do you know the name of the editor or reporter to send press releases to at your local newspaper?
- Do you know how to draft a press release that will be read and not tossed away with the dozens of others that are received each day by the media?
- Do you know if your newspaper prefers to have press releases faxed or e-mailed?
- Do you know the e-mail addresses of the media movers and shakers in your town?
- Do you know why working with the media is important?

Hopefully, you were able to answer "Yes" to most of these questions. But if you couldn't, or if there are some aspects of working with the media that you still do not understand, relax. It's never too late to learn Media Relations 101.

Ways to Work with the Media

- **Obtain an up-to-date media list**–By getting your hands on an up-to-date media list, you are helping yourself in all of your publicity campaigns and efforts. The Department of Tourism

Send a Thank You

When your business receives attention in the media, make sure that you send a thank you to the person who covered the story. It doesn't take more than a postcard, a thank you card, or a short note to let them know you appreciate the coverage they gave you. Learn how to become a friend of the media, and not their enemy. You never know where that relationship will lead, and those contacts may come in handy some time in the future.

(also known as the Convention and Visitors Bureau in some states), your local United Way office and even the Chamber of Commerce should be able to supply you with a free copy of their media list. You should also check their Web sites to see if they have their media list posted. The media list will contain the names, telephone and fax numbers, and nowadays even e-mail addresses of reporters, editors, program managers, and other public relations personnel. (*Important note:* Media lists can change frequently, due to the turnover in personnel and job assignments. Double-check to make sure the person you are sending that press release to is still in charge. If you're not sure, a quick telephone call to the newspaper or other media outlet will confirm it for you.)

- **Use your media list**—Once you get that all-important media list, don't just hang it on your bulletin board or file it away somewhere. Use it. Aren't sure what to use it for? Well, for one thing, it is a useful tool when you are ready to send out press releases. And if you want to hold a press conference, you'll know who to invite and how. (*Important note:* Many media lists don't include newsletters that are published by large corporations for their employees. You might want to contact the human resources department manager at all of the major businesses in your town. See if they publish any type of employee newsletter or bulletin, and if they include press releases and other information from local businesses. Many of them will be glad you called, because they are usually struggling for news to include.)

- **Keep the media informed**—Let the media world know exactly what is taking place at your small business. This is your chance to toot your own horn, and to tell the world about what is happening with your company.

- **Return telephone calls promptly**—Want to get bad press? Then don't worry about returning that reporter's or editor's telephone message that's been sitting on your desk. Ever

Media lists can change frequently, due to the turnover in personnel and job assignments. Double-check to make sure the person you are sending that press release to is still in charge.

read this in your local newspaper: "Efforts to reach the business owner were unsuccessful." Now, doesn't that make great newspaper copy? Wouldn't you rather the general public read something positive about you and your business? Of course you would. Then make sure you return those telephone calls immediately.

Working Against the Media

Believe it or not, there are some people who choose to ignore the media. And if you are a small business owner who has adopted that attitude, then my friend, you will reap what you sow. Ignore the media, and you never know what the consequences might turn out to be.

Rules to Remember to Prevent You from Working Against the Media

- When things go wrong, don't avoid the press. It's best not to sidestep their questions. Sooner or later, they will find out the information they are looking for. The more you avoid them, the worse off it will be. You don't want to be the lead story on page one or the big story on the six o'clock news—unless of course, it's good publicity.
- Have a disaster plan ready. If you have a problem with your business that might be the focus of a media inquiry, then you'd better have a disaster plan ready. Have someone appointed *before* there is a problem who will act as the official spokesperson for the media. Instruct other employees not to comment or answer any questions. Instead, tell them to politely guide the media to your official spokesperson.
- Use only the facts. Don't give theories, or any other information that you're not absolutely, 100 percent sure is the truth.
- Maintain a professional attitude at all times. The media is only doing their job, and by cooperating and having a professional attitude toward them, it will go a long way in helping them to fairly report a news story.

> Have someone appointed *before* there is a problem who will act as the official spokesperson for the media.

There's nothing wrong with being prepared. You never know when something will go wrong, and you certainly don't want to earn a reputation as a business owner who works against the media. Work with them, and things will go a lot smoother.

Planning a Dynamic Public Relations Campaign

Want to be a very successful small business owner? Then take the time necessary to learn how to craft a dynamic public relations campaign that is just right for your business. Budget enough money to hire a professional public relations or advertising firm to create a campaign for you. Let them do their job; it's what they get paid to do.

Sit down with them and explain to them what it is that you are trying to accomplish with your public relations campaign in the local community. Are you trying to enhance your image? Tell them. Are you trying to increase sales? Tell them. Are you trying to be recognized as a leader in your community? Tell them. If you don't communicate your needs to the public relations professionals, they won't be able to help you.

Results a Dynamic Public Relations Campaign Can Produce

- **Increased awareness**—How many times have you thought that business might be better if only more people realized you were there, or knew about everything you offer? Studies have shown that most buying decisions are made on the basis of a selection between three or fewer alternatives, and it's hard to make it to the finals if no one knows you're competing.
- **Increased traffic**—Want to drive more traffic into your business? Then do everything in your power to convince customers and potential customers that your business is worth visiting. And you can do that with a great public relations campaign.

Brainstorm Often

Before you set your PR campaign into motion, make sure you have taken the time to gather your creative team for several brainstorming sessions. Make sure everyone knows what the goals of your PR campaign are, and invite their input and creative ideas to help make it work.

- **Increased sales**–This is probably the best payoff you'll ever get from your public relations activities. And who doesn't want to see an increase in sales? Use your creative public relations campaign to attract customers who want to buy from you.
- **Upgraded sales**–Why not convince your customers to spend more money the next time they visit your business? The cost of your public relations campaign and all of the efforts you put into it will help drive customers toward a better product.
- **Enhanced image**–What business owner doesn't want to be known as the good guy in the community? So sit back, relax, and let the public relations wizards work their magic on you. And watch your image change and improve.
- **Increased morale**–Your employees (and yourself, too) will benefit from a dynamic public relations campaign through increased and upbeat morale. And happy employees can show customers what a great place they work for, and those customers will feel good about making purchases from your business.

Public relations should be a part of your business plan if you want to have a successful operation. Don't skimp when it comes to public relations; your future, and your bottom line, depend on it.

Some Valuable Resources

Here are some resources that will help you as you plan your PR campaign:

Public Relations Society of America
33 Irving Place
New York, NY 10003
212-995-2230
www.prsa.org

Council of Public Relations Firms
11 Penn Plaza, Fifth Avenue
New York, NY 10001
877-PR-FIRMS
www.prfirms.org

For more information on this topic, visit our Web site at www.businesstown.com

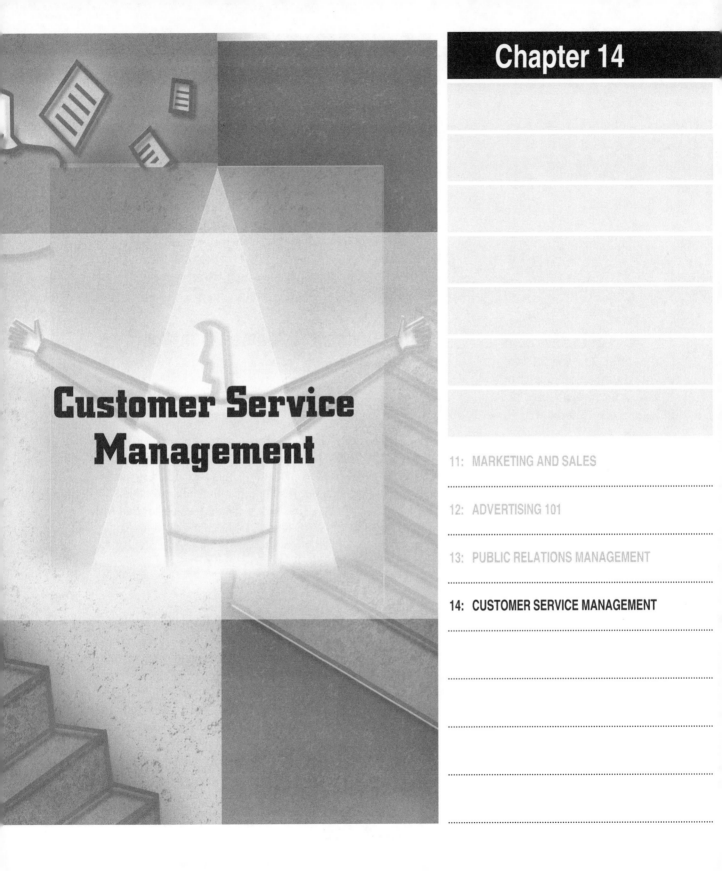

What's all the fuss about customer service, anyway? In these fast-paced days, who has time to treat their customers like royalty? I mean, the customers should be thanking us for being here, right?

How did you feel when you read that paragraph? Hopefully it made you feel uncomfortable. But guess what? Too many small business owners take that attitude about their customers. They don't take the time to get to know them, to find out what their needs are, or to even thank them for the opportunity to serve them.

> "I would advise small business owners to remember that without customers there is no business."

Without Customers, Where Would Your Business Be?

Walter Perkins, customer service manager at E-Commerce Exchange in Irvine, California, focuses his department on customer retention and the building of customer loyalty. "We reward our customers every time we answer the phone," he said. He strives to reward customers with credibility, attractiveness, responsiveness, empathy, and reliability. To his credit, response has been noted by a number of his customers, who regularly follow up a service session with letters of appreciation.

"I would advise small business owners to remember that without customers there is no business," said Perkins. "I would go further to advise that if they do not retain customers, there is no long-term business. It is now, as it has always has been, 'The customer is king.'"

Customer Service Management Advice

The best customer service management advice to follow is to simply get into the trenches so you will understand the types of issues your representatives and customers are facing. Whether or not you understand these issues often tells you if you are fulfilling your customers' needs. If your product or service is not desired by the customer, what is the point in your offering? If you cannot support what you have sold to your customer, why should they stay with you? Acquiring customers is nice; keeping customers is a living.

In this new century, business owners need to take steps to develop a customer-driven culture throughout their organizations. This holds true for product offerings as well as after-the-sale support. Technology has and will continue to affect business. With technology and the ease and affordably of acquiring technology, customers are demanding more. The point is, if you cannot deliver to the customer what they desire, when they desire it, and help them when things go wrong, another organization is merely a "drag and click" away.

Providing Cost-Effective Customer Service

Business owners can provide the best customer service in the most economical way and still stay in business by understanding and embracing the fact that every person in their organizations is responsible for customer service. This means that during the sell, proper expectations have been set. Once the sell has been made, everyone should be able to train and/or provide assistance on the products and services sold. Finally, there should be proactive follow-up to ensure the customer is getting what he or she paid for. Not every business needs a customer service department, but every department should have customer service as their business.

Small business owners can use technology to their advantage by ensuring that the technology they use is there for the purpose of alleviating or reducing mistakes, break-downs, rework, inefficiencies, and variances. Technology is a tool, a tool used to better serve and retain customers.

Not every business needs a customer service department, but every department should have customer service as their business.

More Advice from a Pro

Diane Stokes is vice president of worldwide marketing at Braxtel Communications, a leading provider of customer contact systems that provide the necessary tools for companies to service their customers easily, productively, and economically over any medium the customer chooses. "The best advice I can give on providing better customer service is to re-evaluate your business model so that your priorities are more focused on your customers rather than around your products or services," she said.

"Organizations that create a more customer-centric business model find that they are able to respond and interact more positively with customers because they have a greater understanding of their needs and buying habits. Invest in a technology that can help you centrally manage all your interactions with customers—it will enable you to build better, more long-lasting, and productive customer relationships," she said.

Stokes thinks that small business owners need to be addressing new ways of thinking in this new century.

> Invest in a technology that can help you centrally manage all your interactions with customers—it will enable you to build better, more long-lasting, and productive customer relationships.

The Effects of the Internet and New Technology

"The Internet has changed everything. Using e-mail and the Web, customers are taking a more active role in their interactions with businesses. As a result, more and more customers are demanding online as well as traditional support from those organizations they do business with," Stokes said. "Businesses that can offer their customers a variety of means of 'entering' their organization, rather than just telephone access, will have the upper hand. This is because so few companies today offer these choices," she said.

Stokes believes that small businesses can provide the best customer service in the most economical way and still stay in business. "Today, there are an increasing number of all-in-one, multimedia customer contact solutions that can help businesses improve their customer service. The best of these solutions incorporates a full range of features, which are typically more cost-effective because they include lots of functionality in one complete package, and require very little middleware integration services to work," she said. "The better ones can also integrate with your existing databases and applications without the expense and hassle of purchasing additional technology or copying all of the information to one central location. Many of them even have built-in reporting and monitoring capabilities, which allow you to track anything from how long it takes to process a request to the history of a customer's specific buying habits," she said.

She also believes that small business owners can use technology to their advantage, but just how do they develop successful technology plans to help their businesses succeed?

"There are many technology solutions available today that can help small business owners meet their customers' demands and expectations more efficiently," Stokes said. "Developing a successful technology plan involves taking steps that allow you to be more in tune with your customers. If you've already invested in a form of customer contact technology, make sure that you leverage your current investment. By choosing a technology that integrates into your existing infrastructure, you can save yourself some money. If you plan to invest or have already invested in a multi-channel communications solution, make sure that you have the ability to deliver the same level of service to your online customers as you do to those who contact you by phone," she said.

Pay Attention to Who Your Customers Are

"And lastly, arm yourself with information about your customers by taking a more active interest in who they are. Whether that's keeping customer records up-to-date or investing in a technology that enables you to track their buying history, you'll automatically be more prepared to satisfy their needs and keep them coming back to your business," Stokes said.

So by now you have learned the obvious: in order to provide the best customer service on the planet, you need to hire people who actually care about their job and the customers that they are servicing. Hire the right people for the customer service areas, otherwise, you soon won't have to worry about customer service management, because there won't be any customers to service or manage.

But Do Your Customers Really Like You?

As a successful business owner, it's your job to make sure that everyone is happy. That includes employees, vendors, and of course, your customers. You have many options and ways you can make your employees happy. You may not have as many choices when it comes to keeping your vendors happy (but when you think about it, you are their customer, so shouldn't they be worried about keeping you happy?), but they are still available.

As a successful business owner, it's your job to make sure that everyone is happy. That includes employees, vendors, and of course, your customers.

But the true test is to find ways to make your customers happy, because a happy customer can be your biggest asset, especially in a tight economy. So what is your attitude about customer service, anyway? Do you treat your customers like royalty? Or do you consider them to be a royal pain in the keister? For your sake, you'd better be giving them the royal treatment, otherwise, you run the risk of losing them to the competition, and then where will you be?

One way to gauge if your customers really like you is to ask if they are happy. Ask them if they really enjoy buying from you, and if they would consider recommending your business to their friends.

If you are lucky enough to find someone who is honest and who tells you that they didn't have the greatest shopping experience on earth, then take the time to find out what went wrong. Analyze the problem, and come up with a solution to make sure that it doesn't happy again!

> One way to gauge if your customers really like you is to ask if they are happy.

Employees and Customer Service

How well do your employees handle customer service? Not only customer service complaints, but customer service in general? In no particular order, here are some common problems that employees run into when it comes to customer service issues:

Employees don't embrace "customer service" as everyone's job and responsibility.

Employees have not been trained in the latest customer service techniques.

Some employees tend to ignore customer complaints because they feel there is nothing they can do to make them happy.

Some employees think that customer service is not that important of an issue.

Employees develop an "attitude" (the wrong one, too) when it comes to dealing with customer service problems and issues.

What Customers Really Mean by Customer Service

Customers have their own ideas about what good customer service really means to them. Here are some comments from customers who participated in an anonymous survey:

"Customer service means that the customer is always right."

"Customer service means that I should be treated special."

"What I expect from good customer service is a fair price, a polite salesperson, and quality merchandise or service."

"Customer service means I shouldn't have to ask dumb questions."

"I never shop a second time at a store that has lousy customer service."

"When I visit a business that makes me feel like I'm king, I'm going to return. And I'm going to tell my friends all about them."

> Customers have their own ideas about what good customer service really means to them.

How Customer Service Works in a Successful Company

Mary Naylor began her entrepreneurial career while a student at University of California, Santa Barbara. From holding career planning seminars for fellow students to launching an innovative new service in the nation's capitol, her desire to create an entity of substance while upholding high standards of professionalism has earned her marked respect form the business community. Among Mary's assets are a deep personal regard for honesty and fairness, a "just do it" attitude, and a good sense of humor, counting for a few of the many reasons employees and clients hold her in high esteem.

Mary Naylor is the Founder and CEO of VIPdesk, a company that provides a one-stop service that assists customers with a variety of tasks—from the ordinary to the extraordinary. Via e-mail, live chat sessions, telephone service, and pre-crafted "Instant Answers," VIPdesk makes reservations, arranges purchases, provides information, offers recommendations, conducts research, organizes the delivery of services, and much, much more. In short, VIPdesk is in the business of making life easier for busy people. "VIPdesk has developed a personal service platform that facilitates the processing of personal assistance requests," said Naylor. "VIPdesk processes and fulfills requests for purchases, referrals, research, and reservations through a nationwide remote concierge network."

The company maintains a dedicated concierge staff in its centralized Communication Center in Bend, Oregon, and while the Concierges fulfill service requests on a national level, VIPdesk also has a remote concierge service infrastructure network to enhance the level of expertise.

"VIPdesk hires and trains remote, home-based concierges to process requests via e-mail and live one-on-one chat sessions," she said. "These concierges are highly skilled professionals who provide additional, unparalleled local knowledge. For example, a customer requesting a recommendation of a sushi bar in Atlanta receives response from an Atlanta-based concierge."

Naylor has built her business around customer service. "As a concierge, you must be very resourceful, customer service-oriented, and constantly on the lookout for ways to go the extra mile for the customer. The concierge role is fun, exciting, challenging, and ever-changing to meet the needs of our fast-paced world. You can make the difference to a customer," she said.

Reward Your Customers

Ever wonder why some businesses seem to get more business than they can handle at times? Odds are it's because of the way they reward their customers. Whether it's an occasional "customer appreciation day," or a "frequent buyer discount," or some other creative endeavor, that's the reason. The businesses that take the time to reward their customers will live to see those customers return another day.

What's Your Customer Service IQ?
Take Our Quiz and Find Out!

1. I believe that my customers are my biggest priority.
2. I believe that my customers deserve to be treated royally.
3. I believe that my customers come first in my business.
4. I believe that my customers deserve nothing but the best.

5. I believe that without my customers, there would be no business.
6. I believe that my customers deserve the best customer service on the planet.
7. I believe that my customers should feel special.
8. I believe that my customers can help spread the good news about my business.
9. I believe that my customers deserve a fair market price.
10. I believe that my customers will come back in the future if I've made them feel good.

Well, how did you do? Are you a believer? Unless you said "Yes" to all ten statements, then you need a refresher course in Customer Service 101.

Some businesses have learned from personal experience how to provide good customer service.

Get Everyone Going in the Same Direction

Roxanne Emmerich, the President of The Emmerich Group, Inc., a firm that helps organizations grow by aligning everyone and everything in the same direction, really does believe that "customer satisfaction is not enough."

"Your customers may think you're fast enough and friendly enough, and that your quality is acceptable. They are satisfied. However, when a competitor offers a better price, the customer is gone," she said.

"Many small businesses focus on customer service, but the focal point is in the wrong place. They need to turn that point from customer satisfaction to customer success. Your job as a small business is to help your customers and clients be successful. That's what they really want. Then, when a competitor offers a better price, your customers will say 'Sorry. I wouldn't think of leaving the company I'm doing business with now.'

"Satisfaction is certainly a part of success. To be satisfied, customers want you to provide your product or service in a timely manner. They

> Your job as a small business is to help your customers and clients be successful.

expect you to be empathetic and friendly. They want your product to be high in quality. However, you need to go to the next step," Emmerich said.

No Simple Solution

But just how can you help your customers and clients be successful? "There is no easy answer. The only way to know is to look at your customers individually and ask them how they define success and how you can help them achieve it. It isn't enough to have the right phone skills, correct correspondence, and fast turnaround. How do you begin to define what your customers need to succeed? It's simple. Ask them. They will give you ideas that you will find carry over to other accounts as well. Then, take it one step further. Think outside the box and ask yourself what you would need to be successful if you were the customer," Emmerich said.

"For a window manufacturer whose customers are the lumber yards, it may be training their customer on how to sell the manufacturer's product thereby increasing the lumber yards' revenues. For a bank, it may be a one-stop person whose position doesn't turn over yearly (imagine that), and who completely understands a customer's financial savings and borrowing needs and makes transactions easy. For a health care organization, it may be educating family members on how to nurture their ailing loved ones back to health," she said.

> How do you begin to define what your customers need to succeed? It's simple. Ask them. They will give you ideas that you will find carry over to other accounts as well.

Developing the Strategy

"It is not the role of the owner to develop the strategy for customer success. It is the role of everyone within the company. Not only do people need to look at how to help the outside customers succeed, but they also need to look at how they can help their internal customers do their jobs better," she said.

"To help your customers succeed, you need to love them. You need to care about them and protect them and nurture them as we would a family member. Love does not mean giving your teenager all the money he asks for and letting him set his own curfew. Nor does love for your customers mean you give away the store. It simply means that you are so wrapped up in helping them succeed that you then receive even more of what you need," Emmerich said.

Seek Out Your Best Customers

Jim Stoddard is a consultant with Hook Mountain Marketing, a B2B marketing consultant with 30-plus years of experience in creating strategic and tactical business development programs to small- to medium-sized companies.

He believes that most small businesses need to define and refine their marketing or sales target. "One way to accomplish this is to clone your best customers. Cloning your best business customers is based on the principle that your best prospects will always closely resemble your best customers. So, the best place to start when looking for new, quality prospects is to look at your best existing customers and find out what characteristics (like industries, sizes, and locations) they have in common.

"Then use this information to find prospects (i.e., mailing lists, special interest groups, business associations) that look just like them. This will target your marketing and sales efforts, limit your costs and provide you with the opportunity to contact prospects that have a high probability of interest in your product or service," Stoddard said.

Everyone Counts

You need to make sure that everyone in your business understands the importance of an individual customer. Every customer that walks in your door, or places an order from your catalog or Web site, is important to you and your business. And the sooner that everyone in your business understands that, the better off everyone will be.

Customer Service Problems and How to Handle Them

Having a customer focus means that business is handled so that the customer doesn't have to make multiple calls, visit numerous places, or explain his or her problem to more than one person. All of the small businesses that are successful in this area use one-stop processes so they can be as responsive as possible to their customers. These organizations have internalized a culture in which everything starts with the customer and ends with the customer. As one organization's newsletter aptly noted in its customer service quote of the month section, "Customer satisfaction comes from treating the customer the way we'd expect to be treated if the roles were reversed."

Best-in-business organizations do not settle for customer *satisfaction*, but instead seek to gain customer *loyalty* as well. Private

Smile

One of the hardest things you or one of your employees will have to do is to smile when you are dealing with an obnoxious customer. But once you have embraced the idea that even this particular customer is helping to increase your profits and meet your payroll, it won't be that hard. Smiles are contagious; with any luck, that problem customer will catch one from you.

organizations are focusing on lifetime customer value rather than on the quick sale or one-time deal. In the public sector, customer loyalty can mean committed customers who spread the word about the quality of service they receive from their government; this directly translates to increased public confidence.

One-stop customer service reflects an organization's customer focus; it is an attempt to meet customer demands and needs, to generate customer satisfaction, and to instill customer loyalty. But one-stop service and the organization providing it can only be successful if this approach is truly responsive to the customer. To this end, the successful organizations each employ their own version of a basic, but highly effective, formula:

- They listen to their customers; they make changes to their processes based on what their customers tell them;
- They use a variety of listening and learning strategies to continually obtain customer feedback about performance, expectations, and preferences; and
- They improve their operations based on the feedback received a continuous and ongoing process.

This process underlies best practices in customer service in general, as well as in one-stop customer service in particular.

Measuring Customer Satisfaction/Loyalty

In general, customers expect the companies they do business with to be accessible, accurate, timely, and responsive. Successful managers are very much aware of these key "drivers" of satisfaction, and they continually measure their progress with respect to these drivers using a variety of mechanisms.

Survey, Survey, and Survey Again

Best-in-business organizations use surveys extensively to gauge customer expectations, preferences, and satisfaction. Moreover, many organizations have institutionalized a system of survey techniques to capture "whole picture" information.

Successful managers conduct such surveys both by phone and by mail. The survey instruments are perfected over time based on customer feedback. Some of the different survey techniques we observed in use by our partner organizations are:

- Quarterly or semiannual national surveys to cover broad topics, including customer satisfaction, at a high level;
- Daily call-back surveys to provide specific, immediate customer feedback;
- Fixed-interval mail surveys (for example, surveys of every twentieth customer to assess such factors as timeliness, accuracy, and quality); and
- A fixed number of surveys sent out on a monthly basis (for example, one company mails out 2,000 surveys each month).

Some small businesses conduct periodic surveys every eighteen months of its top 300 customers in terms of dollar and volume. Among other questions, the survey asks what is not being done that customers want to be done, what is not being done well enough, and what useful practices of the organization's competitors could be adopted. Another manager conducts specialized phone surveys every few months for a period of one to two weeks. Survey data are captured both via online surveying tied to the customer's on-screen data file during a call, and through a call-back conducted within twenty-four hours of service.

Focus Groups for Focusing Organizations

Focus groups are another vehicle used to listen to customers and to get their input in creating or modifying services. One company holds focus sessions with high-level representatives of key customer organizations as its focus group "partners" every three years for one full week. These sessions provide a good forum for ensuring that the company is attuned to customer needs and for generating new ideas for future improvements.

> Successful managers conduct such surveys both by phone and by mail. The survey instruments are perfected over time based on customer feedback.

Customer Feedback Systems

"Fix first; count and analyze later." This sentiment conveys the urgent need in today's fast-paced business environment to address problems swiftly. Customer loyalty can easily be built on an organization's rapid and efficient response to customer feedback.

Because successful managers and organizations espouse feedback as critical to good service, they tend to have highly developed feedback systems dedicated to collecting, facilitating, integrating, and helping the organization learn from feedback. Some small businesses are using a variety of innovative systems that channel feedback to help solve problems, improve service, and remove business barriers.

The key component of one organization's call center feedback system is an electronic "nerve center" called ECHO (Every Contact Has Opportunity). All customer contact representatives are tied to ECHO via their computer terminals. They can input, on a voluntary basis, any comments, problems, and/or issues emerging from a specific customer contact that are beyond their power to fix. Essentially, this feedback is then put into a large data file that everyone from the customer contact representatives to top management can access. From there, feedback is directed electronically to action agents in departments throughout the company. These groups act on the feedback and then report on what they have done. Later, the groups analyze the longer range implications of the feedback. The process is supervised to ensure that all feedback loops are linked and that all fixes and actions are shared.

Other organizations, whose customers are companies contracting for specific products/services, use a customer satisfaction program matrix. This document is developed by the program and customer managers at the outset of a contract to capture the specific performance expectations that are important to the customer. Each matrix is customized for the individual contract. The customer provides periodic ratings in each of the performance objective areas. This not only provides feedback to the program managers on how they are doing, but also provides an opportunity for mid-course corrections.

Some companies provide early customer feedback across all functional divisions via an automated tracking system. Feedback is

> Customer loyalty can easily be built on an organization's rapid and efficient response to customer feedback.

used for root cause analysis. Action items are addressed within two days. The tracking system can be accessed by all employees.

Other Listening and Learning Strategies

While much can be learned about customers by direct questioning, best-in-business organizations do not rely solely on this input. They also turn to market and trend analyses that reflect and monitor among other things the technological, societal, economic, and competitive factors that may affect customer requirements, expectations, and preferences.

One factor many successful small business managers have in common is their ability to listen to their customers. But at the same time, when it comes to new and better products for the future, the customer doesn't know enough to tell us what to do. The minivan is a good example. The American public didn't know it wanted minivans until they were out on the market, and then it seemed that nearly every family had to have one. Sometimes your job is to anticipate what customers will want three or four years from now, before they articulate it.

Best-in-business organizations also look to their employees as a source of information about customer service. To provide the best service, an organization must have a good sense of its employees and of their attitudes toward the organization and its customers. This approach reflects the concept that "you can't have satisfied customers without satisfied employees." For this reason, partner organizations have incorporated employee survey programs that measure employee satisfaction with the work environment, communication, and empowerment, as well as target areas for improvement.

> Sometimes your job is to anticipate what customers will want three or four years from now, before they articulate it.

Using Feedback for Results

Successful organizations recognize that soliciting and receiving feedback is useful only if it is subsequently used to instigate action. Some successful managers use what customers tell them to drive their operations. In fact, their one-stop processes themselves evolved from feedback.

Read and Heed

Whenever you get customer feedback, make sure you pay attention to every little detail. Don't just file the forms in a drawer and think "Well, the customers responded, but I'm too busy to act upon their input." Take their feedback seriously. After all, they took time to respond to your questions, so you should take time to respond to their answers.

For example, people in one state said they were tired of having to obtain multiple maps to plan recreational activities in parks because the agencies involved produced maps of only the territories they individually controlled. To solve the problem, the agencies worked together to create a single user-friendly recreational map covering all the area's parks. Furthermore, these agencies, each of which had separate responsibilities for the use and protection of parks, found that customers did not like to deal with separate agencies for similar services. So they reinvented themselves and their operations to enable seamless service that crosses functional lines. The customers don't care that services such as fire fighting and the issuance of tree-cutting permits cross agency lines; now, because the agencies heeded the feedback received, customers don't need to know that, either.

What Successful Managers Do with Customer Feedback

- Implement changes that improve processes by making them more customer-friendly and efficient. This may involve working with other organizations to streamline processes that cross functional boundaries
- Provide daily feedback to managers for them to share with employees, thereby getting everyone involved in solution building.
- Recognize and reward exemplary service behavior and initiate celebrations.
- Help managers evaluate employee and unit performance, and justify salary increases and promotions.
- Assess training needs.
- Formulate action plan goals for the coming year.
- Help identify success stories showcasing real, tangible benefits of services or products.

Good customer service doesn't happen by accident. Make customer satisfaction a priority in your business, and you will be doing your part to help it succeed and prosper.

The Manager and Money

Always a favorite in everyone's book, this section about money will be of interest to both newbies and experienced managers. You're never too old to learn about the basics of accounting, how to plan cash flow, as well as how to stay debt free while you grow your business. Also included is a section on risk taking, and you will learn if you have what it takes to be a risk taker in the new millennium.

Chapter 15

Managing Your Finances

E very small business owner and manager needs to have a good handle on the finances of the business they are responsible for. Whether it's understanding how to manage cash flow better, or making sure that you don't fall too far into debt, managing your finances is an important aspect of your job.

As the owner of a growing business, you may feel that you alone should handle all aspects of your company's finances. Depending upon the nature of your business, you might want to consider outsourcing your accounting and financial needs.

If you think that outsourcing might be a good idea, here are some things to consider before hiring an outside firm to handle your company's finances:

> Depending upon the nature of your business, you might want to consider outsourcing your accounting and financial needs.

Assess your needs—It is very important that you assess and identify your company's needs before you pick up the telephone and call someone. How large is your company and how many different types of financial transactions do you handle on a daily basis? Companies with frequent transactions, both in purchasing and sales, have a greater need for precise accounts payable and accounts receivable that might be better served if handled by an outside specialist. How about your inventory? Do you deal with international currency issues? Or how many small cash transactions does your business handle on a daily basis?

What services do you really want?—You have a wide range of choices about how often an outside person or organization works for your small business. A good bookkeeper can manage accounts payable, accounts receivable, and cash management. If you want all of your financial services handled from an outside firm, don't feel you have to hand over all of the control of your company. You are still responsible for the financial aspects of your small business. But with outside help, you can now focus on the tasks that need you in order to make your business a success.

Do you have the proper equipment to handle the job?— If you have no computerized accounting system, such as QuickBooks or Peach Tree, it is worth hiring an accountant to see what systems might be beneficial to your small business.

What is the impact on your budget?—Before you hire someone to handle the company's finances, assess the potential impact that decision might have on your cash flow. Put a value on what you think the outside financial help is worth and create a budget to see if you can live with the bottom line.

When hiring an outside firm, you can find someone who offers accounting services, bookkeeping services, tax preparation services, or a combination of all three.

Accounting Services

There are many levels of accounting services provided by a wide range of accounting firms. A good accountant can set up your books and offer solid advice when it comes to such issues as tax planning and cash flow problems. He or she can help you select a good retirement plan and help you when setting up employee benefit packages. Accounting procedures can seem like a foreign language at times, but a good accountant can help translate everything into terms you can understand.

Features Provided by Accounting Services Firms

- Payroll, including all payroll tax filings (Forms 941, 1099, W-2, etc.)
- Accounts payable and vendor files
- Accounts receivable and billing services
- General ledger and financial statements
- Cash flow management
- Tax preparation

Ask Associates for Referrals

If you're in the market for an accounting or bookkeeping firm to handle your financial transactions, don't let your fingers do the walking in the yellow pages. Your first step should be to ask business associates for referrals. There's nothing better than a good old-fashioned word-of-mouth recommendation to find a firm that is just right for your company.

Things to Consider

- Develop a list of potential accountants or accounting firms. Ask a friend who is also in business who they are using.
- Make an appointment and interview the owners of the accounting firm. Remember, they are competing for your business, so ask them any tough questions you might have and get the right answers you are searching for.
- Share your business plan and philosophy with them. Ask them if your business is one that they would be able to help.
- Ask about prices, and what is included. Watch out for hidden prices, which may suddenly surface at a later date.
- If you are interviewing an accounting firm, ask to speak to the accountant who will be handling your account. Spend some time talking with that person to make sure you are comfortable with them.
- Don't forget to ask for references, and make sure that you contact them and check them out.

Bookkeeping Services

If your small business is not going to hire a bookkeeper as a staff position, then searching for a good bookkeeping service will certainly be a wise decision for you. Don't try to handle the day-to-day bookkeeping activities that occur, because before you know it you will be spending too much of your valuable time on going through bank statements instead of concentrating on expanding your business. Let a professional bookkeeping service provide you with the answers that you need.

Bookkeeping Services Offer a Variety of Services

- **General ledger services**–They record all of the transactions and details into the correct ledger account.
- **Accounts receivable services**–They will monitor all incoming receivables and ensure that proper payment is received on time.

- **Bank reconciliation services**–This is especially helpful for small businesses that have multiple checking accounts.
- **Inventory services**–They will maintain good inventory records, using either the FIFO (first in, first out) or the LIFO (last in, first out) method.

Remember that a bookkeeper will record business transactions while an accountant will analyze the transactions that have actually taken place. Ask prospective providers about the computer systems that they currently have in operation, and think about how you will make your and their data compatible for backups, and reviewing for accuracy.

Tips for Selecting a Bookkeeping Service

- Ask to see how they store and back up copies of your financial records.
- Ask them what accounting firms they normally deal with.
- When asking for references, make sure that you ask for businesses that are similar in size to your own.
- Ask them how long they have been in business. Avoid hiring a bookkeeping firm that has just opened its doors.
- Ask to see a complete schedule of fees. Make sure that there will be no surprises later, if an unexpected situation occurs.
- Check to see if any complaints have been filed against them at your local office of the Better Business Bureau.

> Remember that a bookkeeper will record business transactions while an accountant will analyze the transactions that have actually taken place.

Tax Preparation Services

Three groups of people can prepare an income tax return on a professional basis for your small business.

Certified Public Accountants–CPAs must be licensed by the state in which they reside and are required by law to maintain their level of efficiency through continuing education. A good CPA is usually proficient in a wide range of finance and tax issues and can provide a wealth of valuable information to help your small business reduce the amount of tax you have to pay each year. Be advised, however, that not all are tax specialists, so when choosing a CPA make sure that you ask about their level of experience in the tax area. Some CPAs will operate as independent consultants, running their own shop as a sole owner, while others may have a partner or a fairly large accounting firm.

Tax Preparers–Anyone can take a course and become a certified, licensed tax preparer. Again, a quick glance in the telephone book and you will no doubt find dozens of listings. Many financial planners also advertise the fact that they provide tax services. Their fees will be substantially lower than those of a CPA or an accounting firm. However, don't let pricing be the only consideration you have when choosing someone to handle all of your business tax needs.

Enrolled Agents–An enrolled agent is someone who is certified by the Internal Revenue Service to prepare taxes. Like CPAs, enrolled agents must continue with additional financial education to maintain their license. Many enrolled agents are former IRS agents, and like CPAs, are authorized to represent taxpayers in IRS hearings and audits.

Consider the Following Questions

- How many years of experience do they have?
- How many other similar businesses do they handle?
- Have they successfully challenged any IRS problems? And were those problems corrected without any additional fees?
- Do they participate in continuing education programs and stay current with new tax laws and accounting procedures?
- Can they provide three references? And will you check out those references?
- Have any complaints been filed against them (either by other clients, or government agencies, like the IRS)?

> Be advised, however, that not all are tax specialists, so when choosing a CPA make sure that you ask about their level of experience in the tax area.

Avoid Problems

The term "buyer beware" is still a good rule of thumb when hiring an accounting, bookkeeping, or tax preparation firm.

- Be careful hiring a firm that claims to provide all of the services you need. Large CPA firms usually have this breadth of capability, but few smaller firms do.
- Never sign a blank tax return and let your accountant or tax person say, "I'll take care of this for you."
- If a firm has had a complaint filed against it in the past, think twice before signing on the dotted line. However, if you still feel strongly about using that particular firm, ask the firm's representative to explain what the complaint was all about, and pay attention to his or her answers.
- Think about the location of the firm. Do you anticipate having to visit its offices often? Or are you comfortable sending paperwork through the mail or via FedEx?

It cannot be stressed enough that you must establish what fees you will be paying before you sign any type of a contract. Many a small business owner has been stung by a whole flurry of extra fees that he or she didn't make sure were included in their original agreement.

Make sure you shop for value that translates into service for a fee. When comparing two offers, make sure you also compare the level of service you will receive. And remember, paying for a service that really does lead to more time for you and increased cash flow for your small business will be a very worthwhile investment.

401(k) Plans

A 401(k) plan is an important tool to help your employees achieve a secure retirement. This type of plan reduces income taxes. When employees put their money into 401(k) plans, their income is reduced dollar for dollar. Therefore, the amount of tax withheld from each paycheck is lower.

> When comparing two offers, make sure you also compare the level of service you will receive.

A 401(k) delays taxes owed on investments. Ordinarily, if you make a profit from investments, you must pay taxes on those earnings right away. Contributions to 401(k) plans are pretax, and taxes are deferred until funds are withdrawn from the retirement savings account.

Employers are able to match the contributions of its employees. Some companies match amounts ranging from ten cents on the dollar to a dollar-for-dollar match. Employer matching is an effective way to ensure broader participation and avoid discrimination. The end result is the employee is able to retire with peace of mind. Employees who are not worried about their retirement are usually more productive and satisfied workers.

Types of 401(k) Plans

Bonus plans—Contributions are not made until the end of the year, when an employee typically receives a bonus. An employee may elect to receive the bonus in cash, or deposit it into their 401(k) account.

Thrift plans—Gives an employee the option of receiving a reduced salary and having the difference contributed to the plan. A fixed percentage of the employee's salary is then withheld from each paycheck and contributed to the plan on the employee's behalf.

Common Features of a 401(k) Plan

The rules and regulations associated with a 401(k) plan are complex and stringent. You should consult with a pension specialist or plan provider to help design your plan. In the design, you will need to choose a mix of features that is best suited for you and your employees.

Employees will want to know how soon they can become a participant of the plan. Many companies require a waiting period of one year, to ensure that the employee has achieved a more permanent status. Some companies might allow an employee to join right away, but they may delay any contributing funds until a later date.

The amount of money an employee will contribute to the 401(k) will vary. Contributions are made on a pretax basis, and are usually a percentage of an employee's paycheck.

Employers are not required to participate with matching funds, but it will make your plan more competitive. The employer may match up to 100 percent of the employee's contribution.

An employer may put some restrictions on matching funds. This is called a vesting requirement. An employee becomes vested in a retirement plan upon completing the years of service required to receive retirement benefits. Vesting means the employee has the right to their retirement benefits at a specific age, even if the employee does not stay with the company their entire working career. The most common type is graded vesting, where an employee has an increased amount of money each year he or she is with the company. The other type is cliff vesting, where an employee must wait a certain period of time before receiving matching funds. The law states that any money an employee puts into a 401(k) plan is always 100 percent vested.

Nearly 80 percent of all 401(k) plans offer loans as an option for employees who find themselves in need of their money right away. The law states that an employee can borrow half of their account balance, and that it must be repaid within five years.

The IRS recognizes that an employee may need money for a bona fide emergency so it does allow withdrawals under certain circumstances, but the employee will pay a penalty for early withdrawals.

> The law states that any money an employee puts into a 401(k) plan is always 100 percent vested.

How to Select the Best 401(k) Plan for Your Company

When selecting the best plan for your company, you need to decide who will perform each of these functions:

Design—Decide how the employer's 401(k) contributions should be allocated and determine the matching contribution. You will also need to decide the availability of loans, hardship withdrawal, and distribution options.

Administration and record keeping—Competent administration is needed to ensure compliance with government regulations, especially for nondiscrimination testing. It's critical to ensure that employees' monies are correctly allocated to their accounts, especially for participant-directed accounts. All providers or consulting firms will have computer systems for tracking and administration. Fees are usually negotiable.

Investments—Investments can be participant-directed or pooled. Part of your choice of investments should be the range and breadth of investment options available to you (the administrator) and your employees. You need to take their overall financial sophistication into account. Most firms provide a range of funds with different risk profiles and investment objectives. Ask your consultant or provider about action you can take to increase employees' return, and reduce the company's potential liability.

Employee communication and participation—Showing employees how participation can help plan for retirement will increase participation. Providing clear, simple to understand printed material, along with access to Internet-based information can also help.

Options When Looking for Qualified Providers

- **Using a full-service 401(k) provider that offers a complete 401(k) package (Fidelity, Merrill Lynch, Smith Barney, etc.).** These integrated providers may lack some skills in 401(k) plan design and overall administration. There may be limited negotiation in fees since they keep fees down using the profits they make on investments.
- **Using a pension-consulting firm to install a 401(k) plan.** You will need a separate investment company, so you lose the benefits of one-stop shopping. Pay particular attention to their record-keeping system. Fees are often negotiable, but they lack the investment income of investment

> Part of your choice of investments should be the range and breadth of investment options available to you (the administrator) and your employees.

providers, so they may often start with a higher fee schedule.

- **Building your own capabilities in-house.** For most small businesses, this is seldom worth the time and effort because the rules are complex, and compliance requirements for nondiscrimination still apply.

Fees and Costs

Direct employer expenses can be reduced by limiting employer contributions or by delaying the way in which employees are eligible for matching contributions. However, pay attention to the rules regarding discrimination. Indirect expenses can be reduced by managing more of the process in-house and by negotiating with your consultant or provider on service and administration fees.

The Department of Labor's Pension and Welfare Benefits Administration gives ten questions to consider when comparing fees from consultants and providers:

1. Have you given each of your prospective service providers complete and identical information with regard to your plan?
2. Do you know what features you want to provide (e.g., loans, number of investment options, Internet trading, etc.)?
3. Have you decided which fees and expenses you, as plan sponsor, will pay, which your employees will pay, and which fees you will share?
4. Do you know which fees and expenses are charged directly to the plan and which are divided from investment returns?
5. Do you know what services are covered under the base fee and what services incur an additional charge? Do you know what the fees are for extra or customized services?
6. Do you understand that some investment options have higher fees than others because of the nature of the investment?
7. Does the prospective service arrangement have any restrictions or fees?
8. Does the prospective arrangement assist your employees in making informed investment decisions for their individual

> Do you know what services are covered under the base fee and what services incur an additional charge? Do you know what the fees are for extra or customized services?

accounts (e.g., providing investment education, information on fees), and if so, how are you charged for this service?

9. Have you considered asking potential providers to present uniform fee information that shows the fees charged?

10. What information will you receive on a regular basis from the prospective provider so that you can monitor the provision of services and the investments that you select and make changes as necessary?

SIMPLE Plans

Savings Incentive Match Plans for Employees of Small Employers (SIMPLE) allows employers who have fewer than 100 employees to offer a retirement plan.

Employees who are expected to receive at least $5,000, and who did so in the previous two years, are eligible to contribute through a deduction from their paychecks. Employees can receive an employer-matched contribution of up to 3 percent of their pay.

Differences Between the SIMPLE 401(k) Plan and Its Traditional Counterparts

Unlike the standard 401(k) plan, SIMPLE plans require few administrative burdens since the financial institution receiving the funds does most of the paperwork. Also, SIMPLE plans are not subject to the same stringent compliance testing required by the IRS of traditional 401(k) plans.

SIMPLE plans usually have lower maximum employee contribution limits. SIMPLE plans require employers to make contributions to their employees' accounts.

Employer contributions are automatically fully vested.

Show Me the Money: A Lesson in Cash Flow

Cash is a four-letter word that can be scary for some small business owners and managers, because they often seem to be without it. Yet

> Unlike the standard 401(k) plan, SIMPLE plans require few administrative burdens since the financial institution receiving the funds does most of the paperwork.

since cash is probably the most important asset that you will ever own, it will be worth your while to learn as much as you can about cash flow and cash flow planning.

Let's start by examining what cash flow really is. To put it in simple terms, cash flow is simply the relationship between the money coming into your business and the money going out of your business. Sounds simple enough, doesn't it? Yet for some reason, cash flow becomes a problem for many small businesses. Anytime you throw any type of financial equation into a small business, sometimes chaos can result.

The problem really lies in all of those lousy details—details that affect your business's ability to pay their bills next month, and even to meet the payroll. To be a wise and successful small business manager, you need to be a wizard when it comes to understanding Cash Flow 101.

> To put it in simple terms, cash flow is simply the relationship between the money coming into your business and the money going out of your business.

The Five Most Important Rules Concerning Cash Flow

1. Make sure you have enough cash on hand at all times. It's very easy to violate this important rule, but it should be one that you follow to the letter of the law.
2. Make sure you know where your cash is going. It doesn't matter how busy your schedule may be, or what new crisis pops up at the last minute, you better know where your cash is headed.
3. Hold on to your cash for as long as you possibly can. Don't pay an invoice just because you're sitting on a pile of cash this month. Hold on to your cash and let it work for you, not against you.
4. Collect all of the cash that is due to you, when it is due. Your job is also to make sure that people who owe you cash send you the cash on time. Uncollected invoices can put a real drain and strain on your pool of cash very quickly.
5. Spread your cash around your business as it is needed. Keep a close eye on each department or division, and be prepared to pump cash there when it is needed.

Rainy Day Fund

Don't get caught out in the rain because you failed to have a Plan B ready to help smooth the way during times of temporary cash flow problems. A rainy day fund should be a line item in your budget, even if you are enjoying a record year with banner profits. Always be prepared for the worst, and if and when those times surface, you'll be glad that you did.

Anticipating Cash Flow

All right, now that you've learned the five most important rules of cash as it relates to small businesses, it's time to get back to Cash Flow 101. Every business has lean and rich times, and to be financially sound, you must master the skills of anticipating future cash flow.

Forecasting will allow you to anticipate slow cycles and help you to develop a plan to overcome them. In order to accomplish this goal, you will need to make projections for:

Income
Expenses
Budget (where you can compare income to expenses)

Income

Start by putting together a monthly income report from your accountant or accounting system. Make sure to include:

Sales
Credit card sales
Accounts receivable
Investment income
Miscellaneous cash income

It is a good idea to use last year's figures to prepare an income projection for this year. Once you have all of your figures available for each month, record them on a cash flow worksheet.

Expenses

It would be a good idea if your accountant or accounting system can issue reports that will detail your expenses by the various categories for each month of the year. You can also retrieve information from your check stubs, bank statements, and credit card statements.

Enter the total monthly expenses for the previous twelve months on your cash flow worksheet. Important reminder: Don't list any expenses that were a one-time expense. For example, if you were paying off a loan and no longer have those monthly payments, make sure you omit them from this year's projections.

Once you have calculated your projected monthly income and expenses, calculate the total cash surplus or shortage for each month. The final calculation is your "running" or "cumulative" cash flow, which takes into account the previous month's surplus/shortage.

Now you will have a fairly accurate projection of month-to-month cash flow. Check your projected amount against actual figures each month and fine-tune your budget where it's needed.

The Key to Understanding Financial Statements

For some reason, small businesses are notorious for not filling out their paperwork. They seem to be too busy to create the forms that are a necessary part of their business life. That's too bad, too, because this lack of attention to paperwork, when combined with a lack of understanding simple financial statements, can spell disaster.

The Most Common Financial Statements Most Small Businesses Use

Balance sheet–A balance sheet takes a snapshot of your small business and gives you an estimate of its worth on any particular date. Balance sheets are usually prepared on the last day of the month and are built on a simple premise: assets = liabilities + owner's equity.

Profit and Loss statement–Also known as a P & L statement, it compares expenses against revenue over a certain period of time to show the company's net profit or loss.

Cash flow statement–This simple statement shows the changes in the business's working capital since the beginning of the year by listing the sources of funds and the

> Lack of attention to paperwork, when combined with a lack of understanding simple financial statements, can spell disaster.

Resource

For an excellent resource book in helping you understand your finances, read *Streetwise® Finance & Accounting* by Suzanne Caplan.

uses of those funds. However, many small businesses don't bother with such a statement, opting instead to work on a cash budget.

Sales statement—This financial statement will show you at a glance where your small business stands with regards to sales and sales projections.

Schedule some time with your accountant and have her explain the basics of these and other financial statements to you. If there is something you don't understand, have her keep explaining it to you until you do. Understanding simple financial statements can make the difference between success and failure of your small business.

For more information on this topic, visit our Web site at www.businesstown.com

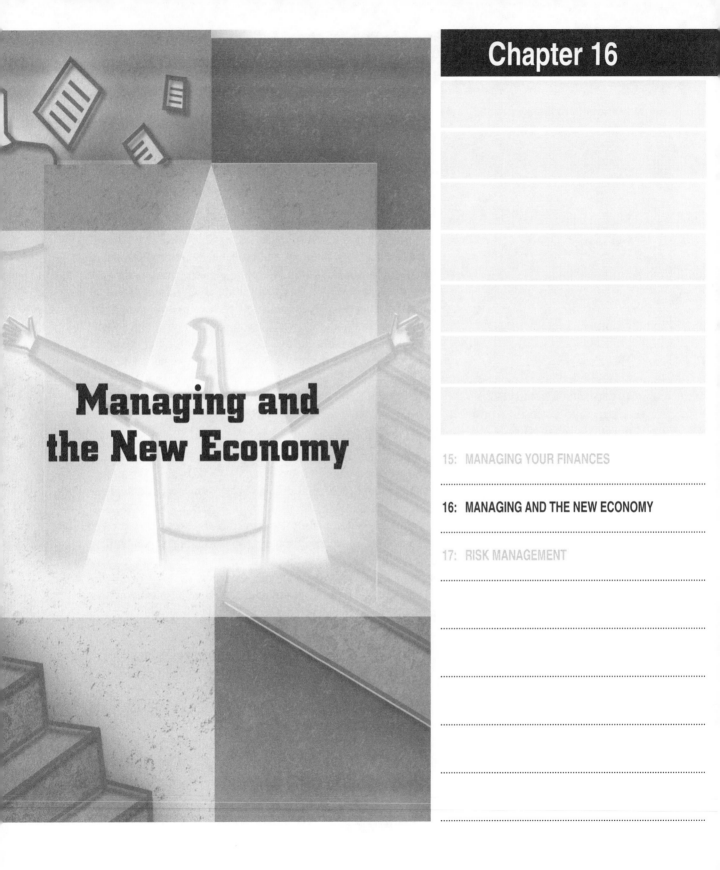

Managing and the New Economy

How well do you understand the new economy? Is there a difference between the new economy and the old economy? Talk to a small business manager who is succeeding, and they will sing praises of the new economy. "It's a super time for the new economy!" or "Don't you just love this new economy?" might be heard from some lucky business owners.

But talk to a few small business managers who are struggling to make ends meet, and they will probably be wanting the old economy back, because odds are, when the old economy was king, they were prospering. It all boils down to that key phrase I wrote about in another chapter: perception is reality. If you perceive yourself and your business to be a winner, you have won half the battle. But the real key to making the new economy work for your business is to understand what the new economy is, and to embrace it with open arms.

> Perception is reality. If you perceive yourself and your business to be a winner, you have won half the battle.

Web Sites

Let's talk about Web sites for a moment or two. Does your small business have a Web site? According to the U.S. Small Business Administration, 25 percent of small business owners said they currently have a Web site.

A Web site can make the difference between success and failure for some small businesses. And for some small businesses that are already doing okay, it can take them to the next level where they can begin to enjoy the fruits of the new economy.

Let's take a look at two examples of small businesses and what happened when they created a Web site.

Case Study Number One: The Squirrel's Nest

For ten years Nancy Kemble had been building The Squirrel's Nest, a place where customers can find all-natural candies. Located in Middletown, Delaware, The Squirrel's Nest grew out of Kemble's love for her son, Jason, who at age two, inspired her to create the candies. Jason, who has since died from cancer, was allergic to artificial flavors and preservatives. "My husband, Jim, and I went grocery shopping and it took almost three hours to read all of the labels," she said. "We were amazed at the amount of foods that contain so many artificial flavors and preservatives."

Kemble realized she had found her niche, and began making all-natural candies with the help of her Pennsylvania Dutch mother-in-law, who shared some of her recipes. Eventually, Kemble hooked up with the Feingold Association in Alexandria, Virginia. The association promotes the Feingold Diet, named after Dr. Ben Feingold, who had studied allergies and observed a link between additives and their effect on people's behavior and ability to learn. Soon her candies were being sold by mail order to parents all across the country that had children with allergies. In addition to having customers in every state, Kemble also gets orders for her candies from Canada, Mexico, and Germany.

Kemble says that being recognized by the Feingold Association has certainly helped her business to grow over the years. "I receive cards and letters from other parents who are thankful that their children now have an opportunity to eat chocolate and other treats, especially around the holidays," she says.

The holidays are her busiest times of the year. Kemble estimates that she processes more than 2,000 pounds of chocolate between Valentine's Day and Easter. "When you cover all natural vanilla wafers, pretzels, nuts, and other goodies with chocolate, it adds up fast," she says.

In the first two months of 2000, Kemble decided to launch her own Web site. "It was the only logical thing to do," she says. "I hoped that by adding a Web site, more parents would learn about The Squirrel's Nest and find the all natural candies they had been searching for," she says. Although she was not familiar with the Internet, she took the time to learn about small businesses and Web sites.

She had read many business articles that advised small business owners to get a Web site, and then be prepared for a huge increase in sales. "So many people believe the myth that if you get a Web site you will become an overnight success. As a business owner, once you make the decision to get your place on the Internet, you need to have patience and take small steps," Kemble says.

> As a business owner, once you make the decision to get your place on the Internet, you need to have patience and take small steps," Kemble says.

As a savvy business owner herself, Kemble knew that she would not become a huge overnight success. "I knew it would take time, so I was prepared to take things a little more slowly," she says.

After working out some technical glitches with her Web site, Kemble began to see orders materializing. "I think by having a Web site, it makes it easier for parents to order. Most of my Internet customers are brand new so far, and they have told me they are glad to have the opportunity to order anything anytime of the day or night. People lead such busy lives these days, so I'm sure that having a Web site makes it easier to order when it is convenient for them," she says. Kemble estimates that it took about six months before her Web site started making a difference in her sales volume. I now receive orders from customers who never knew that I even existed," she says.

Nancy Kemble offers this advice for other small business owners:

"Find something that you absolutely love to do. It's much easier to work long hours if you have a purpose or mission. Your passion and your positive attitude will come across to your customers.

"Thoroughly research the market, and make sure you are offering a product or service that is unique and that there is a demand for. Don't just decide to hang out your shingle or put up a Web site and hope that the customers will beat a path to your door, because that isn't going to happen.

"Next, don't bite off more than you can chew at one time. There's nothing wrong with challenging yourself, but don't push yourself to the limit so much that you are doing more harm than good. And finally, be prepared for and recognize there will be slumps or down times in your business. Very few small businesses get by without short periods of slow sales from time to time."

Case Study Number Two: Global Health and Fitness

Chad Tackett had run a health club and a personal-training business when he began to think about running an Internet site. By 1996 Tackett had realized the potential of the Net for supplying people with information they need to get healthy, right in their own

> "Thoroughly research the market, and make sure you are offering a product or service that is unique and that there is a demand for."

home. The next year Tackett started Global Health and Fitness, designed to help Web users achieve their personal health-related goals. It has received national attention and praise ever since.

Tackett says he "wanted to take the principles and guidelines that [he] taught to my clients to an online program that helped people reach their fitness goals." He grew up in Portland, Oregon, with his parents and two sisters. Although his parents were not involved in the fitness business, Tackett feels they encouraged a health-conscious lifestyle. "Both of my parents were active, competing in marathons and triathlons. They were also very nutrition-conscious, and were always encouraging us to eat healthy," Tackett explains.

After achieving two degrees, one in nutrition and the other in health and fitness, Tackett also became certified as a personal trainer with the American Council on Exercise. From there Tackett went on to manage a health club, then a year later began his own personal-training business. "We've seen a steady growth in the fitness industry since the early eighties, and there's every indication of continued growth," he says.

In preparing to launch his Web site, Tackett worked out hundreds of customized exercise programs and meal plans, developed health recipes and exercise instructions, and wrote five online books. He researched the most reliable fitness sources and developed interactive programs and tools to help Web users in their goals. Because Tackett has a customer-driven strategy for the business he feels it is best to go "above and beyond the customers' expectations." By the time the site was ready to launch in 1997, it was well prepared to help the members.

Because of its comprehensive information, unique offerings, and personal and practical approaches for all ages, sizes, backgrounds, and goals, Tackett says that the site immediately received national attention and praise.

Global Health and Fitness is strictly an online business, which allows for a higher profit margin due to no manufacturing, shipping, or overhead costs. It was designed and continues to be updated by a small design firm in Portland, Oregon, called Webforce Designs. It is a members-only site, which offers a diverse and comprehensive program and benefits to all members. Also,

> Because Tackett has a customer-driven strategy for the business he feels it is best to go "above and beyond the customers' expectations."

because it is online only, Tackett and his two employees are able to update and improve the site with little cost to the members. "A very different scenario from traditional products such as books, videotapes, and other items," Tackett says about the ability to update quickly and effectively.

When looking at Global Health and Fitness's success, Tackett explains that there are three main things that got him where he is today.

> "Word-of-mouth advertising is and always will be the best, most cost-effective form of advertising," Tackett says.

Customer loyalty–"Word-of-mouth advertising is and always will be the best, most cost-effective form of advertising," Tackett says. Because his customers are important to him, the site offers the best information, programs, and incentive programs that it possibly can. The annual membership renewal rate is 90 percent, a number that Tackett finds impressive, but also plans on increasing as he continues to build the site.

Persistence–"As a business owner there will always be ups and downs and you need to continually work hard, stay focused, and remind yourself of the wonderful benefits of owning your own business," Tackett says. "When you are first starting out, there will be a long period of time that you don't reap any benefits from your hard work. However, continually remind yourself that a very worthwhile payoff lies ahead." Tackett's persistence has taken his business from nothing to revenue over $600,000 in only three years.

Constantly improve yourself and your business–"If you're not striving for improvement, your competition will soon catch up with you. Do everything you can to improve your product, and let your customers know about it," he says. The site has grown monthly in visits and revenue since it began. Tackett credits this largely to the continuing supply of new programs, exercise instructions, software features, and special member offers.

Tackett's advice to someone beginning a small-business venture: "If you have the will, dedication, and drive to work through the hard times, there will be a very handsome reward at the finish line. Persist and give it your all, and it will be more than worth all the sacrifice and effort you've endured," he says.

Ten Mistakes To Avoid

Okay, you realize that your small business should have a Web page, and have a good one that will not only attract visitors, but keep them coming back for more. (And it can't hurt to have such a creative-looking site that they can't wait to tell their friends and neighbors, either.) But when you are ready to have your own online presence, there are ten mistakes to avoid. Read these and remember, you have been warned:

1. **Don't bother to update your information**—Want a sure-fire way to keep customers from coming back to your Web site? Don't bother to update any of your information! You wouldn't believe the number of small businesses that go to all of the expense and trouble of finally getting the Web site of their dreams launched into cyberspace, then they never bother to change or update information. Keep the information on your Web site current. Update prices, dates of sales, content, and whatever else your Web site will be featuring.

2. **Clog your site with many banner ads**—Want another way to irritate your visitors and drive away potential customers? Then clog your site with as many banner ads as you possibly can. There's nothing wrong with having a few banner ads, especially if you are working out an affiliate program with Amazon.com, or another Web site that can drive revenue to your coffers. But be careful not to use so many banner ads that your visitors have trouble figuring out just what it is you are trying to say or even sell.

Keep Up

It's important to keep up with the latest business information that becomes available on the Internet. If you don't have time to check out new Web sites each week, assign that task to someone who is fast and very Internet savvy. There is a world of information available to help you and your business to succeed on the World Wide Web.

3. **Have your Web site play Houdini**—I'm sure you have visited other Web sites that are online one day, then gone the next. Then, before you know it, they are back online yet once again. If you want to keep attracting new visitors and turn them into paying customers, stop playing the Houdini disappearing act. Make sure someone in your organization can check to see if your site is up and running each and every day. If you're having problems with your Internet Service Provider, then look for a new one.

4. **Don't let anyone know what you do**—Here's another deadly mistake that many small businesses make when they get their first Web site: They don't let anyone know what it is that they really do. A visitor to the site will be totally confused, and will leave quickly, wondering what the purpose of your Web site really was. From the second your home page loads, your customers should know exactly what it is that you are selling, and how what you are selling will benefit them.

5. **Use a busy background**—For some unknown reason, many small businesses use the wrong type of background graphics when they launch their Web site. (Maybe the same Web page designer is out there?) You know what we're talking about: a really ugly-looking wallpaper design distracts and takes away from the rest of your content. Clean up your act, and get rid of those ugly and busy backgrounds.

6. **Make sure your site loads slowly**—Your visitors and potential customers who stop by your Web site are really pressed for time. Their time is important to them, and they won't waste it by waiting for a slow-loading Web site to appear. Make sure your Web page designer knows and understands that you want a fast-loading site, and you want it now.

7. **Once you launch your site, do nothing else**—Don't fall into the trap of thinking that just because you now have a major Web site for your small business that new customers will beat themselves silly finding you and placing orders for your products and services. Develop a marketing plan that

> Clean up your act, and get rid of those ugly and busy backgrounds.

includes your online presence. Be prepared to spend enough of your time and money to make your Web site work for you.

8. **Don't waste time with photos**—If you think that visitors to your site only want to read text and aren't interested in photos or graphics, think again. Do you use a printed brochure that is nothing but written copy? Of course not. You have splashy colors, graphics, and photos that complement your text. Don't go overboard, but have enough photos and graphics to make your site a fun place to visit.

9. **Don't bother listing your phone number**—Want to really annoy your visitors and potential customers? Then don't bother listing your telephone number, or any other important contact information for that matter. You would be shocked at the number of small business Web sites that have really super looking sites, but for some unknown reason, they have left off the very important contact information. Put an "information box" at the top or bottom of each page, and that way no one will have any trouble finding a convenient way to get in touch with you.

10. **Don't worry about your Web address**—Give your small business Web site the professional look it really deserves by having a professional Web address. A few years ago I was working as a fundraising consultant, and wanted to experiment with a Web site that would allow me to sell a fundraising idea I had developed, which I discussed earlier in this book. The name of the promotion was the "No Go, No Show Fundraising Dinner." I reserved a Web address that was *www.nogonoshow.com*. That way, when people started looking for my fundraising plan, all they had to do was type in *www.nogonoshow.com* and they were directed to my Web site. While it might be nice to take advantage of the Web sites that offer free homepages, many of them will not allow only your business name to be the Web address. Get your own Web address; it's worth more than you will ever realize.

Don't Forget Humor

As you have learned by now, humor is an important factor in advertising and marketing. And the same holds true with Web sites. So don't forget to inject a little humor into your company's Web site. Visitors will love getting a good laugh, and will tell their friends about your business and your Web site.

The Good, the Bad, and the Ugly Side of Web Site Intros

Like every other business on the planet, you have a Web site, and you want yours to be special. You want it to be something that stands out from the crowd and tells your customers to keep on coming back for more. According to Simba Information in Stamford, Connecticut, the number of Internet users will reach 103.5 million by 2002, so major companies are looking for ways to show off their Web site to potential customers.

A study by Andersen Consulting (now Accenture) and Online Insight reports that companies are spending big money on Web brand marketing and advertising in hopes of attracting young and trendy customers to their Web sites.

One method currently being used is the Web Site Intro. Many companies are now using Macromedia Flash intros to provide supplemental information to enhance the users experience. With Macromedia Flash's technology you get a good combination of animation, text, graphics, video, and audio. But are they effective? Are they worth the time and money that it costs to create ones that look good? Industry experts have different opinions about what works, and what doesn't.

"Web site intros tend to add an unnecessary layer of clutter that interferes with the user's access to the main attraction of the Web site," says Charles Fuller, vice president of entrepreneur.com. "With content sites, you want to decrease the steps to the valued content, not build barriers."

Speediness Is Key

If a visitor is coming to your Web site and is searching for information, time is of the essence. No one wants to wait while fancy intros load. "For a Web company, the intro page is absolutely critical," says Steve Yost, owner of Quick Topic. "You have about five to ten seconds to make an impression and give a feel for what the service is about."

Some Web designers get so caught up in the bells and whistles and flashy colors that they forget there are real people wanting real

> The number of Internet users will reach 103.5 million by 2002, so major companies are looking for ways to show off their Web site to potential customers.

information. "If you look at user behavior on Web sites, a huge percentage of visitors only visit the homepage," says Aaron Kassover, chief architect for Ignition State, a digital strategy and solutions firm that builds Web sites and systems for global *Fortune* 500 companies. "You've got one quick chance to draw them in. Do you want to waste it on some cliched phrases fading in and out while your logo rotates behind them?

"Could you imagine consumers' reaction if they were forced to sit through a thirty-second 'intro' before they could walk into a store? Or, if you called a business, and before you were able to choose from the auto-attendant's choices, you were forced to listen to the company theme song? It wouldn't fly."

Intros Can Have a Place

But Meredith Search, director of Macromedia Flash, thinks that the message can be worth the wait. "Intros can do a great job of promoting a corporate brand and communicating a message," she says. "However, people are usually looking to visit a site to garner information, so a 'skip intro' option should always be available."

The longer the intro, however, the greater the chance of the user hitting the skip button. "There's a certain amount of users that will opt to skip out of the intro as soon as it starts to play. There are others that will be curious and watch. But unless the intro is extremely compelling, it should get to the point immediately, otherwise you run the risk of more users hitting the skip button," says Fuller.

Web site intros not only use precious time, but the aren't cheap. "Advertisers will often charge an additional 10 percent or so for developing and deploying Rich Media advertisements as designers create much more advanced and engaging content," says Search.

In the October 2000 issue of useit.com, Jakob Nielsen wrote a column called "Flash: 99% Bad." He wrote that while he agreed that multimedia has a role on the Web, he thinks that Flash technology tends to discourage usability. He feels that the resources would be better spent enhancing a site's core value. Also, he thinks that Flash encourages gratuitous animation. "Since we *can* make things move, *why not* make things move?" he writes.

> The longer the intro, however, the greater the chance of the user hitting the skip button.

Keep It Moving

Remember, visitors to your Web site will decide in the first few seconds if they think it's worth waiting for while your Web site loads before their eyes. So don't make your home page too intense that you lose a potential customer even before the final graphic is displayed.

Even some Web site owners are now rethinking the whole idea of a Web site intro. Glenda Riddick, owner of Rainbow Resource Directory, had a splash page, but then had their site redesigned. "The difference in the old site and the new one is like the difference between night and day," she says. "If anyone thinks the quality of their site doesn't make a difference, our experience will. We are now enjoying more sales since we changed our site and put text on the opening page."

But some companies, like Gráfica Inc., still believe in them. "Depending on a company's industry and target audience, flashy intros can work," says Mark Devaney, director of public relations at Gráfica. "In our case, the flash intro gives visitors an opportunity to preview info that is covered in more detail on the site, which visitors may or may not ever see. The intro is a quick, creative way to literally illustrate our core competencies: advertising, marketing, Web design, and CRM, with animation that helps explain the content in a way that static pages cannot. So in our case, the intro supports our business."

Consumer Reaction

Understanding how consumers make choices has long been a hot topic for social scientists, psychologists, and marketers. But just what has been their reaction to flashy intro pages? Many industry experts feel the reaction is not good.

"Users are becoming much more sophisticated and adept with their Web skills, with some becoming numb to flash Web pages," says Andreas Forsland, CEO of the Rev, an interactive marketing and branding agency. "The Web creator, now more than ever, must do his research in determining who specifically their audience is and what their demographics and lifestyle factors are. And at the same time, they must still consider what action they are requesting from the visitors to their site."

"My take on intro's is usually a big thumbs down," says Kassover. "When a site that puts a 'skip intro' button on their home page, I'm forced to wonder: why put a bandwidth-guzzling intro if it needn't be viewed? Might as well say 'skip gratuitous use of flash.'"

What the Future Holds

"Where appropriate, more sites will adopt intros as part of their mission to entertain and to sell more products or services," said Charles Fuller. "However, I don't think this will be something that impacts the vast majority of sites that rely on quickly delivering their pages and content to users that are trying to accomplish tasks or obtain information and are still accessing the Internet through a dial-up service."

"The wave has crested," said Mark Devaney. "For us it is working, but for other companies that need not be overly creative, the risk and expense of designing and posting an intro may not be worth it."

Companies and consumers will have to decide for themselves if intros are worth creating and viewing.

Tips to Help You Design a Web Site

Remember, as a small business you can have a big impact on the World Wide Web. So if you approach the task with the right focus, and with specific goals in mind, you can create an award-winning Web site.

> Know your true reason for having a Web site before you launch one.

Tips to Keep in Mind When Thinking about Your New Web Site

- What is your reason for having the site? Is it sales? Or is it content with plenty of useful information? Know your true reason for having a Web site before you launch one.
- Decide if you want to hire an outside firm to create your Web site. If someone in your organization has the skills to create an award-winning Web site for your small business, then by all means use the resources you have on hand. But if you need to, hire an outside firm to create your site.
- Make sure that your finished Web site is easy to navigate around and that customers will be able to find everything from A to Z that they are looking for when they stop by to visit.

Look for the Best

Before you design your Web site, start surfing the Internet and look for examples of sites that you feel have been well done. Many Web sites win awards, such as The Webby Awards, and others. Look for those award winners as examples and inspiration for your own site.

- Have a strategy in mind for how you will spread the word about your new Web site. How are you going to get the word out about your new creation? Make sure that you start registering with the major search engines. And make sure your new Web address appears on all of your business cards, letterhead, signs, etc.
- Think about hosting a contest or give something away as a means of attracting visitors. People enjoy getting something for free, or a chance to win something. Be creative and come up with some wacky ideas that will keep customers buzzing about your site and your contest.
- Always remember to keep customer satisfaction as the top order of business. No matter what your reason is for having a Web site in the first place, if you don't make sure that your customers are happy and satisfied, then you could be in for big trouble.

Web sites for small businesses will often level out the playing field and will allow them to compete with larger businesses because viewers and visitors are likely to shop around for the best bargain, or the most informative site. Keep the needs of your viewers and visitors in mind when designing and implementing your site and chances are they are likely to come back again sometime in the near future. As a small business manager, it's in your best interest to utilize every avenue of advertising and sales opportunities, so decide on your goals and get busy creating a Web site that is just right for your business.

The Future of E-Commerce and Your Business

The International Data Corporation (IDC) has conducted some recent research and found that e-commerce is the wave of the future for small businesses. According to their research, the number of U.S. small businesses engaged in e-commerce will increase from 400,000 in 1998 to nearly 2.8 million in 2003.

The Second Annual Small Business Internet Survey conducted by the Gallup Poll for Verizon has some interesting results. Consider these statistics:

- Small businesses that established a Web site to advertise and promote their business increased 123 percent over the past year (21 percent in 2000, compared to 8 percent in 1999).
- Small businesses that established a Web site to sell products decreased 48 percent during the same period (13 percent in 2000 compared to 25 percent in 1999).
- The number of new small businesses with a Web site has not significantly increased (27 percent in 2000 versus 24 percent in 1999).
- Fifty-five percent of the small businesses with Web sites reported that the site has broken even or has already paid for itself in increased business.
- Sixty-three percent of the small businesses with Web sites expect total sales through the Internet to increase within the next twelve months.
- Nearly half of the respondents spent less than $1,000 to create their site, another 21 percent report spending between $1,001 and $5,000.
- Fifty-seven percent found Web site creation easy, rating the process seven or higher on a scale of one to ten.
- More than 60 percent developed their Web site in under three months.

Small Businesses Without an Internet Presence Reported These Results in That Same Survey

- Thirty-five percent of respondents indicate they do not have an Internet site because it is not important to their business, up 7 percent over 1999.
- Many small businesses believe they are too local to benefit from the Internet, with 42 percent reporting this in 2000 and 45 percent reporting this in 1999.

> Nearly half of the respondents spent less than $1,000 to create their site, another 21 percent report spending between $1,001 and $5,000.

- Thirty-three percent of small businesses without a Web site believe their customers won't use it.
- Twenty-nine percent of small businesses without an Internet presence will "definitely" or "probably" develop a Web site within the next twelve months.

Where does your small business fit in the new economy and e-commerce?

How Well Do You Understand the New Economy? Take Our Quiz and Find Out!

1. Are you familiar with the Internet?
2. Do you know the difference between the Internet and the World Wide Web?
3. Does your business have its own Web site?
4. Do you know what in Intranet is?
5. If your business doesn't presently have a Web site, are you planning on launching one in the next ninety days or less?
6. Do you consider yourself an expert in the latest technology that is on the market?
7. Does your business have a technology expert on the payroll?
8. Does your business keep up with the latest computers that are on the market?
9. Do you understand what customers are looking for in the new economy?
10. Do you offer your goods or services over the Internet?

How well did you score? For this quiz, you should have answered "Yes" to at least seven out of the ten questions. That's right. Seven out of ten will make you a "New Economy Guru."

> Do you understand what customers are looking for in the new economy?

For more information on this topic, visit our Web site at www.businesstown.com

---

Chapter 17

Risk Management

How comfortable are you
with risk taking?

How comfortable are you with risk taking? Most people hate to take risks. That's why vanilla ice cream is the most popular flavor sold in America today. Even with exotic flavors like Rocky Road and Fudge Royal available, more people still choose the vanilla flavored ice cream. Why? The answer is simple: They don't want to risk choosing a flavor that they might not like. So they pick the same old, tried-and-true flavor that they have been enjoying for many years. That way they know what it will taste like, how much it will cost, and even how many calories it contains.

That's what it is like for many small business owners. They keep choosing the vanilla ice cream because it's safe. It's comforting. They don't have to worry about any strange tastes. But where would we be without the risk takers of the world?

People Who Weren't Afraid to Risk a Little

The following are some examples of people who were not afraid to take a risk. In many cases the biggest risk takers had little encouragement beyond their own self-determination.

Walt Disney

Probably the most recognizable name in entrepreneur history, Walt had a vision and a dream and wasn't afraid to chase that dream until it became a reality. Even when he was once told he lacked creativity, he didn't quit. He kept dreaming big dreams, and did everything in his power to convince everyone that his dream would one day come true. And it did. But it wasn't always an easy journey along the way.

In 1953 Walt convinced a group of researchers at Stanford University to prepare a feasibility study of his plans for Disneyland. He wanted some expert opinions on whether Disneyland would be a success (even though he knew in his heart that it would be). The answers from the researchers, however, we're not promising. Everyone thought it was a terrible idea, and that he shouldn't go through with his plans and ideas for a new amusement park. But as everyone knows by now, Walt's plan was not "just another amusement park." He dared to dream something different.

Instead of hiring people experienced in designing and building amusement parks, he hired a team that had experience as motion picture art directors. He figured that those people would be able to help him create Disneyland, and it turned out he was right on the money. But what if, when handed that report from Stanford University, Walt had said, "Gee, everyone else thinks it's not going to work, so I'd better listen to them." He didn't, and millions of people who vacation each year both at Disneyland in California and Disney World in Florida are glad he made the decision that he finally did.

Bill Rosenberg

The founder of Dunkin' Donuts had always been a hard worker. He knew it would take hard work and a positive attitude to succeed in business, so in 1946 he founded Industrial Luncheon Services, a company that delivered meals and coffee break snacks to factory workers in the outskirts of Boston, Massachusetts. That venture proved so successful that he thought about opening his first coffee and donut shop, which he called the Open Kettle. By 1950 he opened the first store that was officially known as Dunkin' Donuts; today there are more than 5,000 Dunkin' Donuts franchises in the world. His hard work paid off for him, and he is living proof that you can take a risk and succeed if you stick to your plan and never give up.

> The founder of Dunkin' Donuts is living proof that you can take a risk and succeed if you stick to your plan and never give up.

Ray Kroc

In 1954 Ray Kroc mortgaged his home and invested his entire life savings to market a five-spindled milkshake maker called the Multimixer. One of his customers owned eight of those milkshake machines, so Kroc set out to find out why the customer was so successful. He visited a San Bernardino drive-up hamburger restaurant owned by Dick and Mac McDonald. The two brothers had created an assembly-line production center, selling French fries, milkshakes, and hamburgers in such great volume that they could afford to sell their burgers for only fifteen cents apiece. Kroc was so impressed by their

Create a "Risk List"

Many companies have a wish list, but not too many have a "risk list." Gather your most creative people for a brainstorming session, and ask them to help develop a "risk list" for your company. In other words, come up with a list of ideas that might seem too risky at first, but still might be worth pursuing.

operation, he convinced them to open up several more stores—and he said he would operate them.

Despite friends, bankers, and other people telling him it was too high a risk, Kroc moved forward with his plans and in 1955 opened the Des Plaines, Illinois, McDonald's. The first day's revenues totaled a whopping $366.12. But within five years, the fast-food chain was generating $37 million a year in sales. By the following year, Kroc bought out the McDonald brothers for $2.7 million. Today, there are over 25,000 McDonald's in 117 countries. (Where would all of those people be eating today if Ray Kroc had been afraid to take a risk?)

Mary K. Ash

Mary K. Ash is the founder of Mary Kay Cosmetics, the largest direct-sales cosmetics company in the world. With $5,000 of her own savings, she started the company at the time when men dominated the work force. Her dedication to hard work and never-quit attitude allowed her to eventually prosper in her field. She always wore a bumblebee pin on her lapel, to remind people that the bumblebee should not have the anatomical ability to fly. But it does, and that is her testimony and witness that everyone "can do it." In addition to running the multimillion dollar company, she went on to write two best selling books. Her never-say-die spirit, along with her willingness to put in a hard day's work, proved to everyone that not only wasn't she afraid to take risks, but she took them and made them successful.

Why Risk Taking Is Good for You and Your Business

Small business owners and managers who are not afraid to take risks are sometimes known as "loose cannons" or "hot dogs" to other people. But there are times when you will need to reach out and take a leap of faith to implement your plan.

A risk can help launch a new venture. Remember Ray Kroc? His willingness to risk a little led to some really great things for him, didn't it? In this modern age of so many technological advances, it is easier to risk a little, and gain a lot.

Risks can help you realize your dreams. Remember Walt Disney? His willingness to dream a little and risk a whole lot resulted in Disneyland. Walt was a dreamer, that's for sure, and he wasn't afraid to do whatever it took to see those dreams come true.

Risks can force you to work harder. Sometimes we all need a little push and incentive now and then. By taking a risk, you are forcing yourself to work harder towards the success you are seeking.

By risking a little, people in your organization will begin communicating with each other like never before. It can also create new excitement. And sometimes all it takes is a little excitement and enthusiasm to get the momentum moving forward in a small business.

Strategies to Manage Risk Takers

Do you have a Walt Disney, a Ray Kroc, or a Mary K. working in your small business? Would you even recognize them if they did work there? As a small business manager, it's your job to keep an eye out for those risk takers. We've already established that risk takers can be good for business. However, before you give the risk taker in your organization carte blanche to do whatever they think they want, heed these simple strategies to manage them:

Stay focused—There will be many distractions in your small business every day, so make sure you stay focused on the risk takers at all times. It doesn't mean you have to follow them around, watching their every move and worrying about what they will be doing next. But it does mean that you need to be aware of their plans, activities, and ideas.

Give them room to run free—Risk takers need their space, so make sure you give them what they need. Just like creative types, risk takers tend to operate "outside of the box," and sometimes their ideas may be just a little bit

Hold a Risky Business Contest

Want to encourage risk taking among your employees? Then hold a Risky Business Contest. Have them submit ideas that might be so far out in left field that many people would be afraid to try them. But make sure they create a plan on paper; that way, everyone will have a blueprint to work from. And don't forget to have prizes; what's a contest without rewards?

unusual or even wacky in your opinion. But watch, listen, and learn.

Allow them to break the rules–But not all of the rules. Risk takers, by their very nature, see rules as roadblocks and obstacles to their successes. So by giving them a little leeway, you will be encouraging them to continue on their path to success.

Plan with them–This may sound a little difficult, and at times it will be, but you need to plan with your risk taker. Budget enough time so that everyone can sit down and create a step-by-step approach for the new venture or project. And when those plans are completed, make sure you don't just toss them in a drawer to gather dust. Review those plans frequently, and make adjustments as needed.

Top Ten Ways to Encourage Risk Taking in Your Employees

Are you a good encourager to those employees in your organization who might not be afraid to risk? Or are you quick to say "No!" and squash any dreams they may have? Here are ten ways to encourage risk taking in your employees

1. Provide the right environment. Did you know that the offices of DC comics have a full-sized, lifelike figure sitting in the receptionist area reading a copy of *The Daily Planet*? And that figure looks exactly like Clark Kent. Can you imagine what a fun and creative place that must be to work? Odds are those DC employees are not afraid to risk at all, wouldn't you think?

2. Encourage brainstorming sessions. You just never know what great ideas might come out of that next brainstorming session. If your small business doesn't hold any, you don't know

Suggestion Box

Does your company have a suggestion box? And do you encourage employees to use it, or does it just sit there, collecting dust? One way to encourage risk taking in small businesses is to allow employees to make suggestions in a nonthreatening manner. And a suggestion box will allow that to take place.

what you're missing. They are fun, employees love them, and sometimes some really great ideas are born.

3. Encourage team building. Risk takers who are part of a dynamic team will shine brightly. Encourage the formation of teams among employees who are interested in "taking a leap of faith."

4. Keep some degree of flexibility in the schedule. Don't bother putting everything in writing, because when risk taking is involved, it usually means that the schedule flies out the window. So be prepared to keep some degree of flexibility, not only in the schedule, but in everything else.

5. Ask for a mission statement. If no one knows why they are doing the things they are doing, then why bother doing them in the first place? Write down the mission statement for the new project or venture. (Here's another opportunity for a great brainstorming session.)

6. Learn to accept mistakes and failures. Hey, mistakes will be made. Failures might happen. But as you know, that's all part of the entrepreneurial risk-taking adventure. Don't fret when things go wrong; instead, circle the wagons, and be ready to activate Plan B.

7. Create a network of support. No one can do it alone (even Walt Disney had some help on his side), so create a network of support for anyone involved in risk taking. Networking is very important, and without it, risk taking becomes even more riskier than it needs to be.

8. Create a level of trust. Risk takers need to know that people trust them to run with the ball and make that touchdown. So do whatever it takes to create a level of trust among your employees who are the risk takers in your small business.

9. Look for short-term and long-term results. Before taking a leap of faith and risking a little, make sure you have clearly defined short-term and long-term goals in mind. Remember, without goals and a plan, risk taking can be a dangerous proposition for everyone involved.

Information in Company Newsletters

If your company has a newsletter (and if you don't, you're missing out on many opportunities to communicate with your employees), consider printing articles about successful entrepreneurs who weren't afraid to risk a little. Sometimes all it takes is for an employee to see a success story in writing to encourage them to risk a little, and gain a lot.

10. Learn to defy the odds. As risk takers, people must learn to defy the odds. If you truly believe that you are like Walt Disney, then you must learn to move forward, no matter how the odds may be stacked up against you.

How Comfortable Are You with Risk Taking?

1. I consider myself to be a risk taker.
2. I think all businesses need to risk a little each and every day.
3. Risk taking involves planning, faith, and a little luck.
4. When you risk, you stand to gain more than you stand to lose.
5. People want to risk, but have been trained not to.
6. If you risk, the sky is the limit.
7. You need a blueprint to risk anything.
8. Risk taking can encourage teamwork.
9. Risk taking can be fun.
10. Risk taking has resulted in many successful businesses being launched and expanded.

Okay, how did you do? Hopefully, you said "Yes" to seven or more of those statements. If you did, congratulations, you are on your way to a roller coaster ride of risk taking. Hang on, but believe me, it will be worth it. If you said "Yes" to six or less, then you may still be a little shy about taking risks.

Risk a Little, Gain a Lot

Do you like to gamble? Do you ever go to a casino, or race track, or buy a lottery ticket? When you do, you are risking a little, and you hope to gain a lot. Well, when you risk in business, it's almost the same thing. But guess what? Your odds are better!

Yes, because when you risk a little in the business world, odds are (pun intended) you have done some research and have greater faith in the outcome. In other words, you don't just walk into your office one morning and announce, "Today, I'm going to launch a

> Risk taking involves planning, faith, and a little luck.

Web site and make a zillion dollars!" No one in their right mind would do such a thing, without first carefully considering all of the plusses and minuses.

Using our "launching a Web site" example, a savvy and smart business owner would do plenty of research before moving forward with his or her plan. Sure, it's still risking a little, but during the research phase of the project, you would learn the good, the bad, and the ugly side of launching a Web site, and create a plan that has the highest probability of success.

So don't be afraid to risk a little; after all, you do stand a chance of gaining a lot!

Don't be afraid to risk a little; after all, you do stand a chance of gaining a lot!

For more information on this topic, visit our Web site at www.businesstown.com

Managers and Communication

In this section you will learn why communication is the key to your business's success, and how you can start to communicate more effectively. Time management tips are shared, along with information on how to deal with negative people before they ruin your business. Also included is a chapter on stress management that includes some of the latest techniques you can use to manage work-related stress and stay healthy.

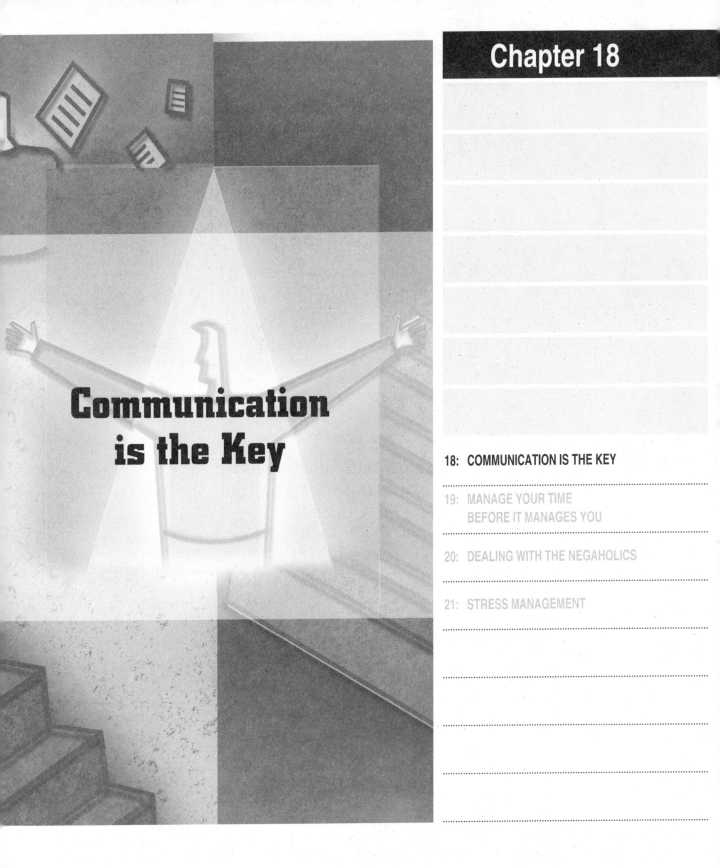

Chapter 18

Communication is the Key

Practice Listening

The next time an employee is speaking with you, don't interrupt. Even if you are pressed for time, spend those extra few minutes listening to that person. Sometimes it takes a few minutes for someone to get their point across. By becoming a better listener, you will become a better boss and manager.

Are you talking so they can listen? When you talk, do your employees listen to you? And how do you know if they are listening to you? On an average day, do you think people really understand what you are trying to communicate to them? If you think you are having troubles in the communication arena you are not alone. Communication problems are the number one problem in businesses today—large and small, it doesn't matter, communication problems can be found there.

Those problems can be solved very easily, but far too many small business manages think that they are too busy to be bothered with such things as a "communication" problem. After all, there are more important things to worry about and take care of, aren't there?

As Zig Ziglar is famous for saying, "That is stinking thinking!" Communication problems should be your number one priority. Because without communication that works, without communication that is understood by everyone involved, your business will soon lie dead in the water, just waiting to sink.

What's Your Communication Style? What Type of Communicator Are You?

The "my way or the highway" type—This type of communicator knows that there is only one right answer: his or hers. Anything else is purely a waste of their precious time, so why even bother asking for someone else's opinion or input on a business-related matter? After only a short time, employees who work for this type of manager will begin to lose all interest in working there, and will soon be hunting for a new position.

The "what I don't know can't hurt me" type—This type of communicator knows that what he or she doesn't know can't possibly hurt him or her. So why bother getting feedback from employees on important business projects?

Let the cards fall where they may; what you don't know can't possibly hurt you, right?

The "I can't make a decision" type—This type of communicator has trouble making a decision. And that can spell trouble for employees of a small business. Think back to the days when you worked for someone else. Did you ever enjoy having a manager who couldn't make a decision? I didn't think so. So get over your fear of making a decision and start making headway today!

The "I will take all the credit" type—This type of communicator is known for stealing everyone else's good ideas and glory. When a job is done well, he or she won't waste time letting everyone know *they* are the brains behind the project. While it's okay to be a good leader and manager, don't be the kind that steals everyone's thunder, or you'll soon find that no one wants to work with you.

The "I don't really care what you're doing" type—These types of communicators are famous for building walls around themselves to keep everyone out of their personal space. If you really don't care what everyone is doing, then you won't mind when your business starts falling apart, will you?

> Get over your fear of making a decision and start making headway today!

Quiz: What's Your Communication Style?

1. When I speak, I expect people to listen.
2. If I don't know about it, it can't affect me.
3. Decision making is for wimps.
4. The glory belongs to ME.
5. You've confused me with someone who actually cares.

How did you score?

1. If you answered "Yes" to this statement, then you are a "my way or the highway" type of communicator.
2. If you answered "Yes" to this statement, then you are a "what I don't know can't hurt me" type of communicator.
3. If you answered "Yes" to this statement, then you are a "I can't make a decision type of communicator."
4. If you answered "Yes" to this statement, then you are a "I will take all the credit" type of communicator.
5. If you answered "Yes" to this statement, then you are a "I don't really care what you're doing" type of communicator.

Common Complaints from Employees

Here are some common complaints from employees at small businesses about communication problems they have encountered:

"I don't know what to do." Clearly, these employees are put out to sea in a rowboat without even an oar or a chart to help guide them along their way. What are you doing to make sure your employees know what their jobs are? Do you provide job descriptions that say more than "additional duties as required?" If not, you shouldn't be surprised when your employees start jumping ship and begin working for your nearest competitor.

"I don't know how to do it." Okay, so maybe you are a pretty good manager, and you do provide your employees with a detailed "to do" list. But what good is that list if they don't know how to perform a particular task? It may be okay in your head to put "develop a marketing plan" on their list of things to do, but if they have never developed one, you're both in big trouble. Make sure your employees have the tools and the necessary training to follow your orders.

Make sure your employees have the tools and the necessary training to follow your orders.

"I don't have the authority to do it." This is a bad situation that will only get worse. If you don't delegate authority to your employees, how do you expect them to get their job done? It doesn't mean that you have to turn over the keys to the vault, but you do have to give them the power to do their jobs, while at the same time holding them accountable for their actions.

"I never get any feedback." Want to keep your employees in the dark and slowly drive them to another place of employment? Then never give them any feedback, and that's what you're sure to get. Employees need feedback, whether it's good, bad, or ugly. Feedback is a way to measure how successfully they have performed. And if you are holding back on the feedback because an employee did a bad job, how will they ever have a chance to correct their mistakes and grow?

Barriers to Effective Communication

Poor communication will slowly eat away at your small business like a cancer. The most common barriers to effective communication in the business world today include:

- People feel afraid to say what they really mean. The bosses at the top of the food chain at many small businesses never get to hear how their employees really feel. Why? Because most people feel afraid to say what they really mean. Put yourself in their shoes: Would you really feel open and honest, and able to tell your manager that you think the decision he or she just made about some customer service issue is wrong, and that you think it will drive customers away? Of course you wouldn't. So why do you expect other employees to feel open and honest? You need to create an environment of trust and respect, one where employees aren't afraid to speak up about an issue. Only then will

> You need to create an environment of trust and respect, one where employees aren't afraid to speak up about an issue. Only then will everyone be on the same team.

everyone be on the same team, and be able to move the business forward.

- People hear something different than what's actually been said. I'm sure you have run up against this problem at different times in your career as a manager. You tell your employees one thing, and they turn around and do something different. But guess what? In their mind, they are doing exactly what it is that you told them to do. Here's an example of what I mean: Suppose you told one of your employees to fax some information to the media as soon as she can. What have you really communicated to her? Well, you told her to do it as soon as she could. But if you really meant to say, "Hey, I think this information should be faxed within the hour so we can make the newspaper's deadline," then you are the one at fault, not your employee. Say what you mean; don't beat around the bush. Don't say things like ASAP when you really have a particular deadline in mind!

- People are suffering from information overload. These days it's not unusual for employees to receive as many as 100 e-mail messages a day; some get many more, too. Add that on top of the faxes, telephone calls, voice mail messages, Post-it notes, memos, and other forms of communication people seem to receive on a daily basis, and it's no wonder people are suffering from information overload. Come up with a strategic plan to help your employees battle the information overload war.

- People block out certain parts of messages. If an employee is hearing something that is upsetting to him (like he has to work overtime when his son or daughter's birthday party is that evening) he might block out certain parts of your message. Defense mechanisms will kick in and selective hearing will take over. Before you have problems in this area, make sure you and your employees know exactly what it is that you want and need. If all else fails, you can always try the "mirror" technique. Train your employees to repeat your instructions to you in this manner. "What I'm hearing you say is that you want me to work on this report tonight?" But

> These days it's not unusual for employees to receive as many as 100 e-mail messages a day.

it works both ways, too. Make sure you find out if your employees are okay with your last minute instructions.

- People hear one message, but your body language conveys something different. I'm sure this has happened to you sometime in your career. A manager gives you verbal instructions, but her body language says something completely different. In most cases, employees will tend to believe the body language, which usually is conveying the truth. So make sure your body language and your verbal messages are on the same wave length.

> **Use Humor**
>
> Use humor to help you knock down communications barriers in your company. If tension is high, people won't be comfortable enough to do their very best. So if you can use humor to "break the ice," then by all means do so.

The Manager as the Great Communicator

If you want to be considered a great communicator (and these days who wouldn't?), then you need to adopt the Ten Rules of Communication.

1. **Thou shalt say what you mean, and mean what you say.** Before attempting to communicate a message to someone else, make sure you understand what exactly it is you are trying to say. Because if you are the least bit confused, don't you think they will be, too?
2. **Thou shalt be empathetic.** Great communicators will put themselves in the shoes of those they are trying to talk with. Make sure they understand and have embraced your instructions clearly and confidently.
3. **Thou shalt match your message to the right audience.** In other words, if you are speaking to clerical workers about an important issue, use language that they will understand and comprehend. Don't use complicated financial terms if the audience doesn't call for it. Learn to recognize who your audience is, and create your message based on that criteria.
4. **Thou shalt organize your thoughts before they come out of your mouth.** Or from the computer, printer, or any other means you use as a way of communicating with your employees. Effective communications and organization go hand in hand.

5. **Thou shalt encourage feedback.** Great communicators will encourage and reward employees who provide feedback. Even if that feedback is something that they really don't want to hear. As a manager, you need to develop a thick skin, and be prepared for all types of feedback: good, bad, and ugly.

6. **Thou shalt not leave anyone out in the dark.** Make sure that everyone stays informed about all aspects of your business, and what's taking place in their particular department. You can issue a daily bulletin, or a weekly bulletin, even e-mail. Or you could hold informal meetings or get-togethers to keep everyone up to speed.

7. **Thou shalt always be truthful.** Want to lose the respect and trust of your employees? Then start by being anything less than truthful to them. Share the news about what's taking place, even if it is bad. At the very least it will keep the rumors from spreading, and sometimes rumors can take their toll on employees and productivity.

8. **Thou shalt have a sense of humor.** It doesn't mean you have to wear clown shoes and a big red, rubber nose. But every employee will appreciate a manager who has a good sense of humor. When you have a sense of humor, people will come to you with their problems and concerns a lot easier than they would if you had no sense of humor at all.

9. **Thou shalt admit when you are wrong and have made a mistake.** Face it, no one is perfect, and no one expects you never to make any mistakes (except your spouse, that is). So if you've made a boo-boo, face up and admit your mistake. Your employees will respect you for it, and will see you as a great leader, rather than one who tries to hide his or her mistakes and never admits when he or she has done wrong.

10. **Thou shalt encourage open communication.** A company that has an open communication policy will leave its competitors at the starting gate in the race for success. Employees who know they can speak their mind and express their opinion without fear of harassment or punishment are more creative, and they will use their imagination to come up with multiple solutions to problems.

Share the news about what's taking place, even if it is bad. At the very least it will keep the rumors from spreading, and sometimes rumors can take their toll on employees and productivity.

Four Ways to Communicate Successfully

There are many ways to communicate these days, but a successful manager will learn the four ways to communicate successfully:

1. **Communicate in person.** There's nothing like an in-person visit to communicate your message to someone. By taking the time to visit with that person, you are not only using the top method of communication (personal), you are also getting an opportunity to witness their reaction to your message. Maybe you thought your employees would be thrilled with the news you are giving them. But their reactions are not what you had hoped they would be. But because you took the time to communicate in person, you now have the opportunity to discuss the issue further and in greater depth.

2. **Communicate over the telephone.** While this is the second best way to convey a message, it's still a good one. You lose the "in-person" reaction, but a smart manager will learn to use the telephone as a great means of communication. Before you pick up the phone and dial, however, make sure your thoughts are organized, and know what you are going to say. And make sure you leave enough time for them to ask questions or discuss anything you just told them.

3. **Communicate in writing.** These days, you have a wide variety of written communication options. A written memo, an e-mail message, a letter, a Post-it note, you name it, you can use it. Again, just like the telephone message option, make sure you have organized your thoughts and put your message in writing very carefully. And before you hit the "send" button or mail that letter or memo, print it out and put it aside for a few minutes. Then read it again. Your mind will sometimes miss an important typo or hidden meaning that you might have accidentally put into your written correspondence.

4. **Communicate through a third person.** While this can sometimes be a risky method, it is one way to communicate. But just make sure that the person who is delivering your message understands exactly what it is you are trying to convey

Who Are Your Heroes?

In your career, who has been your hero? We're not talking about Superman and Batman, but instead, in terms of managers. What manager has been your hero because he or she had been a great communicator? Think back to those times when you worked for that person, and how pleasant it was to serve under them. Then start emulating their communication skills for the benefit of everyone who works under you.

to your employees. If that person is confused, how do you expect your employees to react? Make sure the messenger knows how to deliver your message, exactly the way you intend it to be delivered.

The Written Memo: Why No One Takes Them Seriously

While there's nothing like putting your memo down on paper, there are times when memos are not taken seriously. And if you suddenly start putting out ineffective memos, then before long your employees will begin to ignore *all* of your memos; and that can lead to big trouble.

Examples of Ineffective Memos

You use a memo that doesn't really say anything important—I worked for a major corporation many years ago that used to issue memos that had nothing more than one or two sentences. Here's an example: *Employees should remember to punch in and punch out before beginning and ending their shift.* Well, gee, thanks for the reminder, buddy! But did you really have to waste a whole piece of company letterhead, and print up several thousand of these, so we all got our own personal copy? What kind of a message do you think that is conveying? "We have lots of money and time to waste." Instead of putting out a memo with something like that on it, why not use a "message" on a payroll stub, or a poster in the company cafeteria?

You use a memo to convey bad news—What's wrong, are you afraid to look your employees in the face when you have bad news to share? Conveying bad news by a memo is not a good idea at all.

You use a memo that's not really clear—There's nothing worse than issuing a memo to thousands (or even dozens)

> Conveying bad news by a memo is not a good idea at all.

of employees, and finding out that they really don't understand what it is that the memo is saying. That's a sure-fire way to get the rumor mill grinding, my friend! Review your memos very carefully, and test them out on a few people before you issue them. You'll be glad that you did.

The Future of Communication in Successful Businesses

In the future, it will be a fight for survival among small business managers. With an uncertain economy always right around the corner, and prices that can skyrocket almost overnight, effective communication will be the key to managing a successful business.

Make sure your business is doing everything in its power to be one of those businesses that succeed. Wouldn't it be a shame if you went under because of a lack of communications skills?

Encourage Memo Reading and Writing

If you want memos to be read by your employees, then draft an employee to write one. Just be specific about what message you are trying to pass on, and ask that person to write their version of how they feel it can be put into memo form.

For more information on this topic, visit our Web site at www.businesstown.com

Manage Your Time Before It Manages You

Benjamin Franklin is given credit for this quote: "Time is the stuff of which life is made." He was correct in his thinking, that's for sure. Time is something that we all share equally, no matter how much money we earn or what Ivy League school we graduated from. We all have twenty-four hours a day, seven days a week.

It's how we manage our time that separates us from each other. Many successful business owners learned a long time ago how to master time management techniques. And the best news is: you can learn them as well. And if your response is that you're too busy to learn some new time management techniques, then something is wrong. Because people who have learned how to manage their time well can always find time for something new in their schedule.

Do you manage time, or does time manage you? For many small business owners, it seems as if they are slaves to the monster known as time. They seem to drift from one crisis to another, and can never seem to get caught up with their list of things that really need to be accomplished. You should be required to prove that you have effective time management skills before you are allowed to apply for your business license. Because without those skills, you're making your road to success more rocky than it really needs to be.

> Do you manage time, or does time manage you?

What's Your Time Management IQ? Take Our Quiz and Find Out

1. Do you start each day reviewing your "To Do" list?
2. Do you regularly delegate tasks that can be accomplished by others?
3. Do you set goals for yourself each day?
4. Are you flexible when it comes to your schedule?
5. Do you spend time each day making a plan?
6. Have you learned to say "No" when you need to?
7. Do you acknowledge that you are not perfect?
8. Do you reward yourself when you accomplish a difficult task?

9. Do you know how to eliminate time wasters from your schedule?
10. Do you know when your most productive time is?
11. Do you avoid procrastination?
12. Do you plan useful meetings?
13. Do you schedule some quiet time for yourself each day?
14. Do you avoid missing deadlines?
15. Do you consider yourself an organized person?
16. Do you break large projects into smaller, more manageable ones?
17. Do you take a small tape recorder with you as you travel so you can record important thoughts?
18. Do you make time in your schedule to keep up with professional journals?
19. Can you identify the obstacles that try and keep you from managing your time?

Take a few moments and add up the number of "No" answers you gave yourself. Don't worry about it if you're seeing a lot more "No" answers than "Yes" ones. You are not hopeless, you can change your ways and learn to be a time management wizard.

Let's Review Each Question:

Do you start each day reviewing your "To Do" list? If you answered "Yes," that's great. But if you are like many small business owners and managers, you barely have time to create a To Do list, let alone review it leisurely over a second cup of coffee and a danish. However, if you don't keep a To Do list, how do you know what you need to accomplish each day? You may have a list of things in your mind that you want to get done, but I'm willing to bet that within a few hours, three dozen other problems and activities will pop up that need your immediate attention. Then what happens to that "memo in your mind?" It gets shoved aside, and may be forgotten altogether. So make sure you start each day by reviewing a

> Can you identify the obstacles that try and keep you from managing your time?

list of tasks you would like to have accomplished before the end of your business day. If you've never done something like this before, it may seem strange at first. So if you are new to this whole "To Do" list technique, start out slowly, and list only a few things each day. Then, before you realize it, you will become a master planner and doer, and you will enjoy the fruits of your labor.

Do you regularly delegate tasks that can be accomplished by others? If you answered "Yes," then pat yourself on the back and enjoy a big "attaboy." As you learned in Chapter 4, far too many small business owners and managers fail miserably when it comes to the fine art of delegating. Want to know why so many business owners have trouble delegating? It's because delegation involves passing responsibility for completion of work to another person. And too many business owners find it difficult to put their trust into other people when it comes to managing the affairs of their small business. If you're still having trouble delegating tasks, then reread Chapter 4 before you continue any further.

Do you set goals for yourself each day? If you answered "Yes," consider yourself one of the fortunate ones. Too many small business owners and managers fail to set goals for themselves each day. And since they have no goals, they have nothing to work toward, and they end up spinning their wheels as they watch their competitors succeed in the marketplace. How about you? Do you set goals for yourself each day? And are they realistic goals, ones that you know you can accomplish? And once you have those goals down on paper, do you have a plan of action in mind to help you meet those goals?

Are you flexible when it comes to your schedule? Everyone needs to have some degree of flexibility when it comes to their own individual schedule. How flexible are you? Have you mastered the fine art of juggling your

> Do you set goals for yourself each day? Do you have a plan of action in mind to help you meet those goals?

schedule around when unexpected problems develop? Be flexible, and you will succeed.

Do you spend time each day making a plan? Successful people know the importance of planning ahead, so hopefully, you consider yourself already in that category. But if not, it's not too late to change your way of thinking. Come up with a plan of the day, and brainstorm ways to make those plans happen.

Have you learned how to say "No" when you need to? This is hard for even the most organized executive. But once you learn the fine art of saying "No," it will become a lot easier. Just because someone asks you to do something for them it doesn't mean that you always have to respond with a "Yes." Try saying "No" now and then, and you'll free up more time in your schedule to handle the really important items on your busy agenda.

Do you acknowledge that you are not perfect? Very few people on the planet are perfect, although many would argue that they are, I'm sure. But what does it mean not to be perfect? It simply means that you will make mistakes now and then, but it's not the end of the world. Chalk it up to experience, put it behind you, and move forward in managing your small business.

Do you reward yourself when you accomplish a difficult task? This technique is especially good for managers who are procrastinators. If you find yourself putting tasks off for whatever reason, try the reward system. Select something that you want as a reward, for example, maybe you'll purchase that new Palm Pilot you've seen advertised. Or it can even be as simple as just taking a few hours off from work. Whatever works for you, just do it. When you finish a difficult task, reward yourself. You'll feel good about it.

Do you know how to eliminate time wasters from your schedule? This is a hard one to do, because sometimes a

> Try saying "No" now and then, and you'll free up more time in your schedule to handle the really important items on your busy agenda.

time waster will materialize out of the blue when you least expect it to. But are you any good at eliminating them? For example, are you brave enough to cancel a meeting that really isn't worth your time?

Do you know when your most productive time is? This is the time of the day when you are at your best. Are you a morning person? Do you shine early in the morning and get more accomplished at that time of the day? Or are you an afternoon or evening person? Knowing when your best time to be productive is can go a long way in helping you to accomplish everything on your busy schedule.

Do you avoid procrastination? If you don't, then reread the section on procrastination in Chapter 2. And use some of the tricks in number 8. Don't let procrastination be the kiss of death for your small business.

Do you plan useful meetings? Have you ever stopped and asked yourself, "Why am I at this meeting?" If so, chances are, your presence really wasn't necessary. Stop wasting your time by attending useless meetings. Instead of spending your time there, ask someone to summarize what took place, so you can still be aware of the proceedings.

How many times have you attended a meeting only to find that your attention is elsewhere? Or that you spend most of the time doodling on your note pad? If you find yourself attending too many useless meetings, stop it immediately.

Do you schedule some quiet time for yourself each day? If you don't, you're cheating yourself. Everyone needs to have some quiet time for themselves each and every day, and small business owners and mangers are no exception. Schedule at least twenty minutes where you can shut your door with no interruptions. Have someone answer your telephone, and don't cheat by checking your e-mail. Use that quiet time to catch up on professional reading, or to

> Don't let procrastination be the kiss of death for your small business.

just write down your thoughts in a journal. It may seem strange at first, especially if you're a complete stranger to the idea of quiet time, but after a few days you'll be glad that you put it on your busy schedule.

Do you avoid missing deadlines? If you do, then something is not right. Stop and make a list of the last five deadlines you missed. Try and remember why you missed each particular deadline. Was it because you were too busy working on other projects and it completely slipped your mind? Or were you waiting for information from other people to complete your part of the project? No matter what the cause, make a resolution right here and now that you will stop missing deadlines. Be faithful, start now. And if you need to speak to other people who are part of a project, then do so. Start an office pool and see who can win by meeting all of their deadlines.

Do you consider yourself an organized person? If so, then you really must have enjoyed Chapter 2. If not, then you need to reread that chapter and put some organizational skills into practice. Remember: organized people have time to complete nearly everything on their "To Do" list.

Do you break large projects into smaller, more manageable ones? Or do you let the large projects eat you alive? Every project can be broken down into shorter segments to make them easier to accomplish, so why aren't you taking advantage of that option?

Do you take a small tape recorder with you as you travel so you can record important thoughts? Have you ever had a brilliant idea, or suddenly come up with the answer to a problem that's been bugging you? And then you find yourself without a notebook or pen, or worse yet, you're in traffic and can't really write and drive at the same time. That's when your handy little tape

> Remember: organized people have time to complete nearly everything on their "To Do" list.

recorder comes to the rescue. Get into the habit of carrying one with you, and before you know it, you'll be using it and saving time.

Do you make time in your schedule to keep up with professional journals? If not, then how do you expect to keep up with the latest happenings in your industry? Or how do you expect to find out what your competitors are up to? Make sure you schedule some time to read those professional journals. You can do it during your quiet time (see number 14), or find some other time during your very busy day to get this important task completed.

Can you identify the obstacles that try and keep you from managing your time? Who or what are the time monsters in your life? In other words, what person, place, or thing creeps up when you're not looking and devours a large chunk of your day? Take some time to identify these obstacles, and do everything in your power to remove them. Then you will have the time to manage your small business to the next level of success.

> What person, place, or thing creeps up when you're not looking and devours a large chunk of your day? Take some time to identify these obstacles.

Why Some People Need More Time

Everyone on the planet is wired differently, but that should not be a shock to you. Assign the same task to two different people, and chances are, they will go about doing it completely differently. The result will be the same, but how they got there will be based on their own individual personalities and thought processes.

Some people may need more time than others to complete a project. It's just a fact of life. It isn't right, it isn't wrong, it's just the way it is. Some people thrive on chaos, while others shudder at the very thought of it. Some people are creative, and can come up with five different solutions to the same problem, while other people may struggle to find just the right answer for it.

If you are managing employees who need more time for their projects, make sure you are doing everything you can do help guide them in the process. Ask yourself these questions:

- Am I giving them a realistic deadline? Or have I given them a deadline that is impossible to meet? Sit down and think your timeline through very carefully before you begin your next project.
- Am I giving them the proper tools they need to complete the project? Does everyone on the team have the right equipment? Do they have access to information and databases to help them adequately get the job done? And if not, why aren't I supplying that information to them?
- Are they really qualified to get the job done? Or am I setting up someone for failure, knowing ahead of time that they are out of their league, and are not qualified to get a particular job done?
- Have I given them proper instructions? Does everyone on the team know exactly what it is they are supposed to do? Or are my instructions vague and unclear? Make sure everyone can understand your instructions and that way they can get the job done right the first time.
- Am I giving them the proper supervision? Or am I abandoning them in their time of need? There is a fine line between proper supervision and nagging. Use your common sense when it comes time to playing the role of supervisor, and you will do just fine.
- Do they know they can come to me for help? Do I have a reputation of eating people alive if they come knocking on your door for help? Many small business managers do, believe it or not. So if that's the case in your situation, it's no wonder your employees don't come to you when they need help with a project that they are working on. Be there for your employees, and let them know it.
- Is everyone on the same page and working towards the same goal? From the moment that the project is assigned, does

Time Analysis

Have you ever done a time analysis on your employees? A time analysis is a simple method of determining how fast or how slow an employee can complete a task. By testing employees, you will determine their strengths and weaknesses, and assign tasks accordingly.

everyone have a clear-cut picture of what the goal will be? Do they know what they need to do to arrive at that goal? Or is everyone confused, and working in different directions? Make sure everyone is on the same page and working toward one common goal.

Why Some People Need Less Time

On the other hand, there are some people who can do a project in less time than it takes for others to do the same one. These people have been wired a little differently, and some of them may fall into the Type A personality category. These are the people who hate standing in line for an elevator or for a cup of coffee. They feel as if time is money, and don't want to waste any of it.

These are dedicated employees that you want to have on your team. The future success of your business may depend upon it. The old saying "Surround Thyself With Competence" takes on new meaning when you have these competent and dedicated employees working for you. They are usually great problem solvers, and don't hesitate to brainstorm for creative solutions to any problems they might encounter.

Time Management Tips

Here are some time management tips to help you manage your time before it manages you:

- Spend some time each day planning and organizing your schedule. Organize in a way that makes sense to you. Some people do well with a wall calendar, while others need one of those fancy day planners. Find something that works for you and use it.
- Guard your time. Don't allow others to steal your time away from you. It's yours; you've earned it, now you decide how you are going to spend it.

Flex Time

Consider having flex time in your company. By giving people a flexible schedule, you are allowing them to work at their most productive time. Some people really excel early in the morning, or late in the evening. So give them the flexibility to do so.

- Be proactive when it comes to time management, and not reactive. In other words, don't simply react when something goes wrong. Be proactive and find a way to fix the problem.
- Make a decision and stick with it. But be ready to swerve if there is a bump in the road.
- Don't let paperwork pile up. Remember the rule about handling a piece of paper only one time? It's a very good one to remember and to put into practice.
- Realize that you'll never please 100 percent of the people 100 percent of the time. It's a fact of life; so stop trying to please everyone at the expense of your valuable time.
- Stop trying to respond to every crisis. Let someone else handle the unexpected problem the next time it arises; let them take responsibility instead of you giving up your valuable time to jump in and save the day.
- Have confidence in your ability to manage your own time. If you don't have confidence in yourself, how can you expect others to trust you?
- Keep a time diary for thirty days. Record every fifteen minutes of your workday. Then evaluate everything that took place, and make recommendations to yourself that will improve how well you use your time.
- Clean out your brief case. Get rid of all of those old papers that you have been carrying around needlessly. Learn to live clutter free, and suddenly you will become more organized and have more time on your hands.
- Keep an appointment diary. Make sure you know what is taking place when you begin your workday. And don't overbook yourself.
- Be considerate of other people's time as well. Remember that people work at different paces, and just as you don't want to have someone waste your time, you don't want to be the person who wastes someone else's time either.
- Have an action list. Put things on this list that you want to accomplish each day, no matter what problems or interruptions may materialize.

Time Management Contests

Ask your employees for their best time management suggestions, and offer prizes for the best ones. Sometimes people have a tip or two to share, but never really have a forum in which to do so, and a contest will allow them to share that knowledge they have found that saves them time.

Offer Tips in Unusual Places

Offer your employees time management tips in unusual places; when they read a time management tip that has been taped to the ceiling, it will create quite a buzz around the office. And people will remember the tip that was taped to the ceiling. What other creative places can you put time management tips in your small business?

- Use the 80-20 rule. This rule states that 80 percent of your reward will come from 20 percent of your effort. The trick comes, however, when you try to identify what 20 percent of your effort is really needed.
- Be a good listener. When people are talking to you, don't interrupt them—wait to speak until they are finished talking, even if you have to bite your tongue. Learn to become a good listener.
- Learn how to multitask. Brainstorm on ways you can complete two tasks at the same time. For example, if you take the train to your business, use that time to work on important papers, review trade journals, etc.
- Stop watching the clock. Time will go much slower for you if you stop worrying about what time it is all the time.

For more information on this topic, visit our Web site at www.businesstown.com

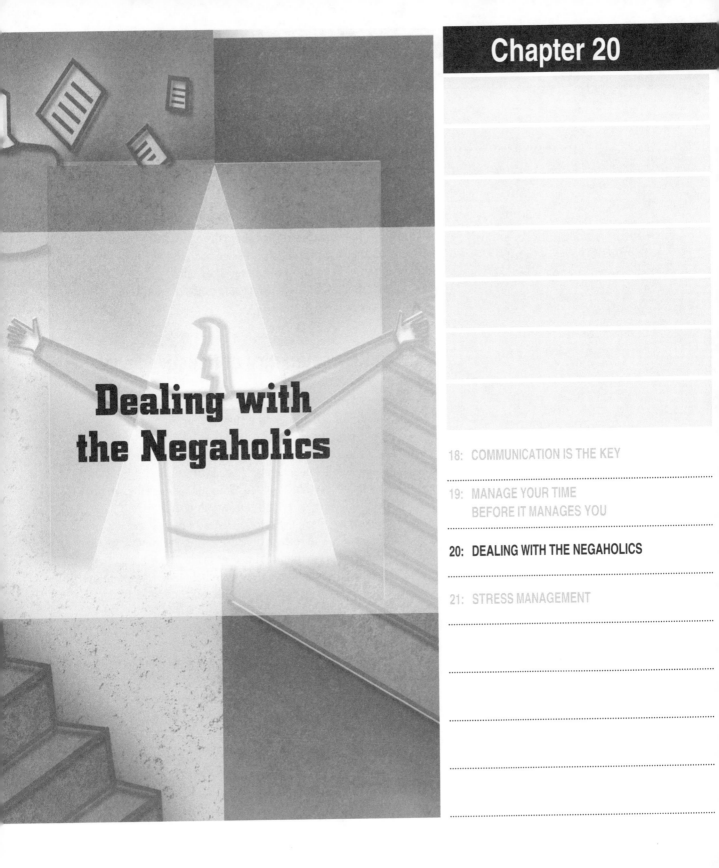

Dealing with the Negaholics

What, or who, is a negaholic? A negaholic is a person who is hooked on negativity. And having a negaholic in your small business can be serious trouble. Why? Because like the common cold, negaholics can spread their "doom and gloom" attitude about everything to anyone who is willing to listen and sympathize with their cause.

I'm sure you've seen your fair share over the years. Those negative people at the staff meetings who seem to find fault with everything you have to say. "That won't work here," they might say. Or, "Are you crazy? I'm not doing that!" and other cute phrases are uttered by negative people everywhere.

> Having a negaholic in your small business can be serious trouble.

Common Characteristics of Negative People

- They always keep to themselves. They never want to participate in any group activities, and if they are forced to do so, morale will take a big nose dive.
- They always act selfishly. They would never, ever, consider thinking about someone else's needs or wants.
- They think everything will fail. They almost never think any project will succeed, even if they are in charge of one.
- They have an "I can't" attitude, instead of an "I can" attitude.
- They spend much of their time criticizing their employer, and every business decision that is ever made.
- They usually come from a dysfunctional family, and want everyone else in the workplace to be miserable along with them. ("Misery loves company" is their motto.)
- They never want to take any risks. Asking them to operate outside of their comfort zone is entirely out of the question.
- They always look for the negatives, when everyone else is looking on the bright side.
- They always want to look for the "lose-lose" situation, instead of a "win-win" situation.
- They have a tendency to be secretive, and avoid communicating with people if they can get away with it.

- They can sometimes suffer from mood swings, and be happy one minute, and miserable the next.
- They like to take control of a situation, but not to make it succeed. Instead, they look for opportunities to make a shambles out of a project (and are quick to blame others for what happened).
- They are impulsive decision makers, and usually end up making the wrong decision (sometimes on purpose).

Are You a Negaholic?
Take Our Quiz and Find Out

1. Are you constantly obsessed with negative thoughts about your small business?
2. Do you have trouble with people in authority?
3. Are you determined to make people see everything "your way"?
4. Are you always looking for the bad in people, instead of the good?
5. Do you have trouble focusing on the whole project as a success, and instead look for little pockets of trouble?
6. Did you have a troubled childhood?
7. Have you drifted from job to job, and still don't feel like you belong anywhere?
8. Do you tend to look at a glass as half empty instead of half full?
9. Do you think of yourself as a "loser" instead of a "winner"?
10. Are you very rarely happy?

If you answered "Yes" to three or more of these questions, then you might be a negaholic. And unlike a chocaholic, that's not really a good thing.

> Do you have trouble focusing on the whole project as a success, and instead look for little pockets of trouble?

Managing Employees Who Are Negaholics

Managing employees who are filled with negativity sometimes seems to take more trouble than what it's really worth. But if you went to the trouble of hiring someone who is (or worse yet, if one of your family members is) a negaholic, it might be worth knowing how to manage them.

Be Firm but Supportive

If you are having difficulty with an employee, remember to be firm and supportive at the same time. If you come across too harshly, the employee will think you have singled them out and are just picking on them. But if you are supportive at the same time, they will view you as a friend, and not as the enemy.

People are human, and humans are known for their unusual and difficult behavior. And sometimes you will find that in your job you may have to deal with difficult people. If you have an employee who is difficult, you can either transfer them to another department, or take the time necessary to help them become a happy, healthy, and productive person. While that first option of transferring them might sound tempting, you should opt for finding ways to modify and reshape their behavior. It may seem like an insurmountable task, but when it is successfully completed you will feel a sense of accomplishment like never before, and your employee will have benefited immensely.

Here Are Some Questions to Ask Yourself

1. Is this person really being difficult? Before you make a big mistake, make sure that the person in question is truly a negaholic. Maybe they are just being difficult and impossible because they have a problem and don't know how to solve it. People are human, and when humans have problems, well, sometimes they tend to lash out at people they work with.
2. Is this a problem that can be solved quietly? Sometimes it's just a matter of pulling the person aside and saying, "Hey, you need to get your act together because you're starting to be a real thorn in people's side." If it can be handled "off the record," then by all means, do so.
3. Is this a problem that really needs my attention? Or can it be handled at a different level? Perhaps a project leader or supervisor may be able to handle it for you. But don't wait so long that the problem escalates further.
4. How can I help this person? While you might be tempted to give the nearest negaholic a one way ticket to Siberia, remember any past successes they may have had. Have they been a team player up until now? Don't give up completely on a negaholic person until you have tried several different creative solutions to fix whatever it is that is wrong.

Tips for Dealing with Difficult People

Be kind and courteous–Remember to treat people like you would want to be treated by them. So extend a kind and courteous attitude when dealing with negative people. Find a way to diffuse an unpleasant situation before things get worse.

Find out what makes them tick–If one of your employees is being difficult, find out what makes them tick. Try and discover why it is they are acting that way, and then go one step further. How well do you really know that person? Some people feel like loners, and when things go wrong in their business or personal life, they really have no one to turn to–no one to talk with about their problem or situation. So why not be that person? Reach out and be a friend today.

Don't be judgmental–Don't jump to any conclusions when trying to figure out why someone is being negative. Collect all of the facts before you draw any conclusions.

Talk to your employee about their attitude and try to figure out what the problem is–Once that person is aware that you have noticed their bad attitude and poor job performance, they may try to curb it or correct it on their own. Believe it or not, often people really aren't aware of their actions or apparent bad attitudes until someone points them out.

As the manager, you are a teacher and a role model– While you may want to avoid point-blank comments and seemingly patronizing statements, you definitely want to have an influence on all of your employees. Take the time to brainstorm about effective ways to educate and mold a problematic employee. Different situations may call for different approaches.

Avoid, at all costs, being patronizing and condescending– People are often not willing to reflect upon what is expressed to them negatively, and may not react in a positive way when they feel they are being criticized.

Don't jump to any conclusions when trying to figure out why someone is being negative. Collect all of the facts before you draw any conclusions.

Kill Them with Kindness

Sooner or later you will be able to win over even the most difficult employee with kindness. So instead of raising your blood pressure and losing sleep over a problem employee, kill them with kindness. That way everyone comes out a winner.

Be sympathetic—Let your negative employee know that you are concerned, while asserting that a bad attitude is unacceptable, and can be changed. People respond better to situations and problems when they don't feel so alone and misunderstood.

Handling Difficult and Negative People Who Are Part of a Team

One of the challenges you will face as a small business manager will take place when you have a group of people working on a project together. Because people will be people, it's bound to happen sooner or later that one or more of those people will become difficult and adopt a negative attitude. And if you don't nip the problem in the bud, it's liable to spread to the rest of the team. Then where will you be?

You should seek to understand everyone's point of view. Gather everyone together for a team meeting and go around the room and ask each person how they feel the project is progressing. Encourage them to be completely honest; if someone is not pulling their weight, it needs to be brought to the attention of the team.

In addition, make an effort to address everyone's problems and concerns. Make sure they understand that you, as their leader, are there for them and that they can point out any problems that are occurring. Ask questions that will force them to come up with solutions to their problems. For example, you might ask: "How do you see this problem, and how do you think we can solve it?"

Make sure you provide the necessary leadership. Without a strong leader, a team will begin to falter and fade, and if an employee has negative vibes that might bring those negative vibes to the surface.

Always remember to keep lines of communication open at all times. Communication is the key to the success of any organization or project. Ask everyone how well they are getting along with other members of the team. Sometimes just having an opportunity to air differences can nip a problem in the bud.

Understanding Negative People and Their Behavior

Understanding negative people and their behavior is a lot like trying to understand the most difficult problem on the planet. Sometimes no matter how hard you try, you never find the answer you are looking for.

Negative people, by their nature, often believe that they have no other choice, that they have to be a royal pain in the neck. They believe that they have some sort of obligation to make life miserable for everyone they come into contact with.

They believe that they have little or not power over the situations in their lives. For them, failure is not an option, it is a way of life. Misery loves company, and so forth.

Common Types of Negative People

The bully–This person can be hostile and angry, and won't hesitate to shout or throw a tantrum to get their way.

The complainer or whiner–This person usually complains about everything they can think of. They aren't interested in fixing any problems; they would rather just complain about them.

The procrastinator–This person will put things off because they really aren't sure how to handle them. They have trouble making decisions.

The "no it won't work" person–It doesn't matter who comes up with the best award-winning idea on the planet, if they are presented with a new idea, they will swear on a stack of bibles that it won't work.

The silent type–This person isn't very talkative, and at times it is difficult to discover what motivates their behavior.

Ask for Their Input

If all else fails, you need to sit down with a difficult employee and ask them how they can come up with a workable solution for their problem. Sometimes all it takes is for a person to realize that they are a valuable part of an organization, and that you do value their input. So don't forget to ask them.

Offer a Time-Out

If you are having problems dealing with a negative employee, the situation might call for a time-out—for both of you. Sometimes all it takes is a little space between you and the problem—and the employee and the problem. So give times-out when you can. Offer a "window of opportunity" that will allow everyone to walk away feeling like a winner.

Things to Consider

Is the person who is being negative in the right job? In other words, do you have every employee assigned to tasks they are qualified for? Frequently in small businesses, people are thrown into an assignment because of a labor shortage. There's nothing worse than putting a square peg into a round hole, and then scratching your head as you try and figure out what went wrong.

If that is the case, what steps can you take to correct the situation before it gets worse? Make a decision and get it over with; when things start operating smoothly again, you'll be glad that you did.

For more information on this topic, visit our Web site at www.businesstown.com

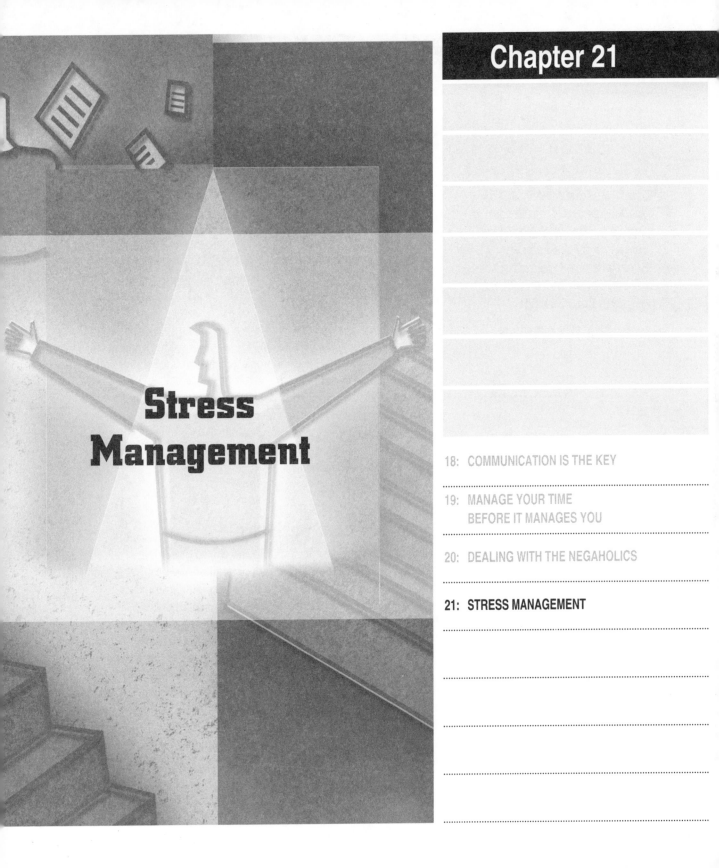

Chapter 21

Stress Management

think stress isn't a problem? According to *USA Today*'s "Snapshots" (December 29, 2000), stress is producing "desk rage" in record numbers at businesses all across the country. Workplace stress and long hours are blamed for this growing phenomenon. Here are some statistics:

- 10 percent of workers have been driven to tears by stress
- 12 percent have called in sick because of workplace stress
- 23 percent report physical violence at work because of stress
- 29 percent say stress causes them to yell at co-workers

And a report issued by the United Nations in the fall of 2000 says that one thing workers around the world have in common is stress. They found that levels of anxiety, burnout, and depression are spiraling out of control.

The U.S. National Institute for Occupational Safety and Health issued a report that says stress-related disorders are becoming the most prevalent reason for worker disability. Researchers estimate that over 100 million people take some type of medication every week for stress-related symptoms.

> The U.S. National Institute for Occupational Safety and Health issued a report that says stress-related disorders are becoming the most prevalent reason for worker disability.

Stress and Your Business

Common signs of stress include increased heart rate, higher blood pressure, muscle tension, depression, inability to concentrate, and fatigue. In a survey conducted by American Demographics in February of 1997, 61 percent of working parents that had survived downsizing felt that morale at work was very low. According to the Gannet News Service (August 16, 1999) four out of ten Americans find that their jobs are the largest cause of stress in their lives.

So as a small business owner, should you be worried about all this fuss over stress? Or is it something to ignore, and hope that it will eventually go away? Well, you'd better not ignore it. Instead, you need to learn how to manage your own stress, as well as how to manage and teach your employees about the basics of stress management.

People from all walks of life have their own definition of stress. What is stressful to one person, however, may be nothing but a minor inconvenience to another. And sometimes an event may be stressful to you at one time, but not another. Let's face it, we all have our good days and our bad days. It doesn't make it right, and it doesn't make it wrong. It's just life, and how we handle the multitude of decisions we must face each and everyday.

The official definition of stress is a *condition that occurs in response to actual or anticipated difficulties in life.* Sounds simple, doesn't it? But unfortunately there's no miracle pill or tonic that can cure your stress. If only it were that simple!

Just How Stressed-Out Are You? Take Our Quiz and Find Out!

1. Are you constantly cranky and irritable with the people you work with?
2. Do you find it difficult to concentrate on your job?
3. Do you feel as if you aren't able to cope with running your business any longer?
4. Have you lost interest in your job or your business lately?
5. Do you have a lack of energy when it comes to work-related tasks?
6. Do you find yourself wanting to take sick days more frequently than any time in the past six months or so?
7. Are you starting to show up late for work, no matter how early you get up?
8. Does your job make you feel angry with people?
9. Do you have trouble sleeping at night?
10. Do you always worry about your job or business at night before you go to bed?
11. Are you exhausted after working all day?
12. Are you dissatisfied with your business?
13. Do you work in a poor environment (excessive noise, isolation, etc.)?

Lunch Time Lectures

Contact a local health center in your town to see if they have speakers available who can come out and offer a presentation during lunch. Invite everyone in the company to participate; even those who think that stress isn't a problem in their life. Stress management skills can be very useful for employees at all levels.

14. Do you get sick more frequently than you ever have in the past?
15. Have you lost your sense of humor?
16. Do you feel like nothing in the world is important anymore?
17. Is your workload overwhelming you?
18. Do you hate owning or managing your own small business?
19. Do you feel like your employees or other people you work with hate you?
20. Do you feel like no one appreciates the hard work you do managing your business?

If you answered "Yes" to five or more questions, then you are probably suffering from some type of work-related stress. But don't get discouraged, there are a million things you can do to help yourself out.

Why Stress Management Needs to Be Taught to Everyone

We've already acknowledged that stress is not good for people and their work environment, so it's no secret that stress management needs to be taught to everyone. The rigors of workplace stress can be deadly, literally. Stress on the job can make you sick and even kill you. According to the American Medical Association, many people suffer heart attacks, strokes, or ulcers as a direct result of workplace stress. Also, the American Heart Association reports that one heart attack occurs somewhere in the United States every thirty-two seconds. And it is estimated that over 50 percent of all heart attacks can be traced back to too much stress.

If you experience job-related stress, remember that you have some control over your own mental health. Make sure that you start the day with the proper attitude. With the proper attitude, you can do just about anything. Think for a moment about a time in your life that you consciously changed your attitude about a situation in your business. Probably you began to feel better, didn't you?

> If you experience job-related stress, remember that you have some control over your own mental health.

Too many people spend 90 percent of their energy on a problem that really warrants only 10 percent. Because we are all only human, that equation will no doubt continue well into the future. However, when you learn the basics of stress management, you can actually begin to learn how to recognize the warning signs of stress. And then you are in a position to do something about the problem before it gets worse.

Successful people have mastered the art of managing stress at work. And if they can do it, then you can too. Now that doesn't mean that the CEO of a *Fortune* 500 company never has a stress attack. What it does mean, however, is that when that stress does attack, they are prepared to do battle—and win!

But don't think you have to be a rich and powerful business leader in order to be successful. You must remember that success has little to do with money. Just because you are rich doesn't mean that you are successful. When Mother Teresa was alive and devoted her life to helping the poor people of Calcutta, she was considered a success. Can you imagine Mother Teresa having a stress attack? I certainly can't.

> Too many people spend 90 percent of their energy on a problem that really warrants only 10 percent.

Ways to Be More Successful and Less Stressful

There are some ways you can become more successful and at the same time, learn how to manage your stress. First of all, believe that you can be successful. When you say "I can," instead of "I can't," half the battle has already been won for you. Take a look at what you have accomplished in the past. By celebrating the events that shaped your life in a positive way you will release any negative thinking that might be hindering your quest for success.

Get rid of excuses that are keeping you from being successful. Instead of thinking that everything is going wrong, and nothing will ever be right again, adopt a personal agenda that includes the following motto: "Can't say can't, won't say won't!" Don't give up too easily. Remember that anything worth doing is worth doing well. You know the old saying: If at first you don't succeed, try, try again.

Dream big dreams. And don't let anything get in the way of those dreams. Walt Disney once said, "If you can dream it, you can do it." Be passionate about improving your life and being as successful as you can possibly be.

List the qualities you think you need in order to lead a successful life, and how you will go about getting those qualities. For example, if you think you need to be more assertive, your goal might be to read a few books or attend a workshop on how to be assertive.

Keep at It

Give your best, no matter what task you are faced with. Even if it's something you'd really rather not be doing. You'll feel better knowing that you gave a full 100 percent worth of energy when it is completed.

Make a plan, but plan carefully. Then stick to the plan, while at the same time remembering how to be flexible. In other words, if you have to deviate from your course to reach your goal and be successful, make sure that you do so.

Don't wait; act now. There's no time like the present to put a plan into action. Stop procrastinating and start living. There is no such thing as the "ideal time" to get something accomplished. There is no time like the present to move forward toward your goal of being a success.

> There is no time like the present to move forward toward your goal of being a success.

Characteristics of a Successful Person:

- Has a sense of humor
- Is a diligent worker
- Is a persistent worker
- Is a committed worker
- Possesses honesty and integrity
- Has a positive attitude
- Practices discipline
- Is a good listener
- Has faith in others

Top Ten Stressful Jobs

Just who has the most stressful jobs in this country? Is it the newspaper editor who's trying to get a story into the production department before the paper goes to press? Or is it the small business owner who's just trying to keep their business open?

You may be surprised to find that there are jobs out there that are more stressful than being the owner of a small business. The National Institute for Occupational Safety and Health (NIOSH) reports the ten occupational groups that are the most stressful. Here is their list:

- Laborers
- Secretaries
- Inspectors
- Clinical-lab technicians
- Office managers
- Foremen
- Managers and administrators (see, you did make the list after all)
- Waiters and waitresses
- Machine operators
- Farm owners

Use Mirrors Effectively

Have you ever thought about using the mirrors in the restrooms as a means of building up your employees' self esteem? A few companies are now putting inspirational and encouraging messages along the tops of the mirrors in the company's restrooms. Simple things like "I'm a winner!" and "I can do it!" can go a long way in inspiring employees to try their very best.

How to Beat Stress Before It Attacks

It's possible to beat stress at work before it attacks and rears its ugly head. The first step is to keep a stress management diary. In your war against stress on the job, one of the most powerful weapons you can carry is a stress management diary. In order to manage your stress you need to know when you are stressed and exactly why you felt stress at that particular moment. And having a stress management diary will help you accomplish this goal.

Your diary should be small enough for you to carry with you to your business. It doesn't have to be anything fancy, no big, black leather journal with gold lettering on the cover. In fact, the best diary is a pocket-sized spiral notebook. It will fit into your pocket, brief case, or purse without taking up too much room. And you can put each day's entries on a separate page.

Make three columns, and label the first column "time," the second one "stress event," and the third one "how I felt." Here's an example of what I'm talking about:

Time	Stress Event	How I Felt
7:10 A.M.	Missed the train	Angry and upset
10:30 A.M.	Computer system down	Annoyed and disgusted
2:30 P.M.	E-mail memo/deadline	Worried

By recording the various times during your workday that you experience stress, you will be able to analyze this information to determine how you can handle that type of situation the next time it occurs.

In the illustration, the first example is "missed the train." Sure, you missed the train and felt angry and upset because you would be arriving at work late. How can you keep this from happening again? It may be as simple as leaving the house five minutes earlier, or even catching an earlier train.

The next incident is "computer system down." Well, of course you were annoyed and disgusted. Anytime the computer isn't available, it can create problems for everyone, even the small business owner. But once you realize that there is nothing you can do to control the computer system (unless you are the computer programmer or technician) then you also realize that it's not worth getting annoyed and disgusted about. (The next time the computer system goes down, take a break, catch up on some professional reading. Or find some other productive task to accomplish instead of fussing and fuming while you wait for the system to be returned to normal.)

Overcome Stressful Obstacles

Throughout your work life you will no doubt be ambushed by stress at different times. For whatever reason, people or situations will sometimes stand in your way of success and a stress-free life. But

> By recording the various times during your workday that you experience stress, you will be able to analyze this information to determine how you can handle that type of situation the next time it occurs.

there are some things you can do to overcome these obstacles that you might run into from time to time. These include:

- Say no when you can. Don't feel as if you have to say "Yes" to everyone else's demands and requests.
- Believe in yourself. Realize that you can solve any problem that life hands you.
- Take time to smell the roses. Life isn't all about just hard work and no play. Find something you like to play, and go for it.
- Recognize that you can't always control other people. But you can control your own actions.
- Look for creative ways to solve all of your problems. Just because it's always been done that way doesn't mean that there isn't a better solution.

Stress Prevention Tips

Make sure you offer stress prevention tips whenever possible. Use space on payroll stubs, posters in the hallways and cafeteria, and even on outdoor signs. The more people are informed about how to prevent and manage stress, the better off they will be—along with your company.

Stressed-Out Employees Are Bad for Your Bottom Line

No one deliberately wakes up and says to themselves, "Today I will let the stress in my job destroy me." But that truth of the matter is that thousands of people do let it happen. They let the stress of their workplace destroy their lives and their professional careers.

The reality of today's workplace is harsh. Organizational loyalty and long-term job security are rapidly disappearing. Employees are being asked to work longer hours for less pay. People are changing jobs and careers more frequently than they did twenty years ago. In short, stress is here, and your employees will no doubt sometimes be bothered by it. And unless you do something to help them manage their stress, it can affect your bottom line.

Think about it: Stressed-out employees won't care about how they are treating customers. And if customers think they are being treated harshly or rudely, they not only won't ever come back to your business, they will tell everyone they know about their bad experience.

Turn Negative Stress into Positive Stress

If you or your employees are under stress, do whatever it takes to turn that negative stress into positive stress. Give everyone the afternoon off, or send out for ice cream, or find some other way of creatively dealing with the problem. Once the stress is gone, you'll be glad that you did.

Some Ways to Relax

- Look in the telephone book and call up a massage therapist. Have them make an emergency visit to your business, and offer everyone a free massage.
- Take everyone to the movies, and pay for their tickets *and* refreshments.
- Hold a contest to see who can write the funniest essay on why they feel stressed out. (Having people put their thoughts down on paper is good therapy, too.)
- Sit down and have a brainstorming session with everyone and ask them to come up with some creative ways to help alleviate the stress they are facing while on the job.
- Send flowers and candy to all of your employees.
- Write a personal note of thanks to everyone, and tell them how much you appreciate them hanging tough during a stressful period at work.
- Rent a funny video, pop some microwave popcorn, and have everyone laugh for the next ninety minutes.

Lemons into Lemonade

Sometimes no matter how hard you try, stress will rear its ugly head and cause problems for you and your employees. So do what you can to turn those "lemon" moments into "lemonade" ones. There's nothing wrong with sitting down, and saying, "Hey, this isn't working, but I'm still okay!" Then laugh a little. And take a breather before you try again.

For more information on this topic, visit our Web site at www.businesstown.com

The Manager, Technology, and the Future

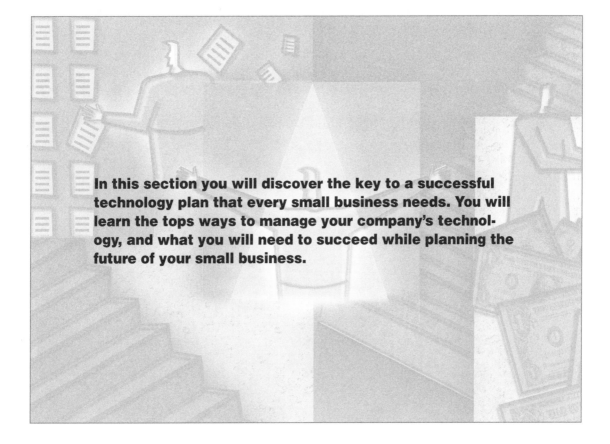

In this section you will discover the key to a successful technology plan that every small business needs. You will learn the tops ways to manage your company's technology, and what you will need to succeed while planning the future of your small business.

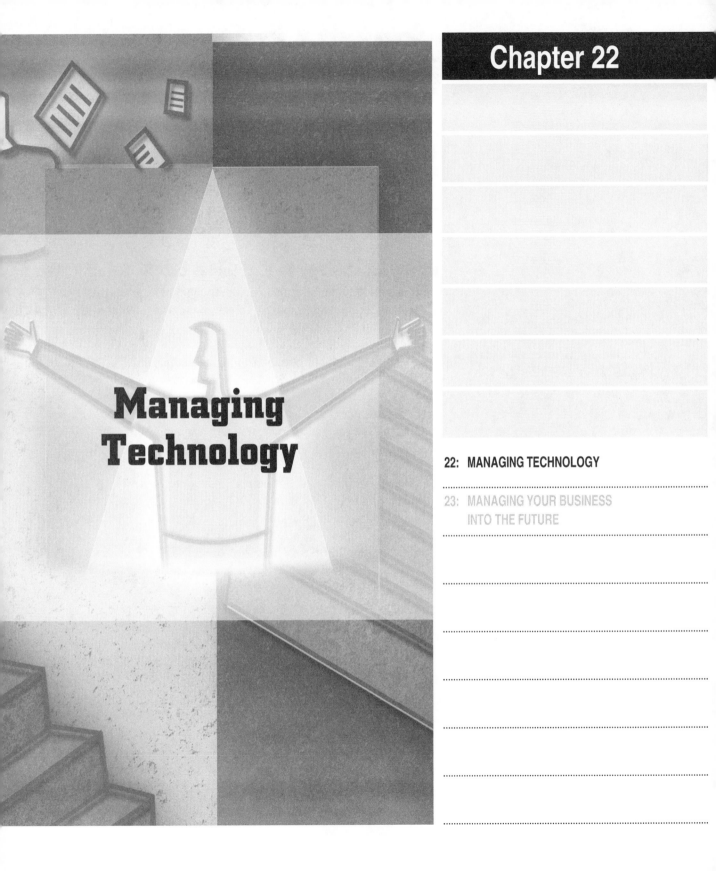

Chapter 22

Managing Technology

oes technology have you scratching your head and trying to figure out which way to go with your small business? Well, don't feel bad, because technology is always moving at the speed of light, and many small business managers sometimes have difficulty making the right decisions.

Using Technology to Its Fullest Extent

According to Mike Foster, founder and president of Foster Success Strategies, a company dedicated to empowering business owners to use technology to increase profit and productivity, many small business managers are in trouble.

"Are you using your computer to its fullest capabilities? If you're like the majority of Americans, the answer is no. According to the U.S. Census Bureau, 92.2 million adults routinely use a computer. Of that number, 63.9 million people use a computer at work, and 37.4 million use one at home. And regardless of whether it's home or business use, the number one computer function is word processing," said Foster.

He believes that small businesses can enjoy a whole new level of productivity when they learn to use their technology to a higher capacity. "Today's technology has expanded and surpassed our old way of doing business. Unfortunately, most people were never taught about these other technology functions, or they're afraid to experiment. As a result, they waste both time and resources by manually doing things that can easily be computerized," he said.

Tools like contact managers, spreadsheets, databases, desktop publishing packages, and "out of the ordinary" Internet capabilities allow your existing investment in technology to better "earn its keep." Here are a few tips from Mike Foster on the different tools that are available to you to leverage as a small business owner.

Contact Managers

Contact management, like the name implies, helps manage the contacts you've made with customers, vendors, and associates.

> Small businesses can enjoy a whole new level of productivity when they learn to use their technology to a higher capacity.

However, instead of simply storing names, addresses, and phone numbers, your contact manger also keeps track of a complete list of pending activities with each person and keeps a history of completed activities. When you use contact management software effectively, you eliminate the need for handwritten notes piled all over your desk and tapes to your computer screen. The contact management software documents each communication with your customers so all your information regarding a project or account is just a click away.

Spreadsheets

The next time you are about to use pencil and paper to create a chart of calculations, stop. Instead, turn to your computer's spreadsheet capabilities to make the process easier. Spreadsheets are useful for small businesses in presentations, when you need to show others how money is being spent or how sales are increasing. Whether you need to keep track of accounting information, production, or any other figures, a spreadsheet saves time and eliminates human error.

Databases

Databases allow you an easy way to track lists of items. This could include customer orders, charts of accounts, employee profiles, and inventory records, etc. Rather than keeping this information in handwritten form in a notebook or legal pad, a database allows you to organize, sort, search your information by specific criteria, and enables you to make quick changes whenever necessary. Database information can also be imported into other applications, such as word processing software, in order to create form letter or envelope addresses.

> Whether you need to keep track of accounting information, production, or any other figures, a spreadsheet saves time and eliminates human error.

Desktop Publishing Tools

Have you ever spent a large amount of money to get a brochure designed and printed in bulk quantity, only to want to change it a few weeks later, before you've eliminated your current supply?

Hire a Techie

If you are technologically challenged (and it's okay to admit if you are), then hire a techie to handle all of your technology issues. A techie is someone who lives and breathes with the latest in gizmos and gadgets. So hire that person, and let him or her show you the way.

Desktop publishing software can help eliminate waste. You can create everything from brochures, booklets, and sales flyers to letterhead, mailing labels, and business cards. And when you invest in a good quality color printer, you can choose to print out the exact quantity you need, thus eliminating waste. Most desktop publishing software programs are fairly simple to learn.

Leverage the Internet

Connect your company to the Internet and you open yourself and your small business to a whole new world of information and services. If you aren't doing it yet, take advantage of other services available (besides surfing and e-mail) that allow you to retrieve you faxes and voice mail while you are away from the office, locate new clients, advertise your services, and research information about other companies. New services are becoming available every day.

The list of capabilities of your existing hardware is virtually limitless. When you learn more about available technology and its capabilities and implement them into you daily routine, you become more productive in you job and more efficient with your time. Sometimes you will need to make a small upgrade or buy some new software, but the payoff can be huge when you reap the rewards of greater job satisfaction for you, and higher profits for your business.

Site Development

If you've developed an e-business site, you're all too familiar with the manic race to design the look-and-feel, assemble the pages, and ultimately launch the site—in many cases in only a few weeks. Unfortunately, in that sprint, companies often overlook important issues. This early step in the e-business marketing cycle is where you make numerous strategic decisions that have enormous implications on your business. Review these key development steps:

- Identify your target audience
- Assemble your team, or skill-sets
- Establish your project timeline
- Determine who will host your site
- Determine if you need e-mail services for your Web site
- Organize your site
- Choose a design for your site
- Determine what type of search capabilities you will provide
- Determine whether you will build or buy a search solution
- Optimize your site for external search engines
- Test and review your site
- Launch your site
- Keep your content fresh and monitor your site

Top Ten Reasons to Have a Web Site

Before you go out and design and launch a Web site, first sit down and come up with the top ten reasons you feel you need to have one. And if you can't come up with ten good reasons, maybe you shouldn't have one at all.

Determine Site Objectives

Not all Web sites are developed solely for the purpose of selling products online. It is important to clearly define your objectives when developing a Web site. Typically, objectives fall into one of three categories:

- Developing or increasing sales
- Reducing cost of doing business
- Improving communications with customers, investors, members, or other "target audiences"

Identify Your Target Audience

Determine who you want to attract to your site in order to guide your planning and define your end-user requirements. Specifically, you need to *know* who is it you need to communicate with and/or sell to. You also need to identify which prospective new groups of people you want to reach to generate new sales. Do not forget your existing customers when designing your site.

The press and other media sources should be considered potential users of your site. Make it easy for them to find what they want and it will help to generate publicity for your business.

Define Your Site Requirements

Identify all functional and technical requirements. Do you want to:

- Provide on-site search capability?
- Use animation?
- Optimize for certain Web browsers?
- Optimize your site for external search engines?
- Provide a means for visitors to get a personalized view of your site?
- Serve live video feeds?
- Encourage a community-building feature, such as a chat room or a discussion group?
- Sell products or add e-commerce components to your site?
- Offer value-added services such as free e-mail, a gift registry, or an online calculator?
- Solicit visitor feedback?

Building Your Site

Establish a budget for site development, and plan for overages. Typically, overages will run between 5 and 10 percent of the total budget. If you have a small budget, consider taking a phased approach. Prioritize your efforts so that you meet the most important objectives first.

If possible, establish a multi-disciplined team with skill-sets in sales, marketing, customer support, product development, design, and engineering. If in-house resources are not available, determine specific needs for outsourcing.

Identify the size, location, experience, services, etc., required from a design firm. Check references, review projects they have completed, and qualify technical capabilities. If you do not have a technical background, employ the help of a colleague or friend with a technical background, and have them help qualify your choice.

Provide a project overview and budget to determine if the project is consistent with the design firm's portfolio and if the firm is capable of performing the job for the allocated budget.

Select a Web Site Design/Development Firm

You should take care to do the following before signing on with a Web site design/development firm:

- Conduct a vendor review
- Talk to references
- Ensure the key members of your team are able to work with the design firm
- Select a design firm that has:
  - A proven track record
  - Qualified skills and services
  - The ability to deliver on time and within budget
  - Commitment to working with you and your team

If you hire an outside design/development firm, you'll need to work out contract terms. Be sure to include all the functional, technical, and budgetary requirements you identified earlier, as well as major technical, design, and development milestones that the firm must meet.

Determine Who Will Host Your Site

Identify your specifications and requirements for your site. Develop a short list of prospective firms based on research and recommendations from colleagues. Once done, send out an RFP (Request For Proposal) to each of the firms. Be sure to ask about connection times, if they are connected to an Internet backbone, if they buy their connectivity through another vendor, administration tools, overall reliability, customer support, fee structures (cost), and service plans.

Check with references on issues such as connection time, amount of downtime, customer support, and overall satisfaction. In general, you'll want to choose a Web host that offers twenty-four-hour-a-day, seven-day-a-week technical support with short hold time, responsive e-mail support, fast connection time (less than three seconds during nonpeak times), good administration tools, and a guaranteed level of service that meets your needs now and in the near future.

> Develop a short list of prospective firms based on research and recommendations from colleagues.

Determine What Features You Need with Your Site

If you want to use your Web address as an e-mail address, make sure this functionality is included by your hosting service. Find out how many mail boxes you can have, and if there is a limit to the size of e-mail attachments. You will also need "dial-up access" to retrieve your e-mail (unless you have a LAN connection). Some providers have these services, but it is most cost-effective to choose one that has a local number.

Determine Site Size Needs

Many ISPs offer packages with a fixed amount of disk space and usage. For a general content site, disk space of 20MB and usage of 50–100MB per month is usually adequate. However, if you plan on utilizing streaming media or other large format files, consider packages with greater capacity. If you find yourself using more than the limit of the package, the ISP will charge additional costs. The costs are usually minimal, but if you find you are paying frequently, you may want to consider upgrading.

Organize Your Site

Your decision about how to organize your site is critical to the usability of the site, and therefore, visitor loyalty. The following tips will help guide you:

> Develop site navigation that is intuitive and easy.

- Group content in a way that makes sense, and as it interrelates. This is called an "Information Architecture."
- Develop site navigation that is intuitive and easy.
- Create clear and complete navigation bars.
- Include a site map and/or a table of contents.
- Include search capability to help your visitors easily locate what they are looking for.
- Conduct usability testing to ensure your site is logically organized.

- External testing should be conducted if your budget allows. Also contract for usability testing services.
- Friends and family, especially those who have little familiarity with the Web, can click through and give constructive criticism on how the site is organized and looks.

Choose a Site Design

Pick a graphic design that is clean—Choose one that easily guides your visitors to your content. Web sites with busy designs can be overwhelming to users and preclude them from coming back.

Do not force your users to click through pages with no content. Long and difficult-to-download pages only annoy users, and provide them with no useful information. If you find most of your customers connect through slow dial-up connections at home, keep streaming media or Flash elements to a minimum.

Choose Search Capabilities

Determine which search capabilities to provide. To increase ease of use and navigation, you will want to include a search capability. Options include:

> Products that search only your site—Present relevant results, but are limited to content found only on your site.

> Products that search the whole Web—Present results that are mostly irrelevant and much too broad to be useful; this may encourage visitors to leave your site because they are unable to find what they are looking for.

> Products that search your site and select external sites— Deliver the relevant content visitors want, and make your Web site a highly sought vertical portal or "vortal."

> Do not force your users to click through pages with no content. Long and difficult-to-download pages only annoy users, and provide them with no useful information.

Once Your Site Is Built

Determine whether you will build or buy a search solution. For all but the largest sites, outsourcing a search solution is generally the most cost-effective route. In addition, a few search engine solution providers will host the search solution, eliminating the need to maintain an additional application, or to purchase additional hardware or software.

Effectively optimizing your site for external search engines requires careful planning. Consider the following tactics:

> Use a Web site tracking and analysis solution to monitor the keywords people are using to find your site.

- **Establish and position strategic keywords** throughout your site. Place them in the site description, keyword and descriptive META tags, Page Title tags, headlines, and in the first few paragraphs of your body text on each Web page.
- **Insert keyword and descriptive META tags** in the header on each Web page.
- **Insert Page Title tags** in the header on each Web page.
- **Insert ALT tags** in the header on each Web page that contains graphics files.
- **Add reciprocal links** to your site to help boost your ranking with a number of search engines/directories that give higher rankings to those sites with many links pointed at them.
- **Submit the site for review** with popular hybrid search engine/directories to help boost rankings with these search engine/directories.
- **Use a Web site tracking and analysis solution** to monitor the keywords people are using to find your site. Change your keywords if they don't map to keywords people are actually using to find your site.
- **Establish a review process** before posting new content to ensure it has been properly tagged, has a headline containing a keyword, and has used the keyword within the first few paragraphs of the body text.
- **You should conduct frequent ad-hoc tests** using your strategic keywords with different search engines. Add a custom gateway page if ranking is low on a particular search engine.

Test Your Site

Once your site has been constructed, conduct comprehensive usability and quality assurance testing before your site "goes live."

- **Test early and test often.**
- **Retest once fixes are made.**
- **Ask friends and relatives** to test the site if your budget does not allow hiring of a testing company.
- Give specific instructions.
- Record successes or failures with each task.
- **Test on different browsers and platforms**, e.g., ask Tester A to use Internet Explorer 5.5 on a Windows 98 machine, while Tester B uses Netscape Navigator on a similar machine.
- **Record the differences** in how each browser responds, and if the design appears cohesive on one, but is broken apart on the other.

Proof all the contents on a staging server (or a local server for smaller operations) prior to going live. It should represent, as closely as possible, the configuration setup at your ISP. Be sure all content that was supposed to be posted is posted, that there are no odd layout issues, that all the links work correctly and as planned, that the navigation works correctly, etc.

After Your Site Is Complete

If you build it they will come—but only if they know where to find it! Promote your Web site address at every opportunity—in press releases, in print collateral, etc. Consider sending an electronic newsletter "direct mail" piece to your target audience announcing your new site. It is far more efficient and cost-effective than direct "snail" mail or advertising. Post notices of your launch to Newsgroups with similar subjects.

Keep your content fresh. Many people view the launching of their site as a finish line when really it's just the beginning. If you want people to come back to your site, you need to constantly serve up new content, features, services, etc. Develop a plan for adding new content, and use feedback provided by your visitors to help prioritize additions.

> Be sure all content that was supposed to be posted is posted, that there are no odd layout issues, that all the links work correctly and as planned, that the navigation works correctly, etc.

Assign a Site Monitor

Consider assigning the task of monitoring your company's Web site to an employee who is using the Internet frequently. Remember, the Web never closes, and if your site is having problems at ten o'clock at night (and the Webmaster is asleep at the wheel), you could be losing valuable sales. By having different people stop by at different times, you are making sure it is up and running for your customers to use and enjoy.

Check your site daily to be sure it is loading at an acceptable speed, that it is "up," and that your links are working properly. If your site contains files, such as banner ads, that are served by third parties, you'll want to take extra steps to monitor your site's performance. Most ISPs provide monitoring and analysis software as part of their package. At the minimum, they should send you weekly status reports that detail hits, unique visitors (the truest indicator of how many people are coming to your site), and the elements of the site being viewed.

(The previous information was provided by Sandy Bay Networks, an E-Marketing Services Provider (ESP) delivering online tools and resources that enable data-driven e-marketing programs. It is used with their permission.)

For more information on this topic, visit our Web site at www.businesstown.com

Chapter 23

Managing Your Business into the Future

How is your crystal ball, by the way? What's that you say, you don't have a crystal ball? Then how can you predict the future of your small business, and determine if it will be a success or a failure? Well, the truth is, you can't. Even if you had a crystal ball, you would still have a hard time predicting tomorrow, because in the business world, you just never know what is waiting for you right around that next corner.

Even if you had a crystal ball, you would still have a hard time predicting tomorrow, because in the business world, you just never know what is waiting for you right around that next corner.

Preparing for the Possibly Rocky Future

Although there is no solid indication that the economy is about to take a turn for the worse and the word "recession" will come back into our common vocabulary, small business owners and sales representatives are beginning to think seriously about how to prepare for a possible downturn, according to Stephan Schiffman, president of D.E.I. Management Group, a New York-based sales training company.

"A recent NBC poll revealed that 23 percent of Americans are concerned that the United States will return to a recession. While there is no financial indication of that—interest rates and unemployment are still low, and inflation has not increased substantially—Americans are seriously considering what will happen if the ten-year boom begins to bust," he said.

Lessons can be learned from the recessions of the '70s and the early '90s, Schiffman says. During both those recessions, it was necessary for small business owners to scale back employees, reduce output, and raise product prices substantially based on inflation. "Wise company owners today are preparing for a similar dramatic change and twist in the economy—prior to being swept up by it," he said.

How are these owners preparing themselves? They are considering all expansion projects carefully since the stock market has reduced the amount of cash flow available for investments.

From the Dot-com Bust to Mega-Mergers

"Dot-com companies are going out of business as quickly as the snow falls in the Midwest this winter; as a result, easy money is no longer in circulation. Brick-and-mortar companies, however, are in a better position since they invested in high technology and the Internet but do not exclusively rely on this industry," he said.

Certain substantial companies in the dot-com world will undergo significant changes immediately after the holidays, predicts Schiffman. "Two examples are Amazon.com and eToys, which both are going through upheavals and evaluating whether or not they can continue without additional financing," he said.

Recent mergers, like the one between AOL and Time Warner, have produced a consolidation of businesses that are more public than the consolidation of the oil and telecom worlds. These alliances represent a huge reduction of the number of companies that are anxious to purchase products from smaller companies. Specifically, the merger of AOL and Time Warner will mean reduction of staff and a reduction of purchasing from a variety of vendors (probably consolidating down to a few large vendors that they can purchase from).

> ### Ask for Predictions
>
> Some companies ask their employees for their predications for the future. This is a very creative means of forcing people to think about where they think your business will be five, ten, or even twenty years from now. Sure, you're bound to get some funny responses, but you will be amazed at some of the other ones.

How Small Businesses Should Prepare

If small business owners accept this prognosis, according to Schiffman, then they will need to prepare on a variety of fronts.

Think strategically about growth plans for the next year. Is it the right time to expand the activity of your operation and hire additional people or are you better off increasing the volume that you get from existing customers rather than trying to get new customers? The warning here is that new customers are the lifeblood of any business, and you cannot afford to depend on existing business.

By 2020, the concept of retaining customers will be substantially more important than obtaining new clients. Companies will be more concerned with keeping customers rather than trying to win clients from the competition.

Today, the long-distance telecommunications market has a 6 percent growth nationwide; there is very little opportunity for the 4,500 long-distance companies to survive. As a result, these firms are taking business away from each other on a regular basis and, in essence, becoming business "churns." In 2020, telecom will consolidate considerably. This also holds true for many other major industries, such as the wireless and the healthcare industries.

Things to Remember

- Know that prices will increase in leases, HMOs, telecom and even paper. As a result, small business owners should increase the cost of their long-term contracts, and give their salespeople an opportunity to put those deals together in 2001.
- Cross-train individuals within your company. Unemployment remains low; retaining your employees is more important than ever. However, be prepared for an eventual layoff if needed. If there should be a shift in unemployment, better employees can be brought in and the weaker 5 percent can be eliminated. Smart companies do this on a regular basis.
- Don't panic! Take into consideration all the necessary information that you receive and evaluate it carefully. Don't be swayed into thinking that an event or situation happened when it did not.

In summary, Schiffman advises that you take proper steps to ensure that your brick and mortar business, your online business, your investments, and your personal accounts are able to weather any sharp downturns.

A Pro's Advice for Small Business Managers

Tom Antion is a small business Internet marketing expert for Switchboard.com's Merchant Education Program. He is a small business expert and owner who says, "I know the difficulties in trying to build and expand a small business."

He offers these tips for managers of small businesses everywhere: Get online: If you are not already online, you're missing the boat. Hordes of people are sick of fighting the mall crowds. You must have a way for them to order from you online or you will lose that share of the holiday business. Remember, having your business online virtually allows you to stay open for twenty-four hours a day, working as an informational site to field questions and process merchandise orders.

Study Business Trends

Sometimes the best way to manage for the future is to look at the past. Study business trends in your industry to see what has taken place over the past two or three decades. You may find some interesting information that will help you manage your business into success as the future unfolds.

Key Word Search: Just because you're online doesn't mean that you have a Web presence. You must know what key words your potential customers are typing to find your products and services. Ask your present customers what search engines and directories they use and what they would type in when looking for what they come up with. If they are unaware of search engines or directories, you may want to send them to a search engine like *www.netscape.com* or directory service like *www.switchboard.com*. Take the results of this test and make sure your Web site is optimized to be found with these keywords.

Customer Service

Get your shipping act together. Because of the immediacy of the Internet, people may wait until the last minute to order and still want guaranteed delivery by Christmas. Make sure you have plenty of FedEx/UPS etc. supplies on hand and that you and your staff know how to correctly use them. Both FedEx and UPS have software that will help you automate your shipping process. A small amount of time learning how to use this software now, will save you mountains of time when the holiday rush is on.

Market Your Web Site

Put your Web site address on all of your vehicles and in-store signage as soon as possible. People will jot down the Web addresses so they can browse your store from home. In your traditional ads you could promote "Web site only" specials. This takes full advantage of your "expensive" advertising space by driving your customers to the "cheap" advertising space on your Web site.

E-mail marketing is a low cost and low risk method to reach out to your customer base. Give your customers an incentive to get on your list. Provide a special, like15 percent off your next purchase, or free x when you buy z. With a tool like Constant Contact, offered directly by Roving Software (*www.roving.com*) or through one of their channel partners like *www.switchboard.com* who integrates with their various advertising and marketing products, small

> Put your Web site address on all of your vehicles and in-store signage as soon as possible.

businesses can add features to their Web sites to collect customer e-mail addresses and information, manage their customer lists, and create e-mail campaigns highlighting special promotions, offers, and coupons to customers.

Organization Will Save You a Bundle

Think ahead: prepackage Internet special items so all you have to do is slap on the shipping label. This will save an enormous amount of headaches when you and your staff are spread thin for the holiday rush. The shipping label can be printed automatically with a sample label printer hooked to your computer. Many Web site shopping carts can be configured to output their results directly to your accounting software. Do everything you can to automate and let the computer do the work for you.

Make sure it is easy to conveniently check your Internet orders ten to twenty times per day during the holiday season. Or simply leave your e-mail application open all day. Many programs can be set to automatically identify an order. The e-mail program will put the order in a special folder and emit an audible tone upon arrival. You can also set these programs to recognize which orders go to which department and automatically forward the e-mails to the appropriate person in that department.

A Success Story

Josh Sinel, president and CEO of Blue Barn Interactive, has these words of advice for small business owners:

"Blue Barn Interactive, an expert organization dedicated to helping companies maximize the value of online communities and other emerging online communication technologies, was founded in 1996 by my partner, Marcy Kaye, and myself, and operated for its first six months in the second bedroom of my cramped NYC apartment. At the end of six months, with our first two employees in tow, we took 500 square feet of office space, installed ISDN lines, and printed business cards. Blue Barn Interactive now has close to forty employees, 10,000 square feet in Silicon Alley, and is aggressively hiring, expanding, and

> Do everything you can to automate and let the computer do the work for you.

multiplying its revenues. Now, moving into the second quarter of 2001, we are accomplishing these things in an environment where most companies in our space—larger and smaller—are cutting back, reassessing their business plans, and in some cases, closing down altogether. In today's environment, especially for the small- to medium-size company, surviving is a key accomplishment.

"I attribute much of the continued success of our company to one small set of guiding principals—traditional business practices, profitable operations, and quality products and services. We took a very conservative approach to doing business, had very traditionally trained advisors, and never "jumped the gun," or grew too quickly—a tendency that can tempt a small- or medium-sized business into very dangerous territory. I think this is much of what we have seen recently in the market—companies being valued solely on potential and rarely on profitability, sound business practices, and real marketable value. Blue Barn Interactive has remained profitable every year, has fed its own growth through those profits, and has built its business with intentional pacing, careful planning, and a real view toward creating something lasting and valuable."

Tips for Making a Small Business Grow

Start at the beginning—Define, for yourself, what your business does, who it is for, and make sure that you can do it. Don't try to sell it before you can do it, or market it before you know it inside and out.

A business's real value is in the quality of the work it does—Value is not in the amount of space, equipment, or employees it has. Expand, hire, and buy when the jobs allow or demand. Revenues exceeding expenses should be the first and most basic goal of any business.

Know when to give it away—Competition for clients and customers is fierce, and early on a company may actually need to give away their products and services for free if it means that they can start a relationship with that client or

> Don't try to sell it before you can do it, or market it before you know it inside and out.

customer. A strong client list or customer base can accelerate a company's opportunities.

Hire slow and hire smart–Do not underestimate the value of each hire, nor the importance of creating a peaceful and collaborative culture. To that end, do not underestimate the time and energy it takes to train, orient, and integrate new employees into the business.

Set reasonable and reachable goals–Reasonable goals allow companies to make more realistic plans, and more realistic plans are better executed. If there are too many contingencies, too many "ifs" in the plans, then there are probably unreasonable goals at the end of them.

Leverage everything–Stay entrepreneurial. Build processes and methodologies, best-practices, role separation, infrastructure etc., but stay entrepreneurial and leverage every asset that the business has collected. From the receptionist, to the controller, to the project manager and designer, the whole will always be greater then the sum of its parts.

Numbers always matter–No matter how large or small the amount, whether Accounts Receivable or Accounts Payable, every dollar counts and every dollar has to be translated meaningfully back into the business. A company should be able to talk about itself in numbers as well as words, and numbers should be able to tell as full and rich a story as words.

Relationships grow businesses–Regardless of technology, or whether a company is selling products and services to other businesses, or to consumers, the quality of the relationship a business can build with its clients or customers speaks directly to the longevity and value of that relationship. Good relationships are built through honesty, fairness, and the delivery of quality and commitment.

> Reasonable goals allow companies to make more realistic plans, and more realistic plans are better executed.

Build to last—Too many small- and medium-sized businesses failed outright because they never had the intention of building an ongoing and lasting business. Regardless of what actually happens, build a business to run on and on, as if it were a family business. Companies who believe things will or should be quick and easy, and who believe they are on a "short run," typically do not build real value, compensate with smoke and mirrors, and for the most part get found out eventually.

Learn and trust your instincts and always ask for help—As an individual running and growing a business you must always trust your instincts—you are a decision maker. Also, seek help. There is a vast amount of people, and resources, such as this book, that can help you to develop your instincts as a businessperson, trust them, and help you to make critical decisions.

Project Management

Robert B. Soudant is a principal in an organization known as PM7Step, and says that small businesses that have rapidly grown from a founder to fifty-plus employees frequently pay scant attention to documented processes. "They will argue that defined processes and their attendant paperwork equate to the bureaucracy they are trying to avoid," he said. "Project management is one such area that calls for written statements of work, expected outcomes, progress reports and eventually, project closure. Most small businesses take the attitude that 'why write when we all know each other?' Then one day they realize things might get out of control," he said.

Seven Steps for Successful Project Management

Conduct a Factor Analysis—Execute a structured and disciplined approach to analyze and understand the effort being requested, through ten elements found in every project.

> Always trust your instincts—you are a decision maker.

Common Sense

Don't overlook good old-fashioned common sense when it comes to planning for the future of your company. Too many business owners get caught up with hectic schedules and everyday problems—and they seem to lose their common sense. If something feels right, it probably is. Listen to your inner voice when it is speaking.

Negotiate a Project Agreement (SOW)—Reach consensus on a written Project Agreement that defines: Scope, Approach, Roles, Responsibilities, Environmental Conditions, Change Control, and Risks associated with the work effort. A Project Agreement authorizes work to begin.

Commit to Change Control—Manage change through a Change Control procedure that is defined in the Project Agreement. Commit to manage through the Change Control process when changes occur during the implementation phase of the project.

Build the Project Plan—Create a project plan by sequentially performing five building steps:

    Build a work breakdown structure
    Determine dependencies
    Develop estimates
    Assign resources
    Finalize the project schedule

Implement the Project Plan—Throughout the life of the project, measure progress and take corrective action, when necessary, to successfully implement the project.

Close the Project—Close the project with sponsor sign-off(s), acceptance reviews, and team recognition. Assess what was done right and what could have been done better. Update all project documentation for future reference

Manage to Changing Expectations—Monitor changing expectations and achieve results by emphasizing deliverables, focusing on risks identified in the planning and scheduling process, and proactively foster open communications at all stakeholder levels.

Tools Needed to Succeed While Planning for the Future

In addition to the latest gadgets, computers and other technological advances, there are some additional tools you will need to guarantee the success of your small business in the future.

You need to be focused on your goals. Without goals, why do you bother to get up in the morning? You need to clearly define what your goals and objectives are and put a strategic plan in place to enable you to meet those goals. The biggest key to remember here is *flexibility*. Without the ability to be flexible and meet challenges head on, you're going to sink fast.

You need to have decision-making capabilities. And you must be able to make snap decisions, almost instantly, while at the same time evaluating all of the options that come into play. You also must maintain a sense of objectivity. You must be able to make good business judgments based on facts, and not on emotions. (This can be difficult for some small business owners and managers of family businesses.)

Be willing to take some risks. It doesn't mean that you're going to bet the whole farm on the blackjack table at the nearest casino, but it does mean that you must be prepared and willing to take some calculated risks. And you must be comfortable with the results, no matter what happens.

Have a clear sense of your business values. And those business values need to be fact based, results driven, and outward looking. Don't settle for anything less.

A high degree of commitment is an absolute must have. Managing a small business into the future, a successful future at that, takes a high degree of commitment. This isn't your typical nine-to-five position, so be prepared to go above and beyond the call of duty in order to meet your goals and objectives.

Sense of Humor

In addition to common sense, you need to keep your sense of humor. Don't let the problems of the business world affect your health and well being. And don't let it affect how you plan the future of your company. A good sense of humor can go a long way in helping you to succeed.

For more information on this topic, visit our Web site at www.businesstown.com

Resources

U.S. Small Business Administration Programs and Services

The SBA is congressionally mandated to assist the nation's small businesses in meeting their financing needs. The agency's finance programs enhance the ability of lenders to provide long- and short-term loans to small businesses that might not qualify through normal lending channels.

There are basically four types of SBA lending and equity investment programs available: the 7(a) Loan Guaranty Program, the 7(m) MicroLoan Program, the 504 Certified Development Company Loan Program, and the Small Business Investment Company Program.

> The SBA is congressionally mandated to assist the nation's small businesses in meeting their financing needs.

Basic 7(a) Loan Guaranty Program

The 7(a) Loan Guaranty Program is the SBA's primary loan program. It is also the most flexible, since the agency can guarantee financing under the program for a variety of general business purposes.

To qualify for an SBA guaranty, a small business must meet the 7(a) loan guaranty criteria, and the lender must certify that it cannot provide funding on reasonable terms except with an SBA guaranty. The SBA can then guarantee as much as 80 percent on loans up to $100,000 and 75 percent on loans greater than $100,000. In most cases, the maximum guaranty is $750,000 (75 percent of $1 million). The International Trade, DELTA, and 504 loan programs, described later, have higher loan limits.

In guaranteeing the loan, the SBA assures the lender that, in the event the borrower does not repay the loan, the government will reimburse the lender for its loss, up to the percentage of the SBA's guaranty. The borrower, however, still remains obligated for the full amount due.

Note: The SBA does not provide grants to start or expand a business.

How it works

You submit a loan application to an SBA participating lender for initial review. If the lender approves the loan subject to an

SBA guaranty, a copy of the application and a credit analysis are forwarded by the lender to the nearest SBA office. Following SBA approval, the lending institution closes the loan and disburses the funds. You make monthly loan payments directly to the lender.

No balloon payments, prepayment penalties, application fees, or points are permitted with 7(a) loans. The lender can tailor the repayment plan for each business.

Use of proceeds

A start-up or existing business may use the proceeds of a 7(a) guaranteed loan to:

- Expand or renovate facilities
- Purchase machinery, equipment, fixtures, and leasehold improvements
- Finance receivables and augment working capital
- Refinance existing debt (with compelling reason)
- Finance seasonal lines of credit
- Construct commercial buildings
- Purchase land or buildings

> To be eligible, a business must be operated for profit and not exceed the SBA's size standards (see the following section).

Eligibility

To be eligible, a business must be operated for profit and not exceed the SBA's size standards (see the following section). Some types of businesses are not eligible, such as those engaged in lending, real-estate development, investment, or speculation. Pyramid schemes and gambling or illegal operations are also ineligible. All loans must be used for sound business purposes.

Maximum size standards

A business is considered "small" if it does not exceed the SBA's established size standards. The size standards are based either on the average number of employees during the preceding twelve months or on sales averaged over the previous three years. The current established size standards are:

- Manufacturing—from 500 to 1,500 employees, depending on the industry
- Wholesaling—100 employees for financial programs (500 for contracting-assistance programs)
- Services—from $4 million to $21.5 million in average annual receipts or 1,500 employees, depending on the industry
- Retailing—from $5 million to $21 million in average annual receipts, depending on the nature of the business
- General and heavy construction—from $17 million to $27.5 million in average annual receipts
- Special trade construction—$11.5 million in average annual receipts
- Agriculture—from $500,000 to $9 million in average annual receipts

What you need to take to the lender

Documentation requirements may vary; contact your lender for the information you must supply. Common requirements include:

- Purpose of the loan
- History of the business
- Financial statements for three years (existing businesses)
- Schedule of term debts (existing businesses)
- Aging of accounts receivable and payable (existing businesses)
- Projected opening-day balance sheet (new businesses)
- Lease details
- Amount of investment in the business by the owner(s)
- Projections of income, expenses, and cash flow
- Signed personal financial statements
- Personal resume(s)

What the SBA looks for:

- Good character
- Management expertise and the commitment necessary for success

> Documentation requirements may vary; contact your lender for the information you must supply.

- Reasonable personal contribution and/or business equity, which along with the loan proceeds enable the borrower to operate the business on a sound financial basis (for new businesses, this includes the resources to withstand start-up expenses and the initial operating phase)
- Feasible business plan
- Adequate equity or investment in the business
- Sufficient collateral
- Ability to repay the loan on time from the projected operating cash flow

Terms, interest rates, and fees

All references to the prime rate mean the lowest prime rate on the day the SBA receives the application. This rate is printed in the *Wall Street Journal* on the next business day.

Your loan-repayment schedule depends on the use of the proceeds and the ability of your business to repay. The general terms are:

- Five to ten years for working capital; and
- Up to twenty-five years for fixed assets such as the purchase or major renovation of real estate or the purchase of equipment (not to exceed the useful life of the equipment).

Both fixed and variable interest rates are available. The maximum rate is 2.25 percent over the lowest prime rate for a loan with a maturity of less than seven years and 2.75 percent over prime for a maturity of seven years or longer. For loans under $50,000, the lender's rate may be slightly higher.

The SBA charges the lender a nominal fee to provide a guaranty, and the lender may pass this charge on to you. The fee is based on the maturity of the loan and the dollar amount that the SBA guarantees. On a loan with a maturity of one year or less, the fee is 0.25 percent of the guaranteed portion of the loan. When the maturity is more than one year, and the SBA-guaranteed portion is $80,000 or less, the guaranty fee is 2 percent of the guaranteed portion. If the maturity is more than one year, and the SBA's portion

> Your loan-repayment schedule depends on the use of the proceeds and the ability of your business to repay.

exceeds $80,000, the guaranty fee is figured on an incremental scale, beginning at 3 percent.

Collateral

To adequately secure the loan, you must pledge sufficient assets to the extent they are reasonably available. Personal guaranties are required from all principals owning 20 percent or more of the business. Liens on personal assets of the principals also may be required. No loan will be declined, however, for insufficient collateral alone.

Special 7(a) Loan Guaranty Programs

In addition to the basic loan guaranty, the SBA has 7(a) programs for specialized needs. Unless otherwise indicated, the rules, regulations, interest rates, fees, and other guidelines of the basic 7(a) loan guaranty govern these programs as well.

CAPLines Loan

Through CAP*Lines*, the SBA helps small businesses meet their short-term and cyclical working-capital needs. A CAP*Lines* loan can be for any dollar amount (except for the Small Asset-Based Line), and the SBA will guarantee up to $750,000, as with the basic 7(a) guaranty. There are five short-term working-capital loan programs for small businesses under CAP*Lines*:

> **Seasonal Line**–This line advances funds against anticipated inventory and accounts receivable for peak seasons and seasonal sales fluctuations. It can be revolving or nonrevolving.
>
> **Contract Line**–This line finances the direct labor and material costs associated with performing assignable construction, service, or supply contracts. It can be revolving or nonrevolving.
>
> **Builders Line**–If you are a small general contractor or builder constructing or renovating commercial or residential

In addition to the basic loan guaranty, the SBA has 7(a) programs for specialized needs.

buildings for resale, this line can finance your direct labor and material costs. The building project serves as the collateral, and loans can be revolving or nonrevolving.

Standard Asset-Based Line—This is an asset-based revolving line of credit designed to assist businesses in need of a short-term line of credit that are also unable to meet credit standards associated with long-term credit. It provides financing for cyclical, growth, recurring, and short-term needs. Repayment comes from converting short-term assets such as inventory and accounts receivable into cash, which is remitted to the lender. Businesses can continually draw down, based on existing assets, and repay as their cash cycle dictates. This line generally is used by businesses that provide credit to other businesses. Since these loans require continual servicing and monitoring of collateral, the lender may charge additional fees.

Small Asset-Based Line—This is an asset-based revolving line of credit up to $200,000. It operates basically like a standard asset-based line. Some of the stricter servicing requirements are waived, however, if the business can consistently show repayment ability from its cash flow.

> Loans can be revolving or nonrevolving.

Terms, interest rates, and fees

Each of the five lines of credit has a maximum maturity of five years, but because each is tailored to your individual needs, a shorter initial maturity may be established. You may use CAP*Lines* funds as needed throughout the term of the loan to purchase assets, as long as sufficient time is allowed to convert the assets into cash by maturity.

You and your lender negotiate the CAP*Lines* interest rate, with the maximum set at 2.25 percent over the prime rate. The guaranty fee is the same as for any standard 7(a) loan. The SBA places no servicing-fee restrictions on the lender for the Standard Asset-Based Line, but it does require full disclosure to ensure the fees are reasonable. On all other CAP*Lines* loans, the additional fee is limited to 2 percent based on the average outstanding balance.

Collateral

Your primary collateral will be the short-term assets financed by the loan.

Defense Loan and Technical Assistance (DELTA) Program

If you own a defense-dependent small business that has been adversely affected by defense cuts or that is located in a defense-impacted community, the DELTA Program can help you diversify into the commercial market. A joint effort of the SBA and the Department of Defense, DELTA provides both financial and technical assistance. The SBA processes, guarantees and services DELTA loans generally through the regulations, forms and operating criteria of the 7(a) Loan Guaranty Program or the 504 Certified Development Company Program.

Eligibility

To be eligible, your business must meet 7(a) or 504 program criteria and have derived at least 25 percent of its total revenue during any one of the previous five operating years from Department of Defense contracts, Department of Energy defense-related contracts, or subcontracts in support of defense prime contracts.

The business must also:

- Use the loan to modernize or expand facilities in order to diversify operations while remaining in the national technical and industrial base, or
- Be adversely impacted by reductions in defense spending and use the loan to retain the jobs of defense workers, or
- Be located in an adversely impacted community and use the loan to create new economic activity or jobs in that community.

> Your primary collateral will be the short-term assets financed by the loan.

Maximum loan and guaranty amounts

The maximum gross loan amount for a DELTA loan under 7(a) is $1.25 million. The maximum guaranty under 7(a) or 504 is $1 million.

Credit analysis

DELTA loans may require special handling due to complicated credit analyses. Because of the transitional state of the business, the applicant may be unable to demonstrate repayment based on past operations despite significant collateral. Revisions to the law allow the SBA to resolve reasonable doubts in the applicant's favor.

Technical assistance

A borrower may also require technical assistance to make the transition to the commercial market. This assistance is provided through the SBA's small business development centers, the Service Corps of Retired Executives, other federal agencies, and other technical and management assistance providers. You will find a directory of technical assistance providers through the SBA home page: *www.sba.gov.*

Community Adjustment & Investment Program (CAIP)

Established in response to changed trade patterns with Canada and Mexico resulting from the North American Free Trade Agreement, CAIP creates new, sustainable jobs and preserves existing ones. The program is a partnership between the federal government (primarily the U.S. Department of the Treasury, the SBA, and the U.S. Department of Agriculture) and the North American Development Bank.

Eligibility

- Business applicants must be located in CAIP-eligible communities. Community eligibility is based upon an analysis of NAFTA-related job losses within the context of local unemployment rates.

> You will find a directory of technical assistance providers through the SBA home page: www.sba.gov.

- For federally funded programs, applicants also must be able to demonstrate that within twenty-four months and as a result of the loan, they will create or preserve at least one job per $70,000 of federally guaranteed funds (the SBA portion) they receive.

Under CAIP, credit is made available primarily through loan guaranties provided either under the 7(a) Loan Guaranty Program or the USDA Business and Industry Loan Guarantee Program. The SBA's 7(a) program typically provides a guaranty of 75 percent of the loan amount or $750,000, whichever is lower. For eligible applicants, NADBank pays the borrower's loan guaranty fee or participates as a direct lender. For more information, call the NADBank Los Angeles office at 562-908-2100, or visit the NADBank Web site at *www.nadbank-caip.org.*

> The SBA can guarantee up to 90 percent of a secured loan or $750,000, whichever is lower.

Export Working Capital (EWCP) Program

The Export Working Capital Program was developed to assist exporters seeking short-term working capital for their transactional financing needs. The loan funds may be used to finance the manufacturing costs of goods for export, the purchase of goods or services, foreign accounts receivable, and standby letters of credit (used for performance bonds, bid bonds, or payment guaranties to foreign buyers).

The SBA can guarantee up to 90 percent of a secured loan or $750,000, whichever is lower.

The EWCP uses streamlined documentation; turnaround is usually within ten days. Borrowers may also apply to the SBA for a letter of preliminary commitment.

You may have other SBA guaranties along with an EWCP loan as long as the SBA's exposure for working-capital loans does not exceed $750,000. When an EWCP loan is combined with an International Trade Loan, the SBA's combined exposure can increase to $1.25 million (with $750,000 as the maximum for the working-capital portion).

Terms, interest rates, and fees

The maturity for an EWCP loan typically matches a single transaction cycle or supports a line of credit, generally with a maximum term of twelve months. With annual renewals, however, it is possible to have a loan maturity of up to three years. The guaranty fee is 0.25 percent of the guaranteed portion of the loan. You and the lender negotiate interest rates and fees.

International Trade Loan (ITL) Program

The International Trade Loan Program guarantees loans to small businesses engaged in international trade, prepared to engage in international trade, or adversely affected by competition from imports. Under this program, the SBA can guarantee as much as $1.25 million in combined working-capital and facilities-and-equipment loans (including any other current SBA loan guaranties). The working-capital portion of the loan may be made according to the provisions of the Export Working Capital Program or any other SBA working-capital program.

To be eligible for the ITL Program, a business must establish that the loan proceeds will significantly expand existing markets or develop new export markets, or that the business is adversely affected by import competition. For fixed-asset loans, a business must also establish that upgrading its facilities or equipment will improve its competitive position.

Use of proceeds

Proceeds may be used for purchasing land and buildings; building new facilities; renovating, improving or expanding existing facilities; purchasing or reconditioning machinery, equipment and fixtures; making other improvements that will be used within the United States for producing goods or services; and working capital. Proceeds may not be used to repay existing debt.

Terms, interest rates, and fees

A loan for facilities or equipment has a maximum maturity of twenty-five years, while a working-capital loan has a maximum

> A loan for facilities or equipment has a maximum maturity of twenty-five years.

maturity of ten years. If the loan proceeds are used for both fixed assets and working capital, the maximum maturity is blended proportionately between the two parts of the loan.

Collateral

The lender takes a first-lien (or first-mortgage) position on behalf of itself and the SBA on items financed under the ITL Program. Only collateral located in the United States, its territories and possessions, is acceptable. Additional collateral may be required, including personal guaranties, subordinate liens, or items that are not financed by the loan proceeds.

Energy and Conservation Loan

Under this program, financing is available for eligible small businesses engaged in the following: engineering, manufacturing, distributing, marketing, and installing or servicing products or services designed to conserve the nation's energy resources. An eligible business may use the loan to buy land for plant construction; convert or expand existing facilities; purchase machinery, equipment, furniture, fixtures, supplies and materials; or provide working capital for entry or expansion into eligible conservation project areas. The loan may not be used for acquiring an energy business or for purchasing energy devices for the business's own use.

The maximum SBA guaranty for loans up to $100,000 is 80 percent. For higher loans up to $750,000, the maximum guaranty is 75 percent.

Pollution Control Loan

This program assists businesses that are planning, designing, or installing a "pollution control facility," which includes most real or personal property that will reduce pollution. Unlike the Energy Conservation Loan, the Pollution Control Loan is for the end-user of the pollution control facility. The program has a maximum SBA exposure of $1 million, less any outstanding balance due the agency on other loans.

> The maximum SBA guaranty for loans up to $100,000 is 80 percent.

Y2K*Action* Loan

The Y2K*Action* Loan is designed to help small businesses recover after January 1, 2000, if they are adversely affected by Y2K problems. These include economic injuries caused indirectly by any other entity, such as a supplier or service, if insurance doesn't cover the loss.

While a Y2K*Action* Loan operates under the general guidelines of the SBA's 7(a) program, there are some differences. The SBA can provide the lender of a Y2K*Action* Loan with a guaranty of up to 90 percent on a loan of $100,000 or less and up to 85 percent on loans greater than $100,000. The maximum SBA exposure in dollars for a Y2K*Action* Loan is $750,000. If you have an existing SBA-guaranteed loan, the maximum total SBA exposure is $1 million.

Streamlined Applications and Approvals

Under the SBA's loan-guaranty programs, the borrower applies to a lending institution, not the SBA. The lender applies to the SBA for a loan guaranty, if it determines this is necessary to approve the loan. The SBA can process a lender's request through a variety of methods. The following methods are used most frequently: Standard, Certified Lenders, Preferred Lenders, SBA*LowDoc*, SBA*Express*, and Community*Express*. You may obtain a list of SBA participating lenders from your local SBA office.

> Under the SBA's loan-guaranty programs, the borrower applies to a lending institution, not the SBA.

Standard Application Process

The lender submits a completed loan application, including a credit analysis, to the SBA field office that covers the territory where the applicant business is located. After receiving all the documentation, the SBA analyzes the entire application, then makes its decision. The process may take up to ten days to complete.

Certified Lenders Program (CLP)

The CLP provides expeditious service on loan applications received from lenders who have successful SBA track records and a thorough understanding of SBA lending policies and procedures. Under this program, the SBA reviews the lender's credit analysis rather than conducting a complete second analysis. This reduces the SBA's targeted response time to three days. Certified lenders, who account for 7 percent of all SBA business loan guaranties, can submit applications under standard processing if they wish.

Preferred Lenders Program (PLP)

The PLP maximizes the use of qualified, private lenders in the agency's financial-assistance delivery system. Under this program, the SBA delegates loan approval, closing, and most servicing and liquidation authority and responsibility to carefully selected lenders. The PLP is designed only for the strongest credits. SBA loan approval is conducted at the SBA's PLP center in Sacramento, California. Turnaround usually takes less than one day. Preferred loans receive the same 75 percent guaranty rate (80 percent on loans of $100,000 or less) as regular and certified SBA-backed loans. Preferred lenders may use certified or standard processing, if they wish. Preferred loans currently account for approximately 33 percent of SBA loans.

Low Documentation Loan (SBA*LowDoc*)

SBA*LowDoc* is the SBA's quick and easy program that provides a guaranty on small business loans of $150,000 or less. Once you have met your lender's requirements for credit, the lender may request an SBA*LowDoc* guaranty for up to 80 percent of the loan amount (75 percent when the SBA's share exceeds $80,000). You complete the front of a one-page SBA application, and the lender completes the back. At SBA*LowDoc* centers, the agency processes completed applications within 36 hours. Loan proceeds may not be used to repay certain types of existing debt. The loan terms are up to ten years for working capital and up to twenty-five years for fixed assets.

> SBA*LowDoc* is the SBA's quick and easy program that provides a guaranty on small business loans of $150,000 or less.

Eligibility

The following businesses are eligible for SBA*LowDoc*:

- Businesses (including affiliates) with average annual sales for the past three years not exceeding $5 million and with 100 or fewer employees;
- If they meet the size standards for their industries—farms; travel agents; real estate agents; engineering, architectural or surveying services; fishing, hunting, or trapping entities; and dry cleaning plants; and
- Business start-ups.

SBA*Express*

SBA*Express* provides selected lenders with a 50 percent guaranty on their loans in exchange for the ability to use their own application and documentation forms. This method makes it easier and faster for lenders to provide small business loans of $150,000 or less. The SBA provides a rapid response—within thirty-six hours of receiving the complete application package. Lenders use their own procedures to approve and service the loans.

Terms

Like most 7(a) loans, the maturity of an SBA*Express* term loan is usually five to seven years for working capital and up to twenty-five years for real estate or equipment (subject to the useful economic life of the equipment). The termination date for revolving credits must be no later than five years after the first disbursement.

Community*Express*

The Community*Express* pilot program is designed to spur economic development and job creation in untapped rural and inner city communities by providing loans and technical assistance. Loan proceeds may be used for most business purposes, including start-up, expansion, equipment purchases, working capital, inventory, or real-estate acquisitions.

> The CommunityExpress pilot program is designed to spur economic development and job creation in untapped rural and inner city communities by providing loans and technical assistance.

To be eligible for Community*Express*, current or prospective small businesses must be part of the SBA's New Markets. Under this program, New Markets are defined as current and prospective small businesses owned by minorities, women, and veterans who are underrepresented in the population of business owners compared to their representation in the overall population, and businesses located or locating in low and moderate income urban and rural areas.

While Community*Express* is similar to SBA*Express*, there are some differences:

- Community*Express* focuses on predesignated geographic areas that primarily serve New Markets.
- The maximum loan amount under Community*Express* is $250,000.
- The SBA's guaranty is 80 percent for loans up to $100,000 and 75 percent for loans between $100,000 and $250,000.
- Community*Express* lenders, together with the National Community Reinvestment Coalition, provide hands-on technical training and support, both before and after loan closings, through community-based, nonprofit NCRC member organizations.

Loan Prequalification Program

Under this program, the applicant goes to the lender preapproved for an SBA loan guaranty. The program primarily assists New Markets with the small business loan-application process. New Markets under this program include segments of the small business community that traditionally may have been underserved by the lending community. Eligible applicants include veterans, exporters, rural business owners, women, minorities, and owners of businesses in selected industries and geographical areas. Local SBA district offices determine their demographic markets for the program and select, train, and monitor intermediaries.

An SBA-designated intermediary assists the prospective borrower in developing a viable loan application package (and may

> While CommunityExpress is similar to SBAExpress, there are some differences.

charge a reasonable fee for this service). The intermediary submits the complete package to the SBA for expedited consideration. The agency usually makes a decision within three days.

If the application is approved, the SBA issues a letter of preliminary commitment stating the agency's intent to guarantee the loan. The maximum loan amount is $250,000. The SBA will guarantee up to 75 percent (80 percent on loans of $100,000 or less). The intermediary helps the borrower locate a lender offering the most competitive rates and terms.

Eligibility factors different from the basic 7(a) program requirements:

- Businesses must be at least 51 percent owned, operated, and managed by members of one of the groups designated as eligible to participate.
- Businesses, including affiliated companies, must employ 100 or fewer workers in total.

Other SBA Loan Programs

7(m) Microloan Program

The SBA's Microloan Program provides very small loans up to $25,000 to small businesses through a network of locally based intermediary lenders. In addition to making the loans, the intermediaries provide management and technical assistance to microborrowers and potential microborrowers.

A small business in need of a Microloan must apply directly to the SBA's local intermediary lender. Contact your closest SBA office to find out if there is one in your area.

Use of proceeds

Microloans may be used to finance furniture, fixtures, equipment, inventory, materials, and supplies. They may also be used to finance receivables and for working capital. They may not be used to purchase real estate.

> The SBA's Microloan Program provides very small loans up to $25,000 to small businesses through a network of locally based intermediary lenders.

Terms and interest rates

The maximum term for a Microloan is six years. Interest rates can be up to 8.5 percent over the intermediary's cost of borrowing from the SBA. Microloans are direct loans from the intermediary lenders. They are not guaranteed by the SBA.

Collateral

Each intermediary lender will have its own requirements regarding collateral and personal guaranties.

Eligibility

Virtually all types of for-profit businesses that meet the SBA's size and type-of-business standards for the 7(a) Loan Guaranty Program may apply for a Microloan.

504 Certified Development Company (CDC) Program

Through certified development companies, the 504 Certified Development Company Program provides growing businesses with long-term, fixed-rate financing for major fixed assets, such as land and buildings. Approximately 270 CDCs nationwide work with the SBA and private-sector lenders to provide financing to small businesses.

CDCs are nonprofit corporations set up to contribute to the economic development of their communities. The CDC program is designed to enable small businesses to create and retain jobs; the CDC's portfolio must create or retain at least one job for every $35,000 of debenture proceeds provided by the SBA.

Typically, a 504 project includes:

- A loan secured with a senior lien from a private-sector lender (covering a percentage of the entire cost),
- A loan secured with a junior lien from a CDC (a 100 percent SBA-guaranteed debenture) covering up to 40 percent of the total cost, and
- A contribution of at least 10 percent equity from the borrower.

> The CDC program is designed to enable small businesses to create and retain jobs.

The SBA-guaranteed debentures are pooled monthly and sold to private investors. The maximum SBA debenture generally is $750,000 (and up to $1 million in some cases).

Use of proceeds

Proceeds from 504 loans must be used for fixed-asset projects such as:

- Purchasing land and improvements, including existing buildings, grading, street improvements, utilities, parking lots, and landscaping;
- Constructing, modernizing, renovating or converting existing facilities; and
- Purchasing machinery and equipment.

The 504 program cannot be used for working capital or inventory, consolidating or repaying debt, or refinancing.

> Proceeds from 504 loans must be used for fixed-asset projects.

Terms, interest rates, and fees

Interest rates on 504 loans are fixed at the time of the debenture sale. The interest rates approximate the current market rate for five-year and ten-year U.S. Treasury issues, plus a small increment. Maturities of ten and twenty years are available.

Fees total approximately 3 percent of the debenture and may be financed with the loan. These include a CDC processing fee of 1.5 percent, a guaranty fee, a funding fee, and an underwriting fee.

Collateral

Generally the project assets being financed are used as collateral. Personal guaranties of the principal owners are also required.

Eligibility

To be eligible, a business must be operated for profit and fall within the size standards set by the SBA. Under the 504 Program, a business qualifies as small if it has a tangible net worth of $6 million or less and an average net income of $2 million or less after taxes for the preceding two years. Loans cannot be made to businesses engaged in speculation or investment.

Franchise Registry

The SBA Franchise Registry eliminates the lengthy review process otherwise associated with a prospective or existing franchisee's application for SBA financial assistance. The registry enables the SBA and its participating lenders to check a franchise's eligibility on the Internet, at *www.franchiseregistry.com*. The Franchise Registry is available to any company with a method of doing business that fits the Federal Trade Commission's definition of a "franchise." This includes both business-format and product-name franchisers.

Loan Repayment Chart

The chart provides the information you need to determine your monthly loan payment. The monthly payment includes principal and interest.

The chart provides the amortization factor necessary to determine the monthly principal and interest payment on your loan. The factor is based on loan increments of $1,000. To obtain the factor, take the following steps:

1. Divide the total (gross) loan amount by $1,000.
2. Using the chart, find the interest rate on your loan in the far-left vertical column, then move horizontally to the column denoting the term of your loan. This number is your amortization factor. Example: A loan at 8 percent interest with a term of 7 years has a factor of 15.59.
3. Multiply your answer in step 1 by the factor in step 2. The result is your monthly loan payment.

Make sure to consult with your lender for the actual loan terms.

> The SBA Franchise Registry eliminates the lengthy review process otherwise associated with a prospective or existing franchisee's application for SBA financial assistance.

Loan Term

Interest Rate	1 yr	2 yrs	3 yrs	4 yrs	5 yrs	6 yrs	7 yrs	8 yrs	9 yrs	10 yrs	15 yrs	20 yrs	25 yrs
8.00%	86.99	45.23	31.34	24.41	20.28	17.53	15.59	14.14	13.02	12.13	9.56	8.36	7.72
8.25%	87.10	45.34	31.45	24.53	20.40	17.66	15.71	14.26	13.15	12.27	9.70	8.52	7.88
8.50%	87.22	45.46	31.57	24.65	20.52	17.78	15.84	14.39	13.28	12.40	9.85	8.68	8.05
8.75%	87.34	45.57	31.68	24.77	20.64	17.90	15.96	14.52	13.41	12.53	9.99	8.84	8.22
9.00%	87.45	45.68	31.80	24.88	20.76	18.03	16.09	14.65	13.54	12.67	10.14	9.00	8.39
9.25%	87.57	45.80	31.92	25.00	20.88	18.15	16.22	14.78	13.68	12.80	10.29	9.16	8.56
9.50%	87.68	45.91	32.03	25.12	21.00	18.27	16.34	14.91	13.81	12.94	10.44	9.32	8.74
9.75%	87.80	46.03	32.15	25.24	21.12	18.40	16.47	15.04	13.94	13.08	10.59	9.49	8.91
10.00%	87.92	46.15	32.27	25.36	21.25	18.53	16.60	15.17	14.08	13.22	10.75	9.65	9.09
10.50%	88.15	46.38	32.50	25.60	21.49	18.78	16.86	15.44	14.35	13.49	11.05	9.98	9.44
10.75%	88.27	46.49	32.62	25.72	21.62	18.91	16.99	15.57	14.49	13.63	11.21	10.15	9.62
11.00%	88.38	46.61	32.74	25.85	21.74	19.03	17.12	15.71	14.63	13.77	11.37	10.32	9.80
10.25%	88.03	46.26	32.38	25.48	21.37	18.65	16.73	15.31	14.21	13.35	10.90	9.82	9.26
11.25%	88.50	46.72	32.86	25.97	21.87	19.16	17.25	15.84	14.76	13.92	11.52	10.49	9.98
11.50%	88.62	46.84	32.98	26.09	21.99	19.29	17.39	15.98	14.90	14.06	11.68	10.66	10.16
11.75%	88.73	46.96	33.10	26.21	22.12	19.42	17.52	16.12	15.04	14.20	11.84	10.84	10.35
12.00%	88.85	47.07	33.21	26.33	22.24	19.55	17.65	16.25	15.18	14.35	12.00	11.01	10.53
12.25%	88.97	47.19	33.33	26.46	22.37	19.68	17.79	16.39	15.33	14.49	12.16	11.19	10.72
12.50%	89.08	47.31	33.45	26.58	22.50	19.81	17.92	16.53	15.47	14.64	12.33	11.36	10.90
12.75%	89.20	47.42	33.57	26.70	22.63	19.94	18.06	16.67	15.61	14.78	12.49	11.54	11.09
13.00%	89.32	47.54	33.69	26.83	22.75	20.07	18.19	16.81	15.75	14.93	12.65	11.72	11.28
13.25%	89.43	47.66	33.81	26.95	22.88	20.21	18.33	16.95	15.90	15.08	12.82	11.89	11.47
13.50%	89.55	47.78	33.94	27.08	23.01	20.34	18.46	17.09	16.04	15.23	12.98	12.07	11.66
13.75%	89.67	47.90	34.06	27.20	23.14	20.47	18.60	17.23	16.19	15.38	13.15	12.25	11.85
14.00%	89.79	48.01	34.18	27.33	23.27	20.61	18.74	17.37	16.33	15.53	13.32	12.44	12.04
14.25%	89.90	48.13	34.30	27.45	23.40	20.74	18.88	17.51	16.48	15.68	13.49	12.62	12.23
14.50%	90.02	48.25	34.42	27.58	23.53	20.87	19.02	17.66	16.63	15.83	13.66	12.80	12.42
14.75%	90.14	48.37	34.54	27.70	23.66	21.01	19.16	17.80	16.78	15.98	13.83	12.98	12.61
15.00%	90.26	48.49	34.67	27.83	23.79	21.14	19.30	17.95	16.92	16.13	14.00	13.17	12.81
15.25%	90.38	48.61	34.79	27.96	23.92	21.28	19.44	18.09	17.07	16.29	14.17	13.35	13.00
15.50%	90.49	48.72	34.91	28.08	24.05	21.42	19.58	18.24	17.22	16.44	14.34	13.54	13.20
15.75%	90.61	48.84	35.03	28.21	24.19	21.55	19.72	18.38	17.37	16.60	14.51	13.73	13.39
16.00%	90.73	48.96	35.16	28.34	24.32	21.69	19.86	18.53	17.53	16.75	14.69	13.91	13.59

Should Problems Arise

If your small business encounters difficulties, the SBA is ready to help with expert business counseling and assistance. In the event that a borrower is unable to meet the obligations of an SBA loan, the agency will work closely with the lender and/or borrower to negotiate a solution. Only when a solution cannot be found will the SBA move to liquidate the assets securing the loan.

If your small business encounters difficulties, the SBA is ready to help with expert business counseling and assistance.

Equity Investment

Small Business Investment Company (SBIC) Program

The Small Business Investment Company Program fills the gap between the availability of venture capital and the needs of small start-up or growing businesses.

Licensed and regulated by the SBA, SBICs are privately owned and managed investment companies that make capital available to small businesses through investments or loans. They use their own funds plus funds obtained at favorable rates with SBA guaranties.

SBICs are for-profit companies whose incentive is to share in the success of small businesses. In addition to equity capital and long-term loans, SBICs provide debt-equity investments and management assistance.

The SBIC Program provides funding to all types of manufacturing and service industries. Some investment companies specialize in certain fields; others seek out small businesses with new products or services because of their strong growth potential. Most, however, consider a wide variety of investment opportunities.

Providing the same services as SBICs, specialized small business investment companies invest in socially or economically disadvantaged small companies; typically, however, they invest in businesses during their growth stages and make smaller investments.

Angel Capital Electronic Network (ACE-*Net*)

ACE-*Net* provides an Internet-based, secure listing service for entrepreneurs seeking equity financing of $250,000 to $5 million from accredited "angel" investors. Using ACE-Net, the angel can negotiate directly with a listed company to provide equity capital funding and advice for a stake in the entrepreneur's corporation.

ACE-*Net* is operated as a partnership between the SBA's Office of Advocacy and a number of nonprofit organizations nationwide. It will ultimately be turned over to a private nonprofit organization. You can access ACE-*Net* at *www.sba.gov/advo/acenet.html.*

Surety Bonds

Surety Bond Guarantee Program

By law, prime contractors to the federal government must post surety bonds on federal construction projects valued at $100,000 or more. Many state, county, city, and private-sector projects require bonding as well. The SBA can guarantee bid, performance, and payment bonds for contracts up to $1.25 million for eligible small businesses that cannot obtain surety bonds through regular commercial channels. The SBA guarantees bonds in two ways:

- Prior Approval Sureties–The SBA must approve guarantees before these sureties can issue guaranteed bonds.
- Preferred Sureties–The SBA authorizes preferred sureties to issue, monitor, and service bonds without prior SBA approval.

The SBA's Web site for surety bond information is *www.sba.gov/osg.*

By law, prime contractors to the federal government must post surety bonds on federal construction projects valued at $100,000 or more.

Federal Government Contracting Assistance

Breakout Procurement

Through this program the SBA promotes, influences, and enhances the breakout of historically sole-source federal government contracts into full and open competition. The goals are to increase the number of federal contracts available to small businesses and achieve significant savings for the federal government.

Prime Contracting

To increase opportunities for small businesses in the federal acquisition process, the SBA initiates small business set-asides, identifies new small business sources, and counsels small companies on how to do business with the federal government. It also conducts surveillance reviews of federal purchasing facilities to assess compliance with the procurement provisions of the Small Business Act.

Subcontracting

The SBA also helps small businesses receive the maximum practical opportunity to participate in federal contracts as subcontractors and suppliers. (By law, certain percentages of large federal contracts must be subcontracted to small businesses.)

Certificate of Competency (CoC) Program

The CoC Program provides an appeal process to small businesses that have been denied contracts with the U.S. government for a lack of "responsibility," or a perceived inability to perform satisfactorily.

Women-Owned Business Procurement

This multifaceted program shows women how to market to the federal government. It also works to increase the pool of qualified women business owners by holding procurement conferences at major federal buying sites. Women business owners registered in PRO-*Net* (see next listing) will have special opportunities in federal procurements of less than $100,000 under an agreement signed between the Office of Federal Procurement Policy and the SBA. For such procurements, the contracting agency can request a waiver from advertising in the Commerce Business Daily if the contracting officer solicits bid information from five small businesses—at least one women-owned and one small disadvantaged business—registered in the PRO-*Net* database. The program Web site is *www.sba.gov/gc/wbpprgm.html*.

> By law, certain percentages of large federal contracts must be subcontracted to small businesses.

Procurement Marketing and Access Network (PRO-*Net*)

An online database of information on thousands of small businesses, the SBA's Pro-*Net* serves as a search engine for contracting officers, a marketing tool for small companies, and a "link" to procurement opportunities and other important information. It also provides links to the online Commerce Business Daily, federal agency home pages, and other sources of procurement opportunities. PRO-*Net* offers free registration to small businesses. Simply access the PRO-*Net* Web site at *http://pronet.sba.gov* and follow the instructions.

SUB-*Net*

SUB-*Net*, an extension of PRO-*Net*, is primarily for prime contractors to post subcontracting opportunities. These opportunities may or may not be reserved for small businesses. They may include solicitations or other notices, such as a search for "teaming" partners and/or subcontractors for future contracts. The SUB-*Net* site enables small businesses to use their limited resources to identify and bid on concrete, tangible opportunities. While the Web site is designed primarily as a place for large businesses to post solicitations and notices, federal agencies, state and local governments, nonprofit organizations, colleges and universities, and small businesses can also use it for the same purpose. You can access SUB-*Net* through the PRO-*Net* home page by clicking on the "Subcontracting Opportunities" bar.

> TM Online is a database of American small businesses that seek to export their products.

Trade Mission Online (TM Online)

TM Online is a database of American small businesses that seek to export their products. It is also a search engine for foreign companies that seek U.S. business alliances through direct product sales, licensing or franchising agreements. You can access TM Online at *www.sba.gov/tmonline.*

Small Business Size Standards

The SBA's Office of Size Standards can tell you if your business meets the federal size standards for a small business. The office develops and prepares regulations on size standards as needed following agency and federal government rule-making procedures. The regulations determine which businesses are eligible for the SBA's financial- and procurement-assistance programs.

You can obtain more information on size standards by logging on to *www.sba.gov/size*.

HUBZone Empowerment Contracting Program

This program encourages economic development in historically underutilized business zones—"HUBZones"—through the establishment of federal contract award preferences for qualified small businesses located in such areas. After determining eligibility, the SBA lists qualified businesses in the PRO-*Net* database. The HUBZone Web site is *www.sba.gov/hubzone*.

Research and Development Assistance

Small Business Innovation Research (SBIR)

Under the SBIR Program, small businesses propose innovative ideas to meet the specific research and R & D needs of the federal government. The program also promotes commercialization of the results generated. Proponents of R & D proposals are awarded federal grants on a competitive basis.

Small Business Technology Transfer (STTR)

This program also awards federal grants on a competitive basis. However, it requires the small company competing for an R & D project to collaborate with a nonprofit research institution from the submission of the proposal to the completion of the designated effort.

Small Business Research, R & D Goaling

The SBA's Office of Technology measures and reports the amount of federal funding for research and R & D (excluding the amounts for SBIR and STTR) awarded to small businesses each year by the major

> After determining eligibility, the SBA lists qualified businesses in the PRO-Net database.

research and R & D federal agencies. You can access *www.sba.gov/sbir* for more information on R & D assistance programs.

Counseling and Technical Assistance

Small Business Development Centers (SBDCs)

Funded and administered by the SBA, SBDCs provide a variety of management and technical-assistance services to small businesses and potential entrepreneurs. SBDCs are a cooperative effort among the SBA, the academic community, the private sector, and state and local governments. Together with the SBA's certified development companies, SBDCs also can help you prepare an SBA loan application. There are approximately 1,000 SBDC locations, primarily at colleges and universities in all 50 states and the U.S. territories. For the SBDC closest to you, call your local SBA office, or check the list of centers at *www.sba.gov/sbdc*.

> SBDCs provide a variety of management and technical-assistance services to small businesses and potential entrepreneurs.

Business Information Centers (BICs)

BICs—supported by local SBA offices—can assist you by providing access to state-of-the-art computer hardware and software, and through counseling by SCORE volunteers. BICs have resources for addressing a broad variety of business start-up and development issues. You can receive help with writing a comprehensive business plan, evaluating and improving your marketing and sales techniques, diversifying into new product and service areas, pricing your products, or exploring exporting opportunities. The BIC Web site is *www.sba.gov/bi/bics*.

Service Corps of Retired Executives (SCORE)

Nationwide, 11,500 SCORE volunteers in 389 chapters provide free, expert advice based on their many years of firsthand experience and shared knowledge, on virtually every aspect of business. SCORE counselors are located at SBA field offices, business information centers, and some of the SBA's small business development centers. Call your closest SBA field office to find the SCORE chapter nearest you, or access SCORE online at *www.score.org*.

Assistance for Armed Forces Veterans

Veterans Business Outreach Program

The SBA's Veterans Business Outreach Program ensures that small businesses owned and controlled by eligible veterans have access to entrepreneurial training, business development assistance, counseling and management assistance. The agency has cooperative agreements in effect with four entities, each serving one of the following SBA regions: two, three, four, and six. The program will be expanded to the agency's remaining six regions in fiscal 2001. Contact SBA to find out the geographic area covered by each region.

Veterans Distance Learning Program

An online resource specifically designed to address the concerns of veterans, the Veterans Distance Learning Program provides training in both English and Spanish on a variety of entrepreneurial topics. Each course requires fifteen to twenty minutes to complete and offers rapid feedback on the student's progress. The curriculum includes courses such as credit repair and financial management, business development planning, and starting a home-based business. You can access the courses by visiting *www.sba.gov/vets*.

> The Veterans Distance Learning Program provides training in both English and Spanish on a variety of entrepreneurial topics.

Assistance for Exporters

U.S. Export Assistance Centers (USEACs)

USEACs combine in single locations the trade-promotion and export-finance assistance of the SBA, the U.S. Department of Commerce, and the Export-Import Bank of the United States. USEACs also work closely with other federal, state, and local international trade-assistance partners. To find the USEAC nearest you, contact your local SBA office or visit *www.sba.gov/oit/export*.

Export Legal Assistance Network (ELAN)

In conjunction with the Federal Bar Association, the SBA and the U.S. Department of Commerce offer to exporters a complimentary initial legal consultation with an international trade attorney. To access this program, contact your local SBA field office.

TradeNet's Export Advisor

TradeNet is an Internet site for exporters created through a partnership of public and private entities led by the SBA. The Web site offers market research, export laws, business opportunities, trade shows and events, research tools, financing information, and forms and documentation. TradeNet also gives you the capability of creating a personalized page called MyExport. You can access TradeNet at *www.tradenet.gov.*

The Export Trade Assistance Partnership (E-TAP)

E-TAP is a program designed to assist small business owners in becoming export-ready and competing in global markets. The program consists of four distinct segments: partnership, training, counseling, and international trade shows or missions. A key component is the customized, intensive international trade training designed to help small businesses not only discover international opportunities appropriate for their companies but also accurately assess the market potential of various countries around the world. The ultimate goal is for U.S. small businesses to participate in trade events in the country or countries with the greatest market potential for the businesses' exports. Contact your local U.S. Export Assistance Center to participate in the E-TAP Program (see also USEACs).

> E-TAP is a program designed to assist small business owners in becoming export-ready and competing in global markets.

Assistance for Native Americans

Tribal Business Information Centers (TBICs)

As SBA resource partners, TBICs offer entrepreneurs access to state-of-the-art computer and software technology, one-to-one business counseling services, and business management workshops. TBICs currently serve Native American reservation communities in California, Minnesota, Montana, North Carolina, North Dakota, South Dakota, and the Navajo Nation. They are operated with individual and tribe-owned organizations; other federal, state, and local agencies; nonprofit organizations; and national Native American organizations. For more information you may access the SBA's Office of Native American Affairs Web site at *www.sba.gov/naa*.

Assistance for Small and Disadvantaged Businesses

Small Disadvantaged Business (SDB) Certification

SDB certification ensures that small businesses owned and controlled by socially and economically disadvantaged individuals meet SDB eligibility criteria. If you own a business certified as an SDB, you may receive a price evaluation credit of up to 10 percent when you bid on a federal contract. To obtain an application for certification, you may contact your local SBA district office, call the SBA Office of SDB Certification & Eligibility at 1-800-558-0884, or access the application on the Web at *www.sba.gov/sdb/forms*.

> SDB certification ensures that small businesses owned and controlled by socially and economically disadvantaged individuals meet SDB eligibility criteria.

8(a) Business Development

The SBA's 8(a) Business Development Program assists the development of small companies owned and operated by individuals who are socially and economically disadvantaged. If you are eligible for this program, you are eligible for federal contracting set-asides and other business-development support to help your company gain access to the economic mainstream. Contact your local SBA district office to apply.

7(j) Management and Technical Assistance

Under Section 7(j) of the Small Business Act, the SBA awards grants to and enters into cooperative agreements with organizations to provide management and/or technical assistance to 8(a) Business Development Program participants and other eligible individuals. The assistance is given in areas such as accounting, marketing, and proposal/bid preparation. The 7(j) Program also provides industry-specific technical assistance and entrepreneurial training. You may obtain additional information on the 8(a) and 7(j) programs at *www.sba.gov/med*.

Assistance for Women

Women's Business Centers

Women's business centers nationwide provide women entrepreneurs with business training and counseling, technical assistance, mentoring, and access to the SBA's programs and services. They also have programs to assist economically and socially disadvantaged women, especially those on welfare. Each center tailors its services to the needs of the local community. To find the WBC nearest you, contact your local SBA district office, or visit the Office of Women's Business Ownership home page at *www.sba.gov/womeninbusiness*.

Online Women's Business Center

This state-of-the-art Web site offers women information about business principles and practices, management techniques, networking, industry news, market research, technology training, and information about the many SBA services and resources available to them. Special features include interactive mentoring and individual counseling; topic forums; newsgroups; information in Spanish, Russian and several other languages; and a data resource guide with a state-by-state listing of the professional services women need to start and build their businesses. You can access the Online Women's Business Center at *www.onlinewbc.org*.

Women's Network for Entrepreneurial Training (WNET)

The Women's Network for Entrepreneurial Training provides mentoring for current and aspiring women business owners through WNET "roundtables." Groups of mentors and protégés meet regularly to provide assistance, support, and networking opportunities. Sponsors include women's business centers, small business development centers,

> Women's business centers nationwide provide women entrepreneurs with business training and counseling, technical assistance, mentoring, and access to the SBA's programs and services.

local business leaders, government representatives, and SCORE. There are now more than 130 WNET roundtables nationwide.

Business Information Services

Answer Desk

A computerized toll-free telephone message system, the SBA Answer Desk provides you with information about starting or running a business and how to get assistance. You can access the Answer Desk toll-free twenty-four hours a day, seven days a week at 1-800 U ASK SBA. Operators are available to answer your questions Monday through Friday from 9 A.M. to 5 P.M. Eastern time. You can also e-mail your questions to *answerdesk@sba.gov*.

A computerized toll-free telephone message system, the SBA Answer Desk provides you with information about starting or running a business and how to get assistance.

Publications

The SBA produces free publications describing the SBA's many programs and services. For copies, call your local SBA field office or the SBA Answer Desk. The Web site for downloadable SBA publications is *www.sba.gov/library*.

SBA OnLine

SBA OnLine is an electronic bulletin board that provides information about the agency's programs and services for starting and running a small business. It also includes many SBA publications. Accessed by modem (9600, n, 8, 1), it operates twenty-three hours a day, seven days a week, and is updated daily. You can access SBA OnLine by dialing 1-800-697-4636 (limited access) or 1-900-463-4636 (full access). The number for the Washington, D.C., metropolitan area is 202-401-9600.

SBA Home Page

Be sure to check out SBA's home page. It offers detailed information on all SBA programs and services, including local resources; other business services; access to SBA OnLine, ACE-*Net*, PRO-*Net* and the

U.S. Business Advisor (see next listing); and SBA Classroom, an online vehicle for reading articles, taking courses, and researching small business issues. The SBA home page also links to many outside resources on the World Wide Web. The home page address is *www.sba.gov.*

U.S. Business Advisor

This Web site provides a one-stop shopping link for small businesses to information and services provided by the federal government. It supplies easy online access to many of the most frequently asked questions about businesses and the federal government. It also provides interactive tools that can be used to find solutions to situations involving the environment, health and safety, and permits you to download many of the forms necessary for regulatory compliance.

The U.S. Business Advisor can also be used to:

- Access electronic commerce services, ranging from loan information to trademark registration, export licenses, payroll benefits, and tax filing;
- Employ Web-based tutorials and online classroom training to find other sources of counseling, education, and training;
- Interact with buyers and suppliers of equity capital, contracting opportunities, trade leads, innovation, and research grants;
- Create a tailored Web page to support international trade activities;
- Access laws, regulations, and guidance; and
- Seek and receive e-mail advice and counseling.

You may access the U.S. Business Advisor through the SBA home page or directly at *www.business.gov.*

Advocacy for Small Business

Office of Advocacy

The SBA's Office of Advocacy serves as a direct link to the small business community and as an advocate of small businesses. It

The SBA's Office of Advocacy serves as a direct link to the small business community and as an advocate of small businesses.

researches pertinent issues, develops policy and legislation, and monitors their effects. The Office of Advocacy produces numerous publications, including an annual report to Congress, *The State of Small Business: A Report of the President*, as well as technical books and statistical and economic reports. It compiles and interprets statistics on small business and is the primary agency within the federal government that disseminates small business data. The office also oversees compliance with the Regulatory Flexibility Act, is a member of the Occupational Safety and Health Administration's and the Environmental Protection Agency's Small Business Advocacy Review panels, and strives to reduce the impact of regulatory proposals on small businesses. The Office of Advocacy's home page is *www.sba.gov/advo*.

> The National Ombudsman annually evaluates enforcement activities and rates each agency's responsiveness to small businesses.

Small Business Regulatory Enforcement Ombudsman

The small business and agriculture regulatory enforcement ombudsman and ten regional fairness boards have been established to receive comments from small businesses about federal agency enforcement actions. The National Ombudsman annually evaluates enforcement activities and rates each agency's responsiveness to small businesses. For more information or to comment on regulatory fairness, call toll-free at 1-888-REG-FAIR, or access *www.sba.gov/regfair*.

Disaster Assistance Loan Program

When a declared disaster strikes, help is close at hand. The SBA's Disaster Assistance Loan Program–the primary federal program for funding long-range recovery for private-sector, nonagricultural disaster victims–provides assistance to businesses of all sizes and to individuals. Interest rates fluctuate according to statutory formulas. A low interest rate (not to exceed 4 percent) is available to applicants without credit available elsewhere. A higher rate (not to exceed 8 percent) is available for those with credit available elsewhere.

Loans for Homes and Personal Property

Real Property Loans

This is the major long-term recovery program for individual disaster losses. Loans are available to qualified homeowners for uninsured losses up to $200,000 to repair or restore a primary residence to predisaster condition.

Personal Property Loans

Loans are available to qualified homeowner and renter applicants for uninsured losses up to $40,000 to repair or replace personal property such as clothing, furniture, cars, and so forth. Loans are not intended to replace extraordinarily expensive or irreplaceable items such as antiques, pleasure crafts, recreational vehicles, or fur coats, etc.

Loans for Businesses

Physical Disaster Business Loans

Loans are available to qualified applicant businesses of any size for uninsured losses up to $1.5 million to repair or replace business property to pre-disaster conditions. Loans may be used to replace or repair real estate, equipment, fixtures, and inventory, and leasehold improvements.

> Loans are available to qualified homeowner and renter applicants for uninsured losses up to $40,000 to repair or replace personal property such as clothing, furniture, cars, and so forth.

Economic Injury Disaster Loans (EIDLs)

Loans of up to $1.5 million are available for small businesses that sustain economic injury as a direct result of a disaster. These working-capital loans are made to businesses without credit available elsewhere. The loans are to help pay ordinary and necessary operating expenses that would have been payable absent the disaster.

Note: When an EIDL and a Physical Disaster Business Loan are combined, the maximum loan amount is $1.5 million, unless the business is a major source of employment as defined by federal criteria.

That means the $1.5 million limit can be waived for businesses that employ 250 or more people in an affected area.

The address for the Disaster Assistance home page is *www.sba.gov/disaster*.

Empowerment Zones/Enterprise Communities

One Stop Capital Shops (OSCSs)

The OSCSs are the SBA's contribution to the Empowerment Zones/Enterprise Communities Program. This federal interagency initiative provides resources to selected distressed communities to address an array of social and economic needs. OSCSs provide access to SBA financial and technical assistance programs as well as to those of other federal agencies, state and local governments, and the private sector. For a list of EZ/ECs and OSCSs, access *www.sba.gov/onestop*.

> OSCSs provide access to SBA financial and technical assistance programs as well as to those of other federal agencies, state and local governments, and the private sector.

Small Business Welfare to Work Initiative

The SBA has a multifaceted role in the President's Welfare to Work Initiative: to connect small businesses with service providers that can provide training to, and support for, individuals leaving public assistance; to provide technical assistance to welfare recipients who have the potential to become entrepreneurs; and to link small businesses with federal resources that can support their welfare to work efforts. You can obtain more information at *www.sba.gov/w2w*.

For More Information

- SBA offices are located in all fifty states, the District of Columbia, Puerto Rico, the U.S. Virgin Islands, and Guam. For the office nearest you, look under "U.S. Government" in your telephone directory, or call the SBA Answer Desk.
- Phone: 1-800 U ASK SBA
- Fax: 202-205-7064

- E-mail: *answerdesk@sba.gov*
- TDD: 704-344-6640
- OnLine Electronic Bulletin Board (modem and computer required)
- 1-800-697-4636 (limited access), 1-900-463-4636 (full access), 202-401-9600 (Washington, D.C., metro area)
- Home page: *www.sba.gov* Gopher: *gopher.sba.gov* Telnet: *telnet.sba.gov* U.S. Business Advisor: *www.business.gov*
- Your rights to regulatory fairness: 1-888-REG-FAIR

Inquire at your local SBA office for the location of the following resources:

- BICs–Business Information Centers
- TBICs–Tribal Business Information Centers
- OSCSs–One Stop Capital Shops
- SCORE–Service Corps of Retired Executives
- SBDCs–Small Business Development Centers
- USEACs–U.S. Export Assistance Centers
- WBCs–Women's Business Centers

Publications
Call your local SBA office or the SBA Answer Desk.
- *The Facts About . . . SBA Publications*–a listing of free SBA publications

> The Facts About . . . SBA Publications—a listing of free SBA publications

Did You Know That in Fiscal 1999, the SBA:

- Maintained a guaranteed loan portfolio of more than $40.5 billion in loans to 486,000 small businesses that otherwise would not have had such access to capital?
- Backed nearly 49,000 loans totaling a record $12.5 billion to America's small businesses?

- Made 3,100 investments worth $4.2 billion through its venture capital program?
- Provided more than 36,000 loans totaling over $936 million to disaster victims for residential, personal-property, and business losses?
- Extended management and technical assistance to more than 900,000 small business persons through its 11,500 Service Corps of Retired Executives volunteers and 1,000 small business development center locations?
- Provided through the HUBZone Program federal contracting assistance to small businesses located in "historically under-utilized business zones"?

> America's twenty-four million small businesses employ more than 52 percent of the private work force.

Did You Know That America's Twenty-Four Million Small Businesses:

- Employ more than 52 percent of the private work force?
- Generate more than 51 percent of the nation's gross domestic product?
- Are the principal source of new jobs?

SBA Field Offices

Alaska	Anchorage
Alabama	Birmingham
Arkansas	Little Rock
Arizona	Phoenix
California	Fresno, Glendale, Sacramento, San Diego, San Francisco, Santa Ana
Colorado	Denver
Connecticut	Hartford
District of Columbia	Washington, D.C.

Delaware	Wilmington
Florida	Coral Gables, Jacksonville
Georgia	Atlanta
Guam	Mongmong
Hawaii	Honolulu
Iowa	Cedar Rapids, Des Moines
Idaho	Boise
Illinois	Chicago, Springfield
Indiana	Indianapolis
Kansas	Wichita
Kentucky	Louisville
Louisiana	New Orleans
Massachusetts	Boston, Springfield
Maryland	Baltimore
Maine	Augusta
Michigan	Detroit, Marquette
Minnesota	Minneapolis
Missouri	Kansas City, St. Louis, Springfield
Mississippi	Gulfport, Jackson
Montana	Helena
North Carolina	Charlotte
North Dakota	Fargo
Nebraska	Omaha
New Hampshire	Concord
New Jersey	Newark
New Mexico	Albuquerque
Nevada	Las Vegas
New York	Buffalo, Elmira, Melville, New York, Rochester, Syracuse
Ohio	Cincinnati, Cleveland, Columbus
Oklahoma	Oklahoma City
Oregon	Portland
Pennsylvania	Harrisburg, Philadelphia, Pittsburgh, Wilkes-Barre
Puerto Rico	Hato Rey
Rhode Island	Providence
South Carolina	Columbia

South Dakota	Sioux Falls
Tennessee	Nashville
Texas	Corpus Christi, El Paso, Fort Worth, Harlingen, Houston, Lubbock, San Antonio
Utah	Salt Lake City
Virginia	Richmond
Vermont	Montpelier
Washington	Seattle, Spokane
Wisconsin	Madison, Milwaukee
West Virginia	Charleston, Clarksburg
Wyoming	Casper

Disaster Area Offices

California	Sacramento
Georgia	Atlanta
New York	Niagara Falls
Texas	Fort Worth

All of the SBA's programs and services are provided to the public on a nondiscriminatory basis.

In addition to SBA field offices, there are approximately 1,000 small business development center locations and 389 SCORE chapters to help you start and/or strengthen your business.

All of the SBA's programs and services are provided to the public on a nondiscriminatory basis.

For more information on this topic, visit our Web site at www.businesstown.com

INDEX

INDEX

managerial qualities for, 6
skills for, 29
Leveraging, 290, 306
Life insurance, 37
Links. *See also* Web site
for Web site, 296
Listening skills, 28, 109. *See also*
Communication skills
"selective listening" trap, 64
Lonesome Dove, 12
Low Documentation Loan
(SBA*LowDoc*), 324-325
Loyalty, 191
Lubin, Jill, 97

M

McDonald's, 233
Macromedia Flash, 224, 225
Management. *See also* Leadership;
Management style; Time
management
change as aspect of, 6-7
self-rating quiz, 7
characteristics of greatness, 6
compared to leadership, 61-62
in general, 4
in new millenium, 14-15
people skills
examples of, 28-30
in general, 28
self-rating quiz about, 4-5
for success, 38-39
Management style. *See also*
Employees
drama style, 12
in general, 11-13
mini-series style, 12
new-school style, 13-14
news program style, 12-13
old-school style, 13
self-test quiz, 55-56

sitcom style, 12
soap opera style, 12
Marketing. *See also* Marketing plan;
Sales
components of, 134
for family business, 97
in general, 134
public relations and, 170
publicity and, 134-135, 136
self-assessment quiz, 143
understanding, 142-143
for Web site, 303-304
writing and, 135
Marketing plan. *See also* Sales plan
components of, 139-140
budget, 140
mission statement, 139
positioning, 140
target audience, 139
in general, 138
Maslow, Abraham, 32
Maslow's theory of needs
discussed, 32-33
implementing, 33-34
Media. *See also* Public relations
public relations and, 173
working against, 177-178
working with, 175-177
Media lists, 174, 175-176
Meetings, 142, 260. *See also*
Interviews
Memo
communicating with, 9, 252
ineffective, 252-253
Mentor. *See also* Training
recommendations for, 123-124, 129
role in business, 121, 271
self-assessment quiz, 122-123
Messy desks. *See also* Procrastination
excuses for, 20
in general, 19
no excuses for, 20-21

Mission statement. *See also* Goals
for marketing, 139
for risk takers, 237
Mistakes. *See also* Failure
acknowledging, 22, 118, 250, 259
delegation and, 44
in family business, 92
risk and, 237
Monitoring process, for delegation, 46
Morale, 276. *See also* Attitude
in general, 38, 179
Motivation. *See also* Encouragement
aspects of, 9
for consumer, 148
employees
in general, 10, 32, 92, 120
incentives and rewards, 35-36
Maslow's theory of needs, 32-34
non-salary rewards, 37-38
other factors, 34-35
inspiration and, 65-66
Multitasking, 266

N

Native American assistance, Tribal
Business Information Center
(TBIC), 339-3340
Naylor, Mary, 187
Needs assessment, for financial
services, 200
Negativity. *See also* Attitude
characteristics of, 268-269, 273
difficult people
common types of, 273
handling, 272, 274
tips for, 271-272
understanding, 273
in general, 268
managing negative employees, 269-270
self-assessment quiz, 269

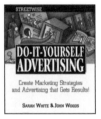
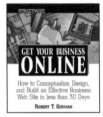
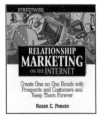
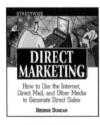

Adams Streetwise® books for growing your business

24 Hour MBA
$17.95
ISBN 1-58062-256-9

Customer-Focused Selling
$17.95
ISBN 1-55850-725-6

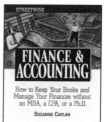

Finance & Accounting
$17.95
ISBN 1-58062-196-1

Hiring Top Performers
$17.95
ISBN 1-58062-684-5

Managing People
$17.95
ISBN 1-55850-726-4

Business Forms w/CD-ROM
$24.95
ISBN 1-58062-132-5

Business Letters w/CD-ROM
$24.95
ISBN 1-58062-133-3

Motivating & Rewarding Employees
$17.95
ISBN 1-58062-130-9

Time Management
$17.95
ISBN 1-58062-131-7

Complete Business Plan
$19.95
ISBN 1-55850-845-7

Small Business Turnaround
$17.95
ISBN 1-58062-195-3

Independent Consulting
$17.95
ISBN 1-55850-728-0

Low-Cost Web Site Promotion
$19.95
ISBN 1-58062-501-0

Internet Business Plan
$19.95
ISBN 1-58062-502-9

Achieving Wealth Through Franchising
$19.95
ISBN 1-58062-503-7

Small Business Success Kit
$19.95
ISBN 1-58062-367-0

FIND MORE ON THIS TOPIC BY VISITING
BusinessTown.com
The Web's big site for growing businesses!

☑ **Separate channels on all aspects of starting and running a business**

☑ **Lots of info on how to do business online**

☑ **1,000+ pages of savvy business advice**

☑ **Complete web guide to thousands of useful business sites**

☑ **Free e-mail newsletter**

☑ **Question and answer forums, and more!**

businesstown.com